Psychosynthesis

Fundamentals in Psychosynthesis

Volume 1

Written and compiled by Joan and Roger Evans

Psychosynthesis

Psychosynthesis

Contents

Psychosynthesis

Psychosynthesis

Psychosynthesis

Psychosynthesis

Foreword The Development of The Institute of Psychosynthesis

Entrance to Il Istituto, Firenze, Italy

Roots of Psychosynthesis

The founder of psychosynthesis, Roberto Assagioli, was an Italian psychiatrist and neurologist. Born in 1888, Assagioli was a highly accomplished scholar, fluent in six or seven languages including Sanskrit. He was also a serious student of eastern philosophies and religions, becoming a student in esoteric studies in the second half of his life. In the psyche of the man himself lay the contradictions that were to effect the development of the psychology he founded; on the one hand he was a scientist bound by rules of empirical study and on the other, a mystic with a profound interest in the healing arts. Assagioli's abiding passion and lifelong search was an empirical study of the underlying spiritual nature of the human being as a willing Self within the complexity, disturbances and sufferings of the human condition. In an interview with Sam Keen, a journalist for *Psychology Today* said: "I believe the will is the Cinderella of modern psychology, it has been relegated to the kitchen...Because modern psychology has neglected the centrality of will it has denied that we have a direct experience of the Self. This is the existential experience of the ultimate connection between the Will and the Self." ('The Golden Mean of Roberto Assagioli', December 1974).

Out of his own search for something beyond his psychiatric training, Assagioli persuaded his doctoral committee in 1910 to allow him to do his thesis on psychoanalysis. He went to Zürich to study with Eugen Bleuler and although he never met Freud, he corresponded with him and on his return to Italy became the first Italian to practise as a psychoanalyst. Within his context of synthesis and his search for understand-

Psychosynthesis

ing the whole person, Assagioli also began to see the limitations of Freud's theories. "Assagioli told me that in one of his letters Freud said, 'I am only interested in the basement of the human building' and Assagioli replied 'Psychosynthesis is interested in the whole building, we try to build an elevator which will allow a person access to every level of his personality.'" (Sam Keen, 'The Golden Mean of Roberto Assagioli', *Psychology Today*, December 1974).

During this time he met and corresponded with Carl Jung as Jung also began to differentiate from Freud. Of all the modern psychologists, he felt that Jung was the closest in theory and practice to psychosynthesis. Assagioli (*ibid*) describes the similarities and differences between Jung and his psychology in the following way, "In the practice of therapy we both agree in 'rejecting' pathologism, that is, concentration upon morbid manifestations and symptoms of a supposed psychological 'disease'. We regard man as a fundamentally healthy organism in which there may be a temporary malfunctioning. Nature is always trying to reestablish harmony, and within the psyche the principle of synthesis is dominant. Irreconcilable opposites do not exist. The task of therapy is to aid the individual in transforming the personality, and integrating apparent contradictions. Both Jung and myself have stressed the need for a person to develop the higher psychic functions, the spiritual dimensions. Jung differentiates four functions: sensation, feeling, thought, and intuition. Psychosynthesis says that Jung's four functions do not provide for a complete description of the psychological life. We hold that imagination or fantasy is a distinct function. And we place the will in a central position at the heart of self consciousness."

From this perspective what is also important is the juxtaposition of the emphasis of science in Freud's work and the mystical implications in that of Jung. As the twentieth century gained momentum, so the world of science became centre stage. The work of Freud became the benchmark for the depth psychologists, with Jung and the more mystical tradition in the background. "It was not until after the second world war in the 1950s that Jung's work began to be more fully recognised." (Jolande Jacobi, *The Psychology of CG Jung*, Routledge, Kegan & Paul, 1962, 6th ed.).

From these early days as modern psychology was developing, Assagioli began to give form and structure to psychosynthesis. In 1926, he founded an Istituto di Psicosintesi in Florence and the focus of his work for the next thirty years was the development of psychosynthesis in Europe. In many ways he was a man before his time and psychosynthesis as a force in psychology remained somewhat hidden and invisible, except in

Psychosynthesis

Italy, until the emergence of the new experiential psychologies and psychotherapies of the Human Potential Movement in the early 1960's. This movement was built on the work of Maslow as he explored the healthy functioning of self-actualising human beings.

"Maslow was the first to create a truly comprehensive psychology sketching, so to speak, from the basement to the attic. He accepted Freud's clinical method without accepting his philosophy. Maslow saw human nature as naturally self-transcending. Healthy satisfied people seek naturally far wider horizons, rather than the near. Freud was unable to go beyond ego satisfaction." (Colin Wilson, *New Pathways in Psychology*, New Amsterdam Library, 1972).

Humanistic practitioners determined that the focus and responsibility for healing and therapy lay with the patient or client themselves; that the healing and self-regeneration process could be more fully accessed through their own direct personal experience and perception of their emotional life as well as through the mind with insight therapy relating to the past.

At the same time, Humanistic Psychology practitioners became more aware that they were also limited in any real description or understanding of the vast realm of human potential which we in psychosynthesis would describe as spiritual.

"One of the reasons for the slow growth and inadequacies of our psychology is that it is culture-bound; it is linked to and frequently limited by the multitudes of (implicit) assumptions that create the consensus reality of the Western World in the twentieth century. It particularly fails to deal adequately with human experience in the realm we call the spiritual, that vast realm of human potential dealing with ultimate purposes, with higher entities, with God, with love, with compassion, with purpose.

"In spite of the fact that science has not dealt adequately with these vital aspects of human experience, I have a deep conviction that science, as a method of sharpening and refining knowledge, can be applied to human experiences we call transpersonal or spiritual, and that both science and our spiritual traditions will be enriched as a result. In particular we will create a scientific transpersonal psychology, or psychologies, a truly Western understanding of the spiritual." (CT Tart, *Transpersonal Psychotherapies*, Harper and Row, 1975).

Psychosynthesis

At more or less the same time the development of Transpersonal Psychology was beginning to emerge in the United States as a force in psychology: "Transpersonal Psychology is the title given to an emerging force in the psychology field by a group of psychologists and professional men and women from other fields who are interested in those ultimate human capacities and potentialities that have no systematic place in positivistic or behaviouristic theory – first force, classical psychoanalytic theory – second force, or humanistic psychology – third force. The emerging Transpersonal Psychology – fourth force, is concerned specifically with the empirical scientific study of, and responsible implementation of the findings relevant to becoming." (Anthony Sutich, *Journal of Transpersonal Psychology*, Spring 1969)

A major turning point in the international development in psychosynthesis came after 1957 when two significant events changed the profile of psychosynthesis as a depth psychology. First, the Psychosynthesis Research Foundation was created in New York under the patronage of the Dupont family which supported research and developed and disseminated the ideas of psychosynthesis and the work of Assagioli. Second, Assagioli's first book, *Psychosynthesis: a Manual of Techniques* (Hobbs, Dorman & Co, 1965) was written and published in English. At the same time practitioners of the Humanistic and Transpersonal disciplines began to study with Assagioli and many went on to found their own centres of psychosynthesis in the United States.

Assagioli and Psychosynthesis

Assagioli did not give his name to Psychosynthesis, and one does not talk of Assagiolian psychology. Rather it is a context for the integration of that which is experienced as immanent – the soul, and that which is experienced as transcendent – spirit. Most of his work was transmitted orally with very little written down from which to interpret the 'master'. He provided the essential framework – he always said that psychosynthesis is a concept, a way of looking at the human being, it is not a thing, an 'ism'. He believed that it was up to each generation to create the forms, to take the theories and develop them, to give substance to the framework and to embody the idea.

A Parallel Process

Essentially, psychosynthesis has the context to synthesise the great contradictions. Perhaps a starting point for looking at the development of psychosynthesis is to remember the contradictions in its founder, Assagioli himself. In his own quest for

Psychosynthesis

meaning, he, like all humankind, had 'religious' yearnings and 'spiritual' experiences which he explored through his studies in the Eastern religions as well as being a medical doctor trained in the objective sciences.

Although psychosynthesis in his own words, is 'a synthesis of many traditions', he himself kept his two methods of inquiry separate and distinct. He even went as far as 'erecting' a wall of silence between his own mystical journey into the unconscious and his explorations as a medical doctor and neurologist. There is a value in things being kept separate so that thought can differentiate coherently within its own context. However, if consciousness and information is suppressed, it will attempt to find different ways to come to the surface, often in ways which were not intended by those who originally suppressed it.

This had its effect in the early years, where attempts to break the wall of silence deflected psychosynthesis from being an important pioneer of transpersonal psychology. Those who followed courses of esoteric teachings attempted to identify Assagioli as a spiritual teacher and 'threatened' psychosynthesis as a psychology in its own right which was developing alongside psychoanalysis (Freud), analytic psychology (Jung), and the humanistic and existential psychologies.

Perhaps it was this 'secretiveness' that contributed to psychosynthesis being so hidden in the years when it might have influenced more positively the development of modern psychotherapy. We find ourselves today having the dialogue with our professional colleagues that Assagioli himself could have had with Freud and Jung. On the other hand it is probably only now, given the spirit of our times, with the humanistic and transpersonal psychologies gaining recognition, that the ground is fertile enough for its reception. We are, therefore, now potentially poised to heal and integrate the contradictions within Assagioli and others of his time. Modern man with all his outer riches, experiences a barren inner world, one where, with the demise of religion, he seeks other references around which meaning can be made.

The London Institute of Psychosynthesis, 1973-1976

In the 1960's and early 70's the United States, and California in particular, was the melting pot for the new psychologies while in Europe, psychology was still held in a tight medical model. The Humanistic and Transpersonal Psychology movements

Psychosynthesis

were being birthed in a culture that was exploring the synthesis between East and West which brought the mystical and the psychological into relationship.

In 1965 Dr William Ford Robertson, a psychiatrist, had created the Psychosynthesis and Education Trust to promote psychosynthesis in the UK. Assagioli was a lecturer and presenter at some of the seminars and this was an important early period providing an intellectual platform for the further development of psychosynthesis. Initially, the ground was not receptive to this psychological approach. The newer therapies of the humanistic movement had not begun and psychiatrists, clinical psychologists and the psychoanalysts were pre-eminent in this field. This Trust ceased to run its activities after three years and until the founding of the Institute of Psychosynthesis, London five years later, there was no centre which acted as a base for psychosynthesis in the UK.

In 1972, the most coherent training programme was being organised by the Psychosynthesis Institute in San Francisco. Psychosynthesis and how it was taught in this programme was a revelation. Here was a context which opened to depths of human suffering and traumas of the past and at the same time honoured the spiritual dimensions of human experience. What was particularly striking was the teaching methodology which combined experiential exercises designed to access unconscious emotional and mental material, with rigorous didactic teaching. It was the beginning of an extraordinary journey.

Assagioli felt it would be more beneficial for us to train in San Francisco , which we did for the next three years, and also work with him as often as we could. This we did until his death in 1974. In the United States, particularly in California, the mind was opening and the new paradigms in science were being explored. In Europe, the thinking around psychology was still more crystallised within scientific doctrines.

We created a simple partnership between us as a vehicle for the Institute and went to study with Assagioli working with him on the creation of an Institute in London.

The aims of the Institute set up in 1973 were as stated in our first brochure: "The Institute is set up with the encouragement and support of Roberto Assagioli to provide in-depth experience in the principles and practice of psychosynthesis through courses, training programmes and publications for the lay and professional public. We are committed to a programme of research as to how the principles of psychosynthe-

sis can be applied to different fields of expression. One of our major objectives is to support and encourage those who are taking initiatives in relation to their spiritual values in service of the larger community."

On introducing the Institute Assagioli said:

For some years I have endeavoured to bring the spirit of psychosynthesis to England. It has been done to some extent but in a partial and limited way. So now I am very glad that the time has come in which, through the co-operation of new friends, an Institute of Psychosynthesis has been founded in England. We have consulted and worked together on its format, scope and policies and we found ourselves in full accord. The gist of our discussion is contained in this brochure which could be called, in a sense, the charter of the Institute; of course subject to development and eventual changes as should happen in every living organism, because I consider that each Institute or Centre of psychosynthesis is not an organisation in the formal sense of the word, but a living centre of light and radiation.

A certain measure of organisation is needed — increasingly with the widening of the activities of the centre — but I think its proper place is to be only instrumental for the main purpose and goal, and I am sure that our friends in England will do that. Therefore I heartily welcome the Institute and express my warm gratitude for the co-operation and help on all levels that has been given by everybody.

As spoken in Florence June 1974.

Roberto Assagioli

We held our own first Basic Training in 1975 in the UK, with practitioners from the humanistic psychology field. This became the first part of a three-part training programme and our first 'crop' were graduated in 1978. Concurrent to the training programme in London in 1976, we started to deliver a programme in Holland comparable to the scale and size of that in the UK. This we continued over the next twelve years until we handed over to a group whom we had trained.

Our professional training programme in psychosynthesis was a departure from the way the majority of humanistic psychology programmes were developing which was through a series of workshops. The Institute was one of the first groups to start a pro-

Psychosynthesis

fessional development programme. At the same time, we also started developing the professional ground for our counselling and psychotherapy training, becoming members of the Standing Conference for the Advancement of Counselling (SCAC), the forerunner of The British Association of Counselling.

1976-1987

Roberto Assagioli died in July 1974 at the age of 87 and the next years saw us sinking the foundations and building the platform for our psychotherapy training. We experimented with different forms, different teachers and different modules. It was a time of outpouring, a period of research, expression, and international connections:

▌ As well as Holland, we supported the development of the Institute of Psychosynthesis in Dublin, Eckhart House, training their students who were to become its faculty. In practice we were coordinating about 250 people all of whom came together to attend an annual International Summer School

▌ We started a Research and Publishing project. Final year students presented their learning about psychosynthesis and its applications to their professional lives. Their papers were published each year in an annual Year Book, which developed into the forerunner of both the Applied Psychosynthesis Programme and the basis for the final thesis of the psychotherapy training

▌ A Psychosynthesis Monograph series was published and we presented papers at International Psychosynthesis conferences which were held during that time in Italy and Canada

▌ We developed a highly competent cadre of trainers which spawned other psychosynthesis training centres in the United Kingdom, France, New Zealand and Scandinavia

▌ The core psychosynthesis psychotherapy courses were fleshed out and tested, and thematic programmes were woven together to provide the basic infrastructure of the training. These were not only the building blocks and foundations of the training programme, they became the fabric of the crucible in which the alchemical process of becoming a psychotherapist is fired. This programme gave a context and a framework which still underpin our psychotherapy training today. In retrospect, it was the beginning of the central theme of what we were later to call a psychospiritual psychology

Psychosynthesis

1988-2002

We began to integrate insights and values from other schools of psychotherapy, seeking to resolve and understand our own contradictions. It was the beginnings of a specific statement by the Institute in the articulation of psychosynthesis which we saw as a psychospiritual psychotherapy. "The notion of soul-making demands more precision, however, when it is used by a therapeutic psychologist rather than a romantic poet. It is not enough to evoke soul and sing its praises. The job of psychology is to offer a way and to find a place for soul within its own field." (James Hillman, *Revisioning Psychology*, Harper Colophon, 1975).

We returned to the foundations of psychosynthesis and psychotherapy and integrated the Freudian perspective and the depth psychologies with the perspective of Jung on which we had been more focussed. By the early 1990s Jarlath Benson, a Group Analyst and Psychoanalyst, and Danielle Roex, a Humanistic and Gestalt Psychotherapist, joined the Academic Staff and became Directors of the Institute, thus broadening our Academic and Clinical base. By 1995, Anne Welsh joined the Directorate, contributing enormously to the Institute's development.

Relationship with Professional Organisations

The United Kingdom Council for Psychotherapy (UKCP)

The widening of our context came at a time when the United Kingdom Standing Conference for Psychotherapy (UKSCP) as it was then called had formed itself as an organisation distinct from the British Association for Counselling. We had spent the previous nine years exploring the identity and boundaries of psychosynthesis psychotherapy and had much more confidence to participate and network in forums with the more traditional psychotherapies. Joan was elected Treasurer and Secretary of the Humanistic and Integrative Section (HIPS) and in 1996, to the Chair, which gave her a seat on the Governing Board of the UKCP for a further three years.

The European Association for Psychotherapy (EAP)

1990 saw the founding of the European Association for Psychotherapy. The Institute then came together with other psychosynthesis centres in Europe to form the European

Psychosynthesis

Federation for Psychosynthesis Psychotherapy and again Joan was elected as its first Chair, taking this organisation through to membership of the EAP.

Association for Accredited Psychospiritual Practitioners (AAPP)

A useful model for cooperation between centres may be seen in the The Association for Accredited Psychospiritual Psychotherapists, which Joan initiated in 1990. In many training organisations there is no differentiation in membership between students and graduates, which sometimes perpetuates transference issues. Given this those members from HIPS who shared a similar context for their work formed an organisation which would go beyond these issues. This was a truly synthetic endeavour. At the level of our training centres there is autonomy and our accredited graduates come together as members of AAPP to appear on the National Register.

The United Kingdom Association for Therapeutic Counselling (UKATC)

A further differentiation occurred with the founding of this Association whereby therapeutic counsellors could also be regulated and registered. The Institute was one of the founding members and its delegates, particularly Anne Welsh, have been active in its development.

Middlesex University – The Synthesis of the Academic and the Experiential

There is in the world today an overwhelming human need for a psychological education, not education in psychology but a psychological education. This means evoking a different type of learning borne out of a psychological awareness, a perception which is not only about the world outside but about the inner world of emotions and feelings as well. By integrating this level of perception, we recognise a dimension of mind beyond the rational and the intellectual, which David Bohm calls the "implicate mind" (*Wholeness and the Implicate Order*, Routledge, 1980).

The question we have asked ourselves over the years is: who is it who is learning? Traditionally education either trains the mind (academic) or is a training in skills (technological). A Psychotherapy education is a training of the person, which requires both clinical and cognitive skills. It is therefore neither the mind nor the body which learns, but the 'inner body', the one who experiences and who learns to distinguish and discriminate between the outer and the inner. In Psychosynthesis terms, the one

who experiences is the soul, and a training through the Institute is a journey of the soul who suffers (undergoes) the process of being trained and who makes meaning of the experience.

At times the bringing together of different theoretical biases from many traditions, both philosophical and psychological, also brings out their contradictions. As an integrative psychology, psychosynthesis provides a context for containing these differences, and comparative study of other schools of psychotherapy serves to illuminate the central thesis of psychosynthesis. In this way psychosynthesis can take its place in the world with its theses strongly supported and open to discussion. With the step into the academic world within a research-based programme, students at the Institute have an opportunity of synthesising these two cultures.

In line with this, in February 1996, we decided to apply to the Middlesex University for validation at the MA level for our psychotherapy programme. To have found a University which honoured work-based learning was important and exciting as it would, we hoped, give academic recognition to the experiential learning methodology which we had developed. In the June of the same year we completed the process and received the validation – this was revalidated in 2001. At the same time the Applied Psychosynthesis Programme was validated, also at MA level, giving students the possibility of studying at the Institute and applying its principles to their field of service. This brought us full circle in relation to our original intentions and commitment to Assagioli in relation to supporting empirical research and evidence-based study.

30 Years On

Every stage of our story poses the question, how do we transcend the contradictions of the past and step beyond our history? That does not mean repressing or denying history, but integrating the learning and therefore redeeming it.

In terms of the spirit of our times, the platform we are establishing is one of a psychospiritual psychotherapy, moving the debate on beyond even the transpersonal psychologies. We believe that tomorrow's world is going to demand a psychology which gives guidance on how we educate our children, on the one hand to help them to look outward to the planet to see their interconnectedness with it and on the other, to look forward towards their future as they seek to understand the aspirations of the human spirit.

Psychosynthesis

We have come to understand more deeply that a psychotherapist is not a spiritual teacher. A spiritual teacher within the contemplative religions prepares the student for psychological and spiritual growth through the received wisdom of the tradition in which he or she is studying. Psychotherapists travel with their clients and prepare the ground for them to receive direct perception of the Self through the integration of their objective and subjective experiences.

As thinking and practice has developed during this century, especially with the new scientific paradigm, psychosynthesis with its principles of Synthesis, has come into its own: "...ideas developed in the West of the individual, his selfhood, his rights and his freedom, have no meaning in the Orient...nor for any earlier civilisations. They are the truly great (new thing) that we do indeed represent to the world and that constitutes our Occidental revelation of a properly human spiritual ideal, true to the highest potentiality of our species." (Joseph Campbell, *Myths to Live By*, Souvenir Press, 1973).

In March 2003, we celebrated our 30th Anniversary. We will have put in place organisational systems to try and ensure ongoing development in the Institute which will continue, hopefully, beyond our own professional lives. The principles which have come out of our learning are:

▮ To have an organisation which is both radiatory and magnetic, that has an identifiable central organising principle as well as one which is open to joining with others in cooperative endeavours

▮ To uphold within the organisation that all members – from students to staff – are understood at the level of their deepest aspirations and are given the opportunity to explore and express them, while at the same time being personally accountable to the organisation in both its limits as well as its potential

▮ To participate actively in research and development projects in the field of transpersonal and psychospiritual psychology and to actively defend the value to humanity of a psychology of the Self

▮ To participate actively in research and development projects in the field of transpersonal and psychospiritual psychology in which 'becoming a moral being' is the outcome of psychotherapy

Joan and Roger Evans, 2002 (founders of the Institute of Psychosynthesis, London)

Psychosynthesis

Introduction Fundamentals of Psychosynthesis

This course introduces the basic methodology and models of psychosynthesis. It is designed particularly to serve those individuals who are attempting to integrate their personal and spiritual experiences. The course creates a context for people to experience and deepen their inner journey of self-realisation and self-expression and to direct their lives more effectively. It will also provide insights and practical ways for obstacles to be transformed into opportunities.

As part of the course, each person will have the opportunity to meet individually with a psychosynthesis guide so that they can explore specific issues and process in depth.

As well as being a comprehensive introduction to psychosynthesis, this course is also a prerequisite for further training at the Institute.

Course Abstractions

The following core abstractions will be the subject of the chapters in this manual which will contain a set of readings on these themes:

- The evolution of the idea of the psyche in psychology
- Psychosynthesis as an holistic model of personal integration and spiritual awakening
- The balance and integration of body, feelings and mind
- Recognising and harmonising subpersonalities
- Identity and personal freedom
- Disidentification and the experience of identity
- Self and duality
- Opening to superconscious experiences, personal crises and spiritual awakening
- The will: freedom of choice and the process of willing
- Wholeness and the process of synthesis in evolution
- Creative expression

Psychosynthesis

Chapter 1 Psychosynthesis Overview

During the Fundamentals course, psychosynthesis is introduced as a concept of the human being and as a relevant psychology for the 21st century. The different levels of the Egg Diagram are explained through a number of basic models and identity is considered through the I/Self relationship.

The Historical Context for Psychology

The reality of inner space and its exploration became as much a scientific endeavour during the 20th Century as did journeying into outer space. The parallel process provided us with metaphors and a plethora of different theories as our understanding of the physical universe dramatically altered from fixed views to relative perceptions.

Psychosynthesis first posited in 1910 by Assagioli, required an expansion of the field of consciousness through these theories before it was able to come into its own as an integrating psychology which spoke to the depths as well as to the heights. As we look to the early roots of psychology in the late 19th Century and its most significant developments in the 20th Century, we observe initially that work on the discovery of the unconscious by Freud in establishing psychoanalysis provided the platform for psychology to look deeply into the inner world. At the same time, it began to turn around the world of the behaviourists who saw phenomena as causal to our existence. Alongside that, psychologists such as Jung, in his work with the Collective Unconscious and the nature of archetypes, provided a deeper way of considering the inner world of the person.

In the second half of the 20th century, Psyche was being wooed by many psychologists as they explored the nature of the human being. In addition, the Freudians and neo-Freudians, the Jungians, and the existentialists began to develop theories about the reality of the human condition in terms of identity and meaning. The humanistic psychologies, also in reaction to the more cerebral and deterministic concepts of the analysts, began to develop a context for emotional life of the person and a reality which dealt with the 'here and now'. This was seen to be as central as a person's historical conditioning.

Psyche was then seen as not only being steeped in her unconscious history and questioning her identity, but at the same time coloured by being alive in the 'here and now'.

Psychosynthesis

Consciousness itself took a leap forward with the expansion in the 1960's where deeper metaphysical and philosophical questions such as 'who are we?' and 'where did we come from?' were asked. The transpersonal psychologies began to acknowledge that each person is also connected to a spiritual essence or divinity and contexts around these questions became conflated, with psychologists, as well as religious leaders, trying to respond. In time, the psychospiritual context, differentiated from that of the religious, has taken its rightful place. This brief overview of the field provides a context within which to consider psychosynthesis. Clearly there is a need for a psychology that integrates or at least attempts to understand Psyche, in a simple way embracing these different approaches.

The Psychosynthesis Core Model of the Psyche

The integrative nature of psychosynthesis is clear from Assagioli's Egg Diagram – explored in depth in the readings which follow this chapter. It delineates a number of different levels of the psyche: the lower, middle and superconscious.

Most particular to psychosynthesis, however, is Assagioli's view of the reality of the Self: that each one of us is a Self, a living divine entity – which simultaneously seeks both to be realised and to express itself. This acknowledgement of Self is both awesome and intensely practical. We see this in the relationship of the Self to its reflection, the personal self or 'I' - that aspect of Self which is in the world, but is not of the world, and expresses itself therefore in both its immanent and transcendent dimensions - both of which affect the experience of identity.

What is Psychosynthesis? (adapted from Synthesis, 1977)

In its most basic sense, psychosynthesis is a name for the conscious attempt to *cooperate* with the natural process of growth – the tendency in each of us and in our world to harmonise and synthesise various aspects at ever higher levels of organisation. Albert Szent-Gyoergyi in his article describes the drive in living matter to perfect itself ('Drive in Living Matter to Perfect Itself', *Synthesis*, 1974, Vol 1, No 1 – reprinted in this book). In human beings, this drive becomes conscious – we feel it as an urge and decide to implement it, to make its progress easier.

Cooperating with evolution in this purposeful way requires conceptual understanding, a framework, and a range of practical techniques. Psychosynthesis integrates both

Psychosynthesis

concepts and techniques into a broad framework, designed to facilitate the natural human drive toward development.

As an inclusive approach to human growth, psychosynthesis dates from 1911 and the early work of the Italian psychiatrist Roberto Assagioli. Though one of the pioneers of psychoanalysis in Italy, Assagioli maintained that Freud had not given sufficient weight to the higher aspects of the human personality. Assagioli recognised the need for a broader concept of man.

Eastern disciplines have often tended to emphasise the spiritual dimension, while Western approaches have usually focused on the personality side. But the human being must be viewed as a whole and each aspect accorded its due importance. Psychosynthesis recognises that each of us has a transpersonal essence, and at the same time holds that our opportunity in life is to manifest this essence, or Self, as fully as possible in the world of everyday personal and social existence.

From this beginning, Assagioli and an increasing number of psychotherapists, physicians, educators, social workers, clergymen and others have worked to develop and refine this view of human growth. The task is considered to be an open one, one that will never be ended.

Over the last sixty years, a number of conceptual points and methods have proven themselves to be fundamental. These provide a working structure for psychosynthesis.

The Self

Assagioli distinguishes psychosynthesis from other psychologies including Jung, acknowledging that the self is; it exists as an ontological reality i.e. as a reality consistent within itself.

The concept of the self as an entity supra-ordinate to the various aspects of the personality, such as body, feelings and mind, is to be found not only in Eastern philosophy and the major world religions, but also in more and more branches of Western psychology. If we examine the concept of the self empirically, we find first of all a centre of awareness and purpose, around which integration of the personality takes place. This is the 'personal self', the 'I', the centre of personal identity.

Psychosynthesis

such qualities as a broad sense of responsibility, a spirit of co-operation, altruistic love, a global perspective, and transpersonal purpose.

Often the two stages overlap, and there can be a considerable amount of transpersonal activity even in the early phases of personal psychosynthesis.

Methods Employed in Psychosynthesis

To be maximally effective in our own psychosynthesis or in helping others, we need to have at our disposal a broad range of methods. As each person is a unique individual, it is important to choose, out of a range of methods available, the ones that are best suited to each person's existential situation, psychological type, specific goals, desires and path of development. A few of the techniques commonly used are guided imagery, self-identification, meditation, development of the will, symbolic art work, journal-keeping, ideal models and development of the intuition, though a complete list would be much longer. The emphasis is not on the techniques, but on fostering an ongoing process of growth that can gain increasing momentum.

The Will

As this process goes forward, it entails developing one's personal will – the will of the personal self. Through this development, we acquire the ability to regulate and direct our many personality functions. We gain the freedom of choice, the power of decision over our actions, and become increasingly able to follow a path in accordance with what is best within each of us.

As we reach towards the Transpersonal Self, we liberate more and more the synthesising energies that organise and integrate our personality. We can make increasing contact with the will of our Transpersonal Self, which provides ever clearer meaning and purpose in our lives. We become able to function in the world more serenely and effectively, and able to relate to our fellows in a spirit of co-operation and good will.

Synthesis and the Psyche

Psychosynthesis, in its fundamental nature, is synthesis of and through the psyche. Here psyche is understood to be not only the human personality, as usually implied by conventional psychology, but much more inclusively, the Psyche or Soul of the ancient

Psychosynthesis

Greek philosophers: the Higher Self. Therefore *psychosynthesis* is that form of synthesis which expresses the will of the Higher Self, and is achieved through wisdom and love – the two fundamental qualities of the consciousness of the Higher Self.

Thus, in its broadest sense, psychosynthesis is a point of view and an attitude, from which we can act with wisdom and love. As such it is well suited to psychology, education and medicine, and also to religion, the social sciences, philosophy, and all other aspects of society and of our world in which *the consciousness of the individual human being* plays a role.

Further Reading

Assagioli, Roberto, *Psychosynthesis: A Manual of Principles and Techniques*, Harper Collins, 1993 (Chapter 1)

Assagioli, Roberto, *The Act of Will*, David Platt, 1999 (Appendix 2)

De Vries, Marco, *The Redemption of the Intangible in Medicine*, Institute of Psychosynthesis, 1981 (pp 28-32 and 34-53)

Psychosynthesis

Psychosynthesis
Research
Foundation

Psychosynthesis: a Way to Inner Freedom

Psychosynthesis appears in embryonic form in the doctoral dissertation of Roberto Assagioli, MD, as far back as 1910. Since then its founder has developed it theoretically, applied it practically and expounded it in more than three hundred papers and two books. It is not a philosophical doctrine. Nor should it be regarded as a specific psychological theory.

It is rather a way of looking at the mystery of man, his inner life, his psyche – a pragmatic approach that strives to take all known facts into consideration and to explore all those that are knowable. It is a method of constructively coming to grips with the complex problems of the psyche, leading to an art of healing, an art of education and an art of living.

Contemporary society, with its bias towards materialism, is inclined to regard as real only what is tangible. Yet a wave of anger is no less real than a wave of the sea. Both phenomena have their causes and create their effects; both can be observed and described. The mental image of a castle is as real as the castle itself. It is real as a subjective experience, and also in the sense that it constitutes the preliminary condition for the construction of the castle.

If we remove our gaze from a material object, it does not cease to exist. If we burn it, chemistry tells us that its substance endures in another form. Some contents of the psyche, such as the experiences of early childhood, seem to vanish without trace. But this is also an illusion, as psychoanalysis has demonstrated in dramatic fashion. The contents of the psyche continue to exist and work in the unconscious, sometimes with disastrous results for the conscious personality.

So, the psyche is just as real as are visible things: in a certain sense even more so, for it is an inner condition which inevitably causes the outer effects. Every attempt to make

Psychosynthesis

men happy by altering their outer conditions of life can be compared to a medicine that combats the symptoms of a disease without eliminating its deeper causes. It possesses value only in so far as it is allied with other and more effective remedies.

Modern physics has routed materialism on its own ground by showing that matter is pure appearance and resolving it into that mysterious something we call energy. Energy can be considered to form a bridge between the psyche and matter. Psychological phenomena, like physical ones, also possess an energy character. We acknowledge this every time we speak of the greater or lesser intensity of our feelings, thoughts, mental images, and so on.

Psychosynthesis fully accepts this point of view, which it shares with several other schools of psychology. It has elaborated techniques that can be used for directing, transforming and sublimating various psychological energies, such as aggressiveness. But it recognises as well the existence of higher energies. These have no need of sublimation, but through an opposite process can descend into the conscious personality with surprisingly integrating, vitalising and regenerating effects. And this process can be induced and facilitated by the intelligent use of appropriate techniques.

Psychoanalysis has demonstrated how dangerous it is to ignore or repress the aspects of the psyche that are connected with the primordial instincts of man, with his biological life and his animal nature. But traditional psychoanalysis has made an omission of a similar but inverse nature. It has ignored or depreciated the higher psychic functions, such as the intuition, altruistic love, and the will – the functions that attain their finest flowering in the genius, the saint and the hero.

These relate to the 'peak experiences' Maslow talks about. In recent years they have started to attract the attention of a growing number of specialists in this field. They originate in that part of the unconscious which has been called the Higher Conscious or Superconscious. So complex and diversified in its contents is the unconscious, this 'behind-the-scenes' of that little stage on which our conscious life unfolds, that to understand something of its nature, it is absolutely essential to make a primary and fundamental distinction – between the lower, the middle and the higher unconscious.

To illustrate, let us consider the following three psychological phenomena – the upsurge of a criminal impulse, the sudden recollection of a matter to be attended to,

Psychosynthesis

and the inspiration of genius. In each of these three cases there occurs an irruption of previously unconscious content into the field of consciousness. But these three unconscious contents are so different in origin and nature as to warrant their being attributed to the lower, middle and higher unconscious respectively.

The lower unconscious contains that which has dropped or been repressed below the threshold of consciousness. It thus corresponds to the individual and racial past. 'Criminal' instincts, for instance, were normal in the caveman just as they are normal in beasts of prey.

The instinctual energies exist in each one of us and are nothing to be ashamed of. They constitute the humus fecundo, the fertile ground into which our personality pushes down its roots. They become injurious and dangerous only when they irrupt and cause confusion and chaos in our consciousness, and form the strongly emotional complexes which psychoanalysis has made familiar to us all.

The middle unconscious contains the memories, thoughts, and feelings with which our everyday life is interwoven. Though at a given moment only a small number of them may be present in the lighted field of consciousness, they come and go, superseding each other with such ease that, in a certain sense, all of them can virtually be considered present. Thus the middle unconscious corresponds to the present time – not to what we have been, and not to what we could be, but to the evolutionary stage we have actually reached.

The basic character of superconscious, transpersonal, or peak experiences, on the other hand, lies in their having little connection with the previous experience of the individual. They present themselves as essentially new, as discoveries or revelations. They are signposts pointing to the paths of the future.

From the superconscious come the stimuli, impulses and energies that mould the evolution of the individual and of humanity in its totality. Most of us have had at some moment of our life a superconscious experience of a mystical, moral or aesthetic nature. The psychological life of great men is characterised by the frequency and the intensity of these experiences. Not only the mystics, but the great poets, artists, scientists and even the great politicians often sense an upsurge of inspiration external to themselves, or to be more accurate, external to their conscious personality. What is the Muse, invoked by the ancient poets, but a personification of the superconscious?

Psychosynthesis

And what the daemon of Socrates? Or the love of which Dante speaks: "I am one who when Love breathes within, Gives ear, and as he prompts takes mode and pitch, From him, and goes and sings his mind to men."

Scientists, less fanciful than artists, do not personify their superconscious, but the phenomenon of inspiration is no less evident in them. It can be the fountainhead of great discoveries. We all remember the 'Eureka' of Archimedes and Newton's apple. A more recent example was Kekule's discovery of the benzene theory.

In a quite different sphere, one of the more significant events of our time, the Ecumenical Council, had its origin in an unexpected inspiration. As Pope John has himself told us, one day, to his great surprise, he heard the word 'council' echo within him, and immediately after, having acquiesced inwardly, he felt himself suffused by a wave of joy.

I have dwelt at some length on this third division of the unconscious, because it is the most neglected and misunderstood. By way of summary, man's psychic structure might be represented symbolically by the diagram on page 17.

The oval divided into three parts represents the unconscious with its three sections – lower, middle and higher. The circle represents the field of consciousness. Outside the oval we may imagine extending what Jung called the collective unconscious. The lines of demarcation are broken as a reminder that the separations are not absolute. The contents of the psyche are continually passing to and from between the unconscious and consciousness, between the different parts of the unconscious, and also between the individual and the collective unconscious, in a manner similar to the phenomenon of osmosis through the semi-porous membranes of cells.

We are now in a position to tackle the central concept of psychosynthesis. As you see, the diagram has a point at the centre of the circle, a star at the top of the oval and a line joining them. The point represents the 'I' consciousness, the sense of personality identity; the star symbolises the Transpersonal Self, our deeper identity, the essence of our being, and the connecting line indicates that we are not dealing with two separate entities, but with two different aspects of one and the same reality. This reality is the central mystery of man.

Psychosynthesis

We make continuous reference to the personal pronoun 'I', as if it were the most explicit word in the whole vocabulary. From a certain very superficial point of view, this is obviously true. If I say, 'I am the writer of this letter', I state something which does not lend itself to ambiguity. In objective terms I could as well say, 'The individual speaking to you is the same as the one who has written this letter.' As everyone knows, small children express themselves precisely in this manner. They say, 'Peter (or Mary) has done so and so', thus showing that they have not yet developed real self-consciousness.

Here is the point. The pronoun 'I' does not indicate solely – and does not indicate primarily – a concept, but an existential experience. Self-consciousness appears at a certain stage of evolution, after a series of other experiences, such as that of one's mother, of one's own body, of hunger, fatigue and fear, and precedes by a long time the experience of abstract thought.

Self-consciousness, then, presents itself as a psychic formation similar to many others and from the dynamic point of view is characterised also by a certain energy charge, a certain intensity – an intensity that varies from one individual to another and from time to time in the same person. It seems to dissolve every night when we go to sleep and we find it again every morning on awakening. It disappears temporarily when we immerse ourselves in action. It is amplified painfully when we feel shame, and pleasantly when our vanity is flattered. It takes on a special emphasis during the act of making a decision, of assuming a heavy responsibility or of rejecting an unfair demand. The negativity of some children at the so-called 'no-stage' may be explained by an instinctive need to develop self-consciousness.

In adolescence self-consciousness undergoes a further tempestuous expansion, which marks the inevitable passage from the submission of the child to the independence of the youth. Lack of wisdom and psychological knowledge on the part of both the young and adults often makes this process pathological and transforms it into the irreconcilable conflict between the two generations.

Let us note that the consciousness of the 'I', like the sexual instinct and the gregarious instinct, like curiosity and every other psychic function, has its dynamics, its rhythms and its own laws of development.

Psychosynthesis

Is all clear now? Everything simple? Unfortunately (or fortunately, according to the point of view), the self-consciousness of the so-called normal man, as an empirical phenomenon, is intrinsically contradictory. Here lies the paradox. From one angle the 'I' is felt to be that which persists throughout all changes of the psychophysical personality. From another it is always more or less confused and identified with one or another of the Protean aspects of this same personality.

It is basically a non-rational and instinctive phenomenon. The young individual knows theoretically that he must grow old and die, but deep inside he does not believe it. When he triumphantly affirms, 'I am young and have a future before me', he identifies his self-consciousness with his youth. That's no crime, but it is certainly an illusion. In his old age perhaps he will sadly smile and murmur, 'I believed my youth need never end and here I am old and my days glide by with monotonous sameness and I've nothing to look forward to but death.' He will be identifying his self-consciousness with his old age, and be unaware that this too is an illusion, the same illusion in a different guise.

The snobbish man of rank will identify himself with his title, the envious proletarian with his plebeian situation. The girl who takes part in a beauty contest identifies herself with her body in its aesthetic aspect, and the same thing can be said of the girl who suffers from feelings of inferiority because of her plainness. Should an accident irreparably disfigure the former, she will feel destroyed. If the latter undergoes plastic surgery that makes her look attractive, she will get the strange feeling of having 'become someone else'. One can identify oneself with a group, like a patriot with his national group, or with a function, as does a woman who strongly accentuates her function as a mother.

One can identify oneself in a more or less complete manner with two or more different functions at different times, and this leads to the formation of true subpersonalities. We can say that each one of us has a number of subpersonalities which are not always well harmonised. Typical is the instance of the general, harsh and authoritarian on the barrack square, who becomes a lamb in front of his wife. Here two subpersonalities co-exist without mutual interference and the result is merely comic. But in other cases they can come to a head-on collision, and then the situation becomes dramatic. St. Augustine, for example, has given us a masterful description of the conflict between the animal man and the spiritual man, both powerfully alive within him, and

Psychosynthesis

of how it was resolved. In other words, he has passed down to us in his confession, the story of his psychosynthesis.

I must resist the temptation to enlarge on this subject, but for the sake of clarity I would like to summarise the conclusions at which we have arrived so far. The self-consciousness of the normal man lacks consistency, because he swings from being more or less identified with the 'I', and therefore experiencing himself as being one and permanent, or being identified, in alternation, with the many, changeable elements in his personality.

Now, this inconsistency is also the characteristic of dreams. So that one might say that normal individuals live in a dream state, that they are more or less asleep. The dream, too, has its function, its value, its beauty. But many, having unpleasant dreams, want to wake up and cannot. Others, in a half-waking state, are vaguely aware that just beyond the boundaries of their consciousness there is a radiant world, full of light and energy, toward which they are drawn. They long to shake off their lethargy and move toward it. But they often don't know how to start, or if they do, they may soon be discouraged by the many obstacles which they see around them.

To all who feel that waking up spells a liberation, a joy, and a promise, psychosynthesis offers a pathway and a method. The general programme of a psychosynthesis can be outlined thus:

▪ Realistic assessment of the psychophysical personality, including as far as possible, the subconscious and the superconscious aspects

▪ Discovery and realisation of a centre of self-identity. This implies some degree of awakening – that is, the realisation of the self as distinct from the psychic contents with which it habitually and illusorily identifies itself

▪ The forging of a personality harmoniously integrated about the awakening self. This calls for the use of the will and the imagination and strengthening of all under-developed qualities. It also includes the integration of the individual with the family and social environment (inter-individual and group psychosynthesis)

This programme is put into practice by means of a number of techniques, more than forty of them, and varies according to the age, psychological development, and constitution of the individual. It varies also according to whether it is applied by a psychotherapist in guiding a client, by a parent in bringing up his children, by a teacher to his pupils, or by an adult to himself.

The general programme I have outlined is so vast that its realisation would require the whole of one lifetime. In fact the lives of some great men could be described in terms of a process of psychosynthesis brought about in part by spontaneous maturation, but also in part as a result of deliberate intention implemented by the more or less conscious use of certain psychosynthetic techniques. I am thinking of such men as Dante and St. Francis of Assisi, Goethe and Rabindranath Tagore.

This means that one can well go on practising psychosynthesis throughout life. On the other hand, devoting a few minutes each day for even a few weeks or months to this work can produce such beneficial effects as to more than compensate for the required effort.

Gabriello Cirinei (reprinted from the Psychosynthesis Research Foundation, 1970, delivered at the International Psychosynthesis Conference, London, 1964)

Psychosynthesis

The New Copernican Revolution

There are many signs that man may be undertaking a systematic exploration of the vast, imperfectly known universe of his own being, a step as epochal as his construction of a science of the galaxies.

As future historians look back on our times what will they conclude to have been the most significant event of the present decade in terms of its impact on the future? The riots in the cities? The Vietnam War? The Great Society programs? The hippie movement? Student protest? Technological and scientific advances? Man to the moon?

None of these, I would make bold to guess. Nor any of the events or trend discontinuities which the in-vogue forecasters are picking out with their current methodologies. I will suggest below that it will be something quite different from any of these, an event perhaps well symbolised by an obscure scientific conference to be held in Council Grove, Kansas, in April 1969.

What follows is a report on research in process. It does not pretend to present demonstrated conclusions. Rather, it raises questions and advances possible interpretations which are so momentous in their possible implications for the future that the fullest possible amount of responsible dialogue is called for.

Let us suppose for a moment that we are back in the year 1600, concerned with forecasting probable future trends. In retrospect it is clear that one of the most significant events in progress was what came later to be called the Copernican revolution. Would our futurist researches have picked this up? They might have, if we were looking at the right things. What was the essence of this remarkable transformation that started with the brash suggestions of Nicholas Copernicus and Giordano Bruno and led to consequences as diverse as a tremendous acceleration in physical science and a decline

Psychosynthesis

in the political power of the Church? One useful interpretation is that a group of questions relating to the position of the Earth in the universe, and the nature and significance of the heavenly bodies, passed out of the realm of the theological and philosophical and into the realm of empirical inquiry. No longer were these questions to be settled by referring to this or that ecclesiastical or scholarly authority; rather they were to be subjected to illumination by systematic observation and experiments. The consequences of such a shift are manifold. New research activities are started; familiar phenomena are given new interpretations; educational approaches are altered; power structures in society undergo change; new bases for consensus are applied to conflicts between belief systems.

A later similar event occurred with the work of the geologists, paleontologists, and biologists of the nineteenth century culminating in the controversial evolutionary hypotheses. Questions relating to the origin of the earth and of man were relabelled 'empirical' instead of 'theological'. Again the consequences reverberated throughout the worlds of research, education and politics.

I believe there is good reason to suspect that we are in the midst of another such salutation today. *Much evidence suggests that a group of questions relating to the commonality of and interpretation of man's subjective experience, especially of the 'transcendental', and hence to the bases of human values, are shifting from the realm of the 'philosophical' to the 'empirical'. If so, the consequences may be even more far-reaching than those which emerged from the Copernican, Darwinian, and Freudian revolutions.*

The evidence is of various sorts. The most obvious kind, of course, is simply the indications that scientists – that is, persons with recognised scientific training, on the staffs of research organisations and universities with high standards, and holding membership in good standing in recognised scientific associations – are manifesting more and more interest in developing an adequate science of ordinary and extraordinary subjective experience. This is not completely new, of course. The phenomena of hypnosis have been studied in a scientific way, off and on, for at least a century and a half. Phenomenology has been a sometime influence in psychology. Freud's psychoanalysis and its offshoots have attempted to probe the unconscious processes. Pioneering books in the exploration of supraconscious processes include FWH Myers' *Human Personality and Its Survival of Bodily Death*, Richard Bucke's *Cosmic Consciousness* (Dutton, 1923), William James' Varieties of Religious Experience

Psychosynthesis

(Collier, 1961), and Pitirim Sorokin's *The Ways and Power of Love* (Beacon Press, 1954), the first three being approximately two-thirds of a century old. Early in 1969 the first issue will appear of the *Journal of Transpersonal Psychology*, dedicated to the systematic exploration of 'transpersonal experience'. The April 1969 Council Grove (Kansas) conference on 'voluntary control of inner states', co-sponsored by the Menninger Foundation and the American Association for Humanistic Psychology, represents an unprecedented assemblage of scientists working with altered states of consciousness through such techniques as autohypnosis and group hypnosis, aural feedback of alpha wave signals, and psychedelic drugs.

In the field of clinical psychology several scientists are proposing to formulate through their researches "a natural value system, a court of ultimate appeal for the determination of good and bad, of right and wrong" (Abraham Maslow, *Towards a Psychology of Being*, Van Nostrand, 1962) and "universal human value directions emerging from the experiencing of the human organism" (Carl Rogers).

An ever-increasing number of students, now in the millions at least, are involved with 'awareness-expanding' activities in free-university courses and elsewhere. This concern is intimately related to student demands for a person-centred rather than scholarship-centred education.

The science of man's subjective experience is in its infancy. Even so, some of its foreshadowings are evident. With the classification of these questions into the realm of empirical inquiry, we can anticipate an acceleration of research in this area. As a consequence there is new hope of consensus on issues which have been at the root of conflict for centuries (just as earlier there came about consensus on the place of the Earth in the universe, and on the origin of man). The new science will incorporate the most penetrating insights of psychology, the humanities, and religion. These developments will have profound impacts on goal priorities in society, on our concepts of education, on the further development and use of technology, and perhaps (as in the case of the Copernican revolution) on the distribution of power among social institutions and interest groups.

Young and incomplete as the science of subjective experience is, it nevertheless already contains what may very well be extremely significant precursors of tomorrow's image of man's potentialities. Space does not permit documenting them here;

however, the following three propositions have accumulated an impressive amount of substantiating evidence:

▌ The potentialities of the individual human being are far greater, in extent and diversity, than we ordinarily imagine them to be, and far greater than currently in-vogue models of man would lead us to think possible

▌ A far greater portion of significant human experience than we ordinarily feel or assume to be so is comprised of unconscious processes. This includes not only the sort of repressed memories and messages familiar to us through psychotherapy. It includes also 'the wisdom of the body' and those mysterious realms of experience we refer to with such words as 'intuition' and 'creativity'. Access to these unconscious processes is apparently facilitated by a wide variety of factors, including attention to feelings and emotions, inner attention, 'free association', hypnosis, sensory depriva-tion, hallucinogenic and psychedelic drugs, and others

▌ Included in these partly or largely unconscious processes are self-expectations, internalised expectations of others, images of the self and limitations of the self, and images of the future, which play a predominant role in limiting or enhancing actuali-sation of one's capacities. These tend to be self-fulfilling. Much recent research has focused on the role of self-expectations and expectations of others in affecting per-formance, and on the improvement of performance level through enhancing self-im-age. On the social level research findings are buttressing the intuitive wisdom that one of the most important characteristics of any society is its vision of itself and its future, what Boulding calls "organising images" (*The Meaning of the Twentieth Century*, Harper & Row, 1964). The validity of the self-fulfilling prophecy and the self-realising image appears to grow steadily in confirmation

Assuming that the evidence substantiating these propositions continues to mount, they have the most profound implications for the future. For they say most powerfully that we have undersold man, underestimated his possibilities, and misunderstood what is needed for what Boulding (1964) terms "the great transition". They imply that the most profound revolution of the educational system would not be the cybernation of knowledge transmission, but the infusion of an exalted image of what man can be and the cultivation of an enhanced self-image in each individual child. They imply that the solution to the alienation and widespread disaffection in our society is not alone in vast social programs, but will come about through widespread adoption of a new image of our fellow man and our relationship to him. They suggest that the most pervasive illness of our nation is loss of the guiding vision, and the cure is to be found in a nobler image of man and of a society in which his growth may be better nurtured. They reassure that an image of fully-human man and of a new social order need not be built of the gossamer of wishful thinking, but can have a sound foundation in the research findings of the most daring explorers of the nature of man and his universe.

It is perhaps not too early to predict some of the characteristics of the new science. Preliminary indications suggest at least the following:

▮ Although we have been speaking of it as a science of subjective experience, one of its dominant characteristics will be a relaxing of the subjective objective dichotomy. The range between perceptions shared by all or practically all, and those which are unique to one individual, will be assumed to be much more of a continuum than a sharp division between 'the world out there' and what goes on 'in my head'

▮ Related to this will be the incorporation, in some form, of the age-old yet radical doctrine that we perceive the world and ourselves in it as we have been culturally 'hypnotised' to perceive it. The typical common sense scientific view of reality will be considered to be a valid but partial view – a particular metaphor, so to speak. Others, such as certain religious or metaphysical views, will be considered also, and even equally, valid but more appropriate for certain areas of human experience

▮ The new science will incorporate some way of referring to the subjective experiencing of a unity in all things (the 'more' of William James (*Varieties of Religious Experience*, Collier, 1961), the 'all' of Bugental (*The Search for Authenticity*, Holt, Rinehart & Winston, 1965) and the 'divine ground' of Aldous Huxley's *The Perennial Philosophy* (Harper and Brothers, 1945))

▮ It will include some sort of mapping or ordering of states of consciousness transcending the usual conscious awareness (Bucke's 'cosmic consciousness', the 'enlightenment' of Zen, and similar concepts)

▮ It will take account of the subjective experiencing of a 'higher self' and will view favourably the development of a self-image congruent with this experience (Bugental's 'I-process' (1965), Emerson's 'over soul', Assagioli's 'true self' (*Psychosynthesis: A Manual of Principles and Techniques*, Hobbs, Dorman, 1965), Brunton's 'over self' (*In Quest of the Over Self*, Dutton, 1938), the 'atman' of Vedanta, and so on)

▮ It will allow for a much more unified view of human experiences now categorised under such diverse headings as creativity, hypnosis, mystical experience, psychedelic drugs, extrasensory perception, psychokinesis, and related phenomena

Psychosynthesis

∎ It will include a much more unified view of the processes of personal change and emergence which take place within the contexts of psychotherapy, education (in the sense of 'know thyself'), and religion (as spiritual growth). This view will possibly centre around the concept that personality and behaviour patterns change consequent upon a change in self-image, a modification of the person's emotionally felt perception of himself and his relationship to his environment

John Platt has argued in *The Step to Man* (1966) – as have Kenneth Boulding (1964) and Teilhard de Chardin (*The Future of Man*, Harper & Row, 1964) before him – that the present point in the history of man may well, when viewed in retrospect by some future generation, appear as a relatively sudden cultural step. The portentous impact of the new technology is the heady yet sobering realisation that we have the future in our hands, that man recognises his role as, to use Julian Huxley's (1945) phrase, "a trustee of evolution on this earth". The new man, "homo progressivus" in Teilhard de Chardin's (1964) words, is described by Lancelot Law Whyte as "unitary man", by Lewis Mumford as the "new person", and by Henry Murray as an "ally of the future". The challenge of our time is whether we make 'the step to man' or our Faustian powers prove our undoing and the whole vast machine goes off the track through the strains of internecine conflict and degradation of the environment.

To become the new man and to construct the new moral order requires a guiding image which is worthy of the task. Man's highest learning has seemed to comprise, in CP Snow's terms, not one culture but two. And the noblest of the images of man to be found in the culture of the humanities appeared somehow alien to the culture of the sciences. The preceding arguments suggest that this state of affairs is probably a temporary one. For example, Ernest Becker proposes that the two cultures can be joined in a true science of man through admission of the universal value statement that that which estranges man from himself is unwholesome. Whether this or something else becomes the unifying principle, the reconciliation may soon take place. On the one hand, we will come to use comfortably many pluralistic images of aspects of man – one for his biochemical functioning, another perhaps for dealing with his pathologies, still another for encompassing his most fully human actions and proclivities. But on the other hand we will find nothing incompatible between any of these and an overarching image of what man can be, or perhaps more accurately, can come to realise that he is already.

Psychosynthesis

The social significance of our dominant basic assumptions regarding the interpretation of subjective experience can be made more specific. At the surface level, so to speak, the nation is beset by numerous social problems which we point to with the terms poverty, crime, racial discrimination, civil disorder, unemployment, pollution, and the like. Experience with attempts to deal straightforwardly with these problems – to tackle discrimination with civil rights legislation, to alleviate the ills of poverty with minimum wage laws and welfare payments, to eliminate ghettos with urban renewal programmes, to deal with civil disorders by increasing police power – indicates that such direct measures typically have unexpected and unintended outcomes. It is as though an 'ecology of situations' were upset by a piecemeal approach.

The reason appears to be intrinsic. It seems that these manifest problems are in a sense symptoms of underlying conditions that are more pervasive and less easy to objectify. At another level these problems reside in the institutions of the society, in built-in power distributions, in the traditional roles to which persons are trained, in the time-hallowed structures and processes. At a still deeper level they involve the most basic assumptions, attitudes, and felt values held by the individual and promoted by the culture. The most carefully designed social measures will not achieve their desired goals unless they involve not only rationally designed programmes and structures, but also changes in deeply rooted beliefs, values, attitudes and behaviour patterns, both of the individuals who constitute 'the problem populations' and of the self-righteous others who assume that they are not implicated.

An analogy with the process of psychotherapy may reassure that in attending to these underlying conditions we are dealing with that which is more, or less, real and relevant. In the end the neurotic discovers that he was divided against himself, and in a sense lying to himself to conceal that condition. So it may be with our social problems that the significant constructive change is first of all an inner one rather than outer, and in the direction of recognising the hidden lies and resolving the hidden divisions. To put it in somewhat different terms, just as it is possible for a person to have a pathological set of beliefs about himself, so it may be possible for our society to possess a dysfunctional belief and value system.

In fact, much of today's student unrest centres around the accusation that the society's operative assumptions about man's deepest desires are indeed not consistent with individual inner experience nor in the long-term interest of man or society. A domi-

Psychosynthesis

nant theme among disaffected students is that the American corporate capitalist system manipulates and oppresses the individual.

Thus it is not solely in an idealistic vein that the new science of subjective experience is hailed as having profound significance. It has survival value as well.

Several recent scholars of the future such as Robert Heilbroner, Kenneth Boulding (1964), and Fred Polak have made much of the concept that it is the *image* of the future which is the key to that future coming into realisation. "Every society has an image of the future which is its real dynamic." As previously noted, much evidence has been accumulated to indicate that the power of the image may be far greater than we have heretofore suspected.

To whatever extent the science of the past may have contributed to a mechanistic and economic image of man and a technocratic image of the good society, the new science of subjective experience may provide a counteracting force toward the ennobling of the image of the individual's possibilities, of the educational and socialising processes, and of the future. And since we have come to understand that science is not a description of 'reality' but a metaphorical ordering of experience, the new science does not impugn the old. It is not a question of which view is 'true' in some ultimate sense. Rather, it is a matter of which picture is more useful in guiding human affairs. Among the possible images that are reasonably in accord with accumulated human experience, since the image held is that most likely to come into being, it is prudent to choose the noblest.

It is strange to observe that at this point in history when we literally have the knowledge and material resources to do almost anything we can imagine – from putting a man on the moon, to exploring the depths of the oceans, to providing an adequate measure of life's goods to every person on earth – we also seem the most confused about what is worth doing. The great problems facing us are a sort where we need belief in ourselves and will to act even more than we need new technologies, creative social programme concepts, and programme budgeting. At a time when the nation may well be in its gravest peril in over a century, and Western civilisation may hang in the balance, it could even come to pass that a new 'Copernican revolution' might provide a missing balance in some four-century-old trends started by the first one.

Willis Harman (reprinted from the Psychosynthesis Research Foundation, 1969, first printed in Stanford Today, Winter 1969)

SYNTHESIS

Drive in Living Matter to Perfect Itself

For quite some time science has recognised the principle of entropy as a fundamental factor in the universe. Entropy causes organised forms to gradually disintegrate into lower and lower levels of organisation. This tendency by itself leads one to consider the world as a whole to be like a great machine running down and wearing out.

But there is mounting evidence for the existence of the opposite principle: syntropy – or 'negative entropy' – through the influence of which forms tend to reach higher and higher levels of organisation, order, and dynamic harmony. In the following essay, Albert Szent-Gyoergyi, research biologist twice awarded the Nobel Prize, describes his conception of an 'innate drive in living matter to perfect itself', and suggests that such a syntropic principle can be found even at the sub-atomic level of matter.

Syntropy is closely related to the process of synthesis, and today many are calling increasing attention to a psychological drive toward synthesis, toward growth, toward wholeness and self-perfection. Szent-Gyoergyi's conception has therefore far-reaching implications not only for the physical and biological sciences, but perhaps even more for psychology and for our view of the human being, of society, and of the world.

Albert Szent-Gyoergyi's paper was originally presented as a lecture delivered for the Symposium on the Relationship between the Biological and Physical Sciences at Columbia University.

I have always been an amateur scientist but a professional poacher. I have never been married to any single principle, and my relations to sciences have been most promiscuous. This is perhaps the reason why I was chosen to discuss here The Relationship Between the Biological and Physical Sciences.

That title suggests some basic difference between the animate and inanimate world, and so at the outset we find ourselves in a contradiction. We probably all feel that there is some basic difference between the living and the non-living, while as scientists we cannot believe that the laws of the universe should lose their validity at the surface of our skin. Life must actually have been created by these laws. So our first step has to be to clear our minds about this contradiction.

They can be so cleared, to a great extent, by the simple fact that things can be put together in two different ways, at random or meaningfully. This is a cardinal point. I would like to illustrate it by an example. Six toothpicks and two corks on a table will be but six toothpicks and two corks. Their qualities are additive. However, if I put these toothpicks and corks together in a specific way, they will make a (somewhat symbolic) horse which can no longer be fully described in terms of the constituents. New qualities are developed which are no longer additive. With a few more pieces I could set a man on this horse; then I would again have something new – neither a horse nor a man but a man-on-a-horse. This is what is called 'organisation'. Putting things together in a meaningful way; it is one of the basic features of nature.

If elementary particles are put together to form an atomic nucleus, something new is created which can no longer be described in terms of elementary particles. The same happens over again if you surround this nucleus by electrons and build an atom, when you put atoms together to form a molecule, etc. Inanimate nature stops at the low level of organisation of simple molecules. But living systems go on and combine molecules to form macromolecules, macromolecules to form organelles (such as nuclei, mito-chondria, chloroplasts, ribosomes or membranes) and eventually put all these together to form the greatest wonder of creation, a cell, with its astounding inner regulations. Then it goes on putting cells together to form 'higher organisms' and increasingly complex individuals, of which you are an example. At every step new, more complex and subtle qualities are created, and so in the end we are faced with properties which have no parallel in the inanimate world, though the basic rules remain unchanged.

Levels of Organisation

Any level of organisation is fascinating and offers new vistas and horizons, but we must not lose our bearings or else we may fall victim to the simple idea that any level of organisation can best be understood by pulling it to pieces, by a study of its compo-nents – that is, the study of the next lower level. This may make us dive to lower and lower levels in the hope of finding the secret of life there. This made, out of my own life, a wild-goose chase. I started my experimental work with rabbits, but I found rab-bits too complex, so I shifted to a lower level and studied bacteria; I became a bacteri-

Psychosynthesis

ologist. But soon I found bacteria too complex, and shifted to molecules and became a biochemist. So I spent my life in the hunt for the secret of life.

It is most important for the biologist to give himself an account of these relations when he asks himself on which level of organisation to work when embarking on research with the desire to understand life. Those who like to express themselves in the language of mathematics do well to keep to lower levels.

We do not know what life is but, all the same, know life from death. I know that my cat is dead when it moves no more, has no reflexes and leaves my carpet clean – that is, no longer transforms chemical energy into mechanic, electric or osmotic work. These transformations of energy are most closely linked up with the very nature of life. We, ourselves, get our energies by burning our food and transducing its chemical energy into heat and various sorts of work.

So for twenty years I studied energy transformations by going to the source of the vital energies and worked on biological oxidation on the molecular level. These studies netted me a Nobel Prize (which was most pleasant) but left me eventually high and dry without a better understanding.

So I turned to muscle, the seat of the most violent and massive energy transformations. This study led me and my associates to the discovery of a new muscle protein, and we could then ourselves make little muscles and make them jump outside the body. To see these little artificial muscles jump for the first time was, perhaps, the most exciting experience of my scientific life, and I felt sure that in a fortnight I would understand everything.

Then I worked for twenty more years on muscle and learned not a thing. The more I knew, the less I understood; and I was afraid to finish my life without knowing everything and understanding nothing. Evidently something very basic was missing. I thought that in order to understand I had to go one level lower, to electrons, and – with greying hair – I began to muddle in quantum mechanics. So I finished up with electrons. But electrons are just electrons and have no life at all. Evidently on the way I lost life; it had run out between my fingers.

I do not regret this wild-goose chase – because it made me wiser and I know, now, that all levels of organisation are equally important and we have to know something about

Psychosynthesis

all of them if we want to approach life. The biologist wants to read in the book of creation. If there was a creator, he could not have been a molecular biologist only. He must have known a great deal of quantum mechanics and mathematics, too, and must have been a good geneticist and physiologist. He must have been all of that, and so if we want to follow his trail and read in the book of creation, we must be a bit of everything. Even if limiting our work to a single level, we have to keep the whole in mind. Naturally, the higher we climb on the ladder of organisation and complexity, the less our material becomes accessible to mathematical analysis, but we must not think ourselves to be scientists only when speaking in equations. [*A holistic attitude is just as important for the psychologist and the educator, who deal primarily with functions and processes which occur at the highest levels of organisation in the individual. A simple reductionist approach will prevent a correct evaluation of such processes and the understanding of their true nature, and might in some cases hide the very fact that they exist.*]

To finish my life's story, now I am climbing up again on the ladder of organisation on which I worked my way down through half a century, and am working on the cellular level – for the cell is the cornerstone, the greatest wonder, of living nature, and is, today, a somewhat neglected dimension. Not only do I not regret my earlier climbing down to electrons; I even feel I might not have climbed down far enough, and it is possible that we have to wait for discovery of new science, some sort of super-wave-mechanics, till we can really approach life; but electrons and quantum mechanics are the limit set to the biologist by physics today.

Quantum mechanics, which deals with the electronic structure of molecules, taught me something most important: how wonderfully subtle and complex is a structure of even a simple molecule. As a student I learned that the benzene ring is a hexagon, and this was all there was to it. Quantum mechanics has taught me that in the simplest aromatic molecule every carbon atom has its individuality which can be described only by half a dozen electronic indices, which give to the molecule a very sharp profile, a very specific individuality, most complex in the very complex molecules of the living edifice.

This brings me to the problem on which I plan to spend the next fifty years of my research. The problem is this: most biological reactions are chain reactions. To interact in a chain, these precisely built molecules must fit together most precisely, as the cogwheels of a Swiss watch do. But if this is so, then how can such a system develop at

---

Fundamentals of Psychosynthesis

all? For if any one of the very specific cogwheels in these chains is changed, then the whole system must simply become inoperative. Saying that it can be improved by random mutation of one link sounds to me like saying that you could improve a Swiss watch by dropping it and thus bending one of its wheels or axles. To get a better watch all the wheels must be changed simultaneously to make a good fit again.

Drive to Improvement

There is no need to descend into the electronic world for examples on this line. In the winter, at Woods Hole, the sea gulls are my main company. These gulls, the 'herring gulls', have a red patch on their beaks. This red patch has an important meaning, for the gull feeds its babies by going out fishing and swallowing the fish it has caught. Then, on coming home, the hungry baby gull knocks at the red spot. This elicits a reflex of regurgitation in mama, and the baby takes the fish from her gullet. All this may sound very simple, but it involves a whole series of most complicated chain reactions with a horribly complex underlying nervous mechanism. How could such a system develop? The red spot would make no sense without the complex nervous mechanism of the knocking baby and that of the regurgitating mother. All this had to be developed simultaneously, which, as a random mutation, has a probability of zero. I am unable to approach this problem without supposing an innate 'drive' in living matter to perfect itself.

I know that many of my colleagues, especially the molecular biologists, will be horrified, if not disgusted, to hear me talk about a 'drive' and will call me a 'vitalist', which is worse than to be called a communist. But I think that the use of such words as 'drive' does no harm if we do not imagine we have found an explanation by finding a name. If we look upon such words as simply denoting great unsolved problems of science, they can even lead to useful experimentation. [Previously the author had spoken of a tendency rather than a drive, as in the following: "My feeling is that living matter carries, in itself, a hitherto undefined principle, a tendency for perfecting itself" ('The promise of medical science', in G Wolstenholme (ed), *Man and His Future*, Little, Brown, 1963, pp 188-195).]

By 'drive' I denote here simply the ability of life to maintain and improve itself. You know this from your daily life. You know well that if you use your car too much and your legs too little, your car gets worn out while your legs atrophy, just fade away. This is one of the most characteristic differences between the living and non-living. The non-living is worn out by use, while the living is improved, developed by it. Life keeps life going, building up and improving itself, while inactivity makes it go to pieces.

An early American physiologist, Bowditch, discovered an unexpected phenomenon which reflects these relations and makes them accessible to experimentation. I am alluding to his 'staircase'. If I ask you what you expect if I make the heart rest for a little while and then make it go again, your guess will probably be that the first beat after the rest will be stronger than the last one before it. But the opposite is true: it will be weaker, and the tension developed will gradually rise to its original level in the subsequent beats. Here is the same problem in a nutshell.

Dr. Hajdu and I have tried to find out what is behind this 'staircase' phenomenon and found that what happens is simply that, in rest, potassium leaks out of the muscle fibres, and is pumped back in the subsequent contractions. For the muscle to work well the potassium must have a high concentration inside the fibres and low outside them. What happens in rest is an increase in randomness; the entropy of the potassium increases in rest and decreases again in function. Function thus keeps the living system on its low entropy state, in its highly specialised spatial structure – puts or keeps everything in its place. Life thus keeps life going, building up itself.

[Entropy, which we described as the tendency of organised forms to gradually disintegrate into lower and lower levels of organisation, is predominant in 'inanimate matter', and is easiest to observe (the machine ultimately breaking down, energy eventually being used up, etc.). It has long been accepted by science and is described by precise mathematical formulations. Syntropy, the opposite principle, the tendency to reach higher and higher levels of organisation, harmony, and order, is predominant in 'living' organisms. It becomes increasingly prominent in the more advanced species – those where consciousness is most developed – thus culminating, as far as we know, in man.

Syntropy is only now beginning to capture the attention of the scientific community and is far from being generally accepted, yet some of the foremost contemporary thinkers consider it a fundamental principle of nature. Buckminster Fuller, for example, states: "The history of man seems to demonstrate the emergence of his progressively conscious participation in theretofore spontaneous universal evolution...My continuing philosophy is predicted...on the assumption that in dynamic counterbalance to the expanding universe of entropically increasing random disorderliness there

must be a universal pattern of omnicontracting, convergent, progressive orderliness and that man is that anti-entropic reordering function..." (RB Fuller, *No More Secondhand God*, Southern Illinois University Press, 1963, p xii).

The concept of syntropy, in such views as Fuller's has, as we have said, the most far-reaching implications, both philosophical and practical, for the full development of the human being, his integration within the scheme of nature, and his ultimate purpose. The fact that syntropy is much more difficult to observe than entropy has been the cause of much perplexity, and an obstacle to its wider acceptance as a principle of nature. An Italian mathematician, Luigi Fantappié, suggested a reason for this difficulty: human consciousness, he observed, is at the top of the organisation ladder of nature, and intimately associated with the syntropy side of the entropy-syntropy polarity. Therefore it is normally oriented toward, and attracted by, its polar opposite, entropy, and able to observe the entropic world from a most detached and objective perspective, with greater ease and precision. In his book, *Principi di una Teoria Unitaria del Mondo Fisico e Biologico* (1944) (Principles of a Unified Theory of the Physical and Biological World), Fantappié offers a clear presentation – based on rigorous mathematical formulations – for both syntropy and entropy, and deals with the implications of syntropy in the physical, biological, psychological, and spiritual dimensions.

These are not merely abstruse problems of biology. We could show, with Dr Hajdu, that if your heart fails in some infectious disease and you die, this is because it behaves like a heart which rested too much; and if digitalis pulls you through, it is by doing to it what work should have done.

But the heart may be too complex to allow a more detailed analysis, and according to the rules of my life I should take you lower down from the molecular to the electronic dimension. So I will talk about 'charge transfer'. It has become clear during the last decades that under certain conditions an electron of a molecule, say molecule A, can go over to...another molecule, molecule B. For this the two molecules must be in very intimate contact...Evidently the electron goes over because by its doing so the free energy of the system decreases and the system becomes more stable. [Other more familiar examples of energy transfer are a boulder rolling down the slope of a mountain, or a piece of iron being attracted by a magnet. In both cases, energy that was initially stored as 'potential energy' becomes transformed into 'kinetic energy' as the two elements (the boulder and the earth, or the magnet and the piece of iron) move toward each other. When the two elements again come to rest, finding a new, more stable point of equilibrium, the kinetic energy is released, and either is dissipated as heat or can be utilised to do useful work.

In general, each time two or more elements come closer together, energy is released. It is interesting to observe that often as the process continues, and all elements in a system come as close as possible to one another, releasing the greatest amount of energy, they arrange themselves not randomly, as an aggregate, but according to specific patterns, determined by geometrical laws, where order, harmony, and often great beauty are readily apparent. Crystals are formed this way. They have qualities and properties beyond those of their component parts, and are thus a true 'synthesis' of atoms.

We can see therefore that synthesis not only does not require energy – except when needed initially, to get the process going – but releases energy that was up to then locked in matter, and makes it available.

This same process is very apparent in the psychological domain. When a number of individuals form a harmonious group, thus becoming psychologically close to one another, much energy is released, which becomes available and can be turned outward to useful purposes. Or within the individual, when, as the result of effort, we 'overcome a psychological block' and feel 'more together' we have supplied the initial energy to allow some of our personality elements to move closer to each other, and form a more harmonious structure. The energy released by such a step toward greater 'psychological synthesis' is immediately experienced, often as a feeling of elation or greater well being, or as the urge to action, sometimes even as a 'peak experience'. Whenever such energy becomes available – and particularly if suddenly, or in large quantity, as in the case of a psychological 'breakthrough' – it can be deliberately channelled and utilised to keep the process of synthesis going, and accelerate it. If this is not done, it will largely dissipate – thus wasting much of the potential benefit of the breakthrough – or even disturbing other aspects of the inner synthesis, occurring in nearby psychological 'space'.] The 'charge transfer energy' will thus contribute to the forces keeping the two molecules together. Without it the system would be less stable, would tend more to go to pieces. Here then is a simple example of function maintaining structure. We could continue this spirited game and add molecules C, D, E and F to the system and imagine the electrons flowing from B to C, and from there to D, E and F continuously.

Psychosynthesis

This is not a meaningless speculation, a 'jeux d'esprit', for all of our vital energies are actually derived from such an electron flow. The energies which are driving you are the energies which these 'flowing' electrons gradually lose in this transfer from one molecule to the other. Finally this energy is translated into 'high energy phosphate', the immediate source of the energy by which your cells live. This flow of electrons can be expected to help keep the molecules of the chain together, in their very specific steric relations, and we can expect the system to tend to go to pieces as soon as the electron flow stops. We have thus a clear-cut example of life being kept in the living condition by life itself, kept by work in good working order. We can even expect the system of our molecules A and B to tend to add further molecules, to decrease free energy further, and thereby to become more stable, better and more complex. So actually we arrive at a 'drive' to improvement, to building up.

In thermodynamics such a system as I just described would be called an 'open system', which reaches its energy minimum – that is, its greatest stability – by working. So the 'drive' can even be expressed in the idioms of accredited science.

'Wisdom' of Living Matter

These problems are so fascinating that I would like to spend a few more minutes with them. Many years ago I proposed, with my colleagues, Isenberg and McLaughlin, that electrons may be transferred by certain molecules at specific points only, and showed that indoles will probably transfer their electron at Carbon no 3. [*The term 'indole' refers to a particular type of ring pattern formed by some of the atoms within certain organic molecules. 'Carbon no 3' is a carbon atom placed at a specific location in the indole ring.*]

Many of the drugs which provoke hallucination, the 'hallucinogens', contain an indole ring. With Karreman and Isenberg we also showed that hallucinogens have a strong tendency to give off electrons, are good 'electron donors'. We concluded that hallucination, in this case, may be caused by transfer of electrons from the drug to the nerve cell. Both our assumptions have found corroboration very recently – the first by Green and Martieu in Pullman's laboratory, the latter by Snyder and Merrill, who showed that the hallucinogenic property goes parallel to the electron-donating ability in a great number of hallucinogens and related compounds.

Psychosynthesis

In order to be able to pass an electron on at a certain point, the molecule must be fitted together most accurately, and linked together strongly in two dimensions to form a 'membrane' as in the case of mitochondria, where all our vital energies are generated by the flow of electrons. So these considerations may lead even to an answer of one of the most puzzling problems of biology: what is a membrane? The knowledge gained might also help to cure mysterious diseases, answer problems of everyday medicine.

Since I was not afraid to use the word 'drive'. I might as well be even more audacious and use the word 'wisdom'. I am not the first to do so. The great American physiologist, Walter B. Cannon, talked and wrote a great deal about the 'wisdom of the body'...

I would like to illustrate with one example what I call 'wisdom'. If you look at a motor nerve cell, which gives the immediate command to your muscles to contract, you will find a great number of fibres from other nerve cells, hundreds of them, ending at its surface. These fibres bring messages from faraway nerve centres and modify the action of this motor nerve cell and the motion this nerve cell will induce.

Perhaps I could make this clearer by a little story about a kitten which shared my tent once in Cornwall, England. One day a snake crept into our tent. My kitten stiffened in horror. When I touched its tail, the kitten jumped up vertically about two feet high. This happened because the nerve fibres which ended on the motor nerve cells conveyed the message that there was danger of life and any motion had to be fast and violent. These messages came, as I said, from faraway complex nerve centres which worked up and evaluated the visual impressions of my kitten.

The problem I want to bring out here is this: how could these hundreds of nerve fibres, coming from faraway nerve centres, ever find the right motor nerve cell? All this could not have been coded into the egg cell from which my kitten grew. Of course, this egg cell must have contained (in conjunction with the sperm) all the information which is necessary to build such a wondrous organism as a cat. But all those excessively complex networks which make a brain could not have been inscribed into the egg cell. The egg cell cannot be a blueprint; it can only be an instruction manual, which contains instructions on how to build macromolecular systems with sufficient wisdom to find their place and function. That all this could not have been inscribed in the egg cell we could show by cutting these nerve fibres and introducing a new factor of which the egg did not know. We could expect that the fibres would again find their severed ends through their own wisdom. As suggested by the experiments of Sperry, even if we should cut a great number of these fibres simultaneously, they would not get mixed up and each of them would find its very own ending again – a really remarkable wisdom.

This 'wisdom' may be even much more difficult to understand than the 'drive', but also must have its well-defined mechanism. Perhaps this 'wisdom' and 'drive' are essentially the same, and may be the property of living matter in general – the property that has driven matter to generate life, which then tends to build its own mechanisms. I feel strongly that, for instance, the human speech centre was not developed by random mutation, but had to be developed as soon as man had something to say – the function generating its own mechanism. Of course I know that to make any such change permanent, the change must be communicated by some sort of feedback mechanism from periphery to DNA. We do not know of any such feedback, but it was only a few years ago that we had not the least idea of how DNA communicates with the periphery either.

Maybe this drive is not an exclusive property of living systems, but is the property of matter in general. We know today that fairly complex organic molecules can be built without the intervention of living matter, while by the word 'organic' our scientific fathers wanted to express the idea that it is only life which can build such molecules. Sidney Fox in Florida even builds protein-like substances without life. It may have been this innate drive of matter which led to the origin of life and played, later, an important hand in its evolution.

Areas of Ignorance

I have tried to show that many of the greatest problems of biology are unsolved, if not untouched, and that we can expect to solve them by applying physics. But whether physics in its present state allows us the analysis of the underlying mechanisms, I do not know. I rather doubt it, and we may have to wait for the discovery of entirely new physical sciences till we can penetrate deeper into the nature of life. In my student days we hardly knew more than the structure of a few amino acids and sugars, and we felt obliged to explain life. It was not so long ago that the young Max Planck was advised by one of the best physicists to become a pianist rather than a physicist because physics was a finished and closed subject to which nothing could be added. So we biologists have to look out most anxiously for any new development in physics and

Psychosynthesis

any new instrument physics may give into our hands. Meanwhile, we must not feel obliged to explain life with our present knowledge, and we should not shy away from admitting our ignorance – the first step towards new knowledge being to recognise ignorance.

I have been often reproached for being a vitalist, mysticist, obscurist, and teleologist while the real situation was clear and simple, there being a complete interdependence between structure and function. Since every function must have its underlying structure which must be of physical nature, all we have to do is to apply physics to structure. This may be so, but, all the same, I feel we must be careful with this interdependence as we don't know how many unknowns our equations still contain. Certainly there is such an interdependence as there is complete interdependence between the needle of your gramophone and the groove on your record; and once the needle follows the groove, your victrola must produce the sound it does. All you have forgotten is only Beethoven or Bach, whose music you might have been playing, and without whose genius your gramophone would be useless. Of course, Bach and Beethoven, too, were built of macromolecules, but, all the same, we do well to keep our reverence before their genius, which is still far beyond the possibility of detailed physical analysis. Such a speechless deep reverence and amazement before the wonders of nature is the main result of my half a century's poaching, and if I were to sum up my summary now, I would do it in Shakespeare's words, saying: "There are more things in heaven and earth, Horatio, than are dreamt of in your philosophy." (*Hamlet*, I, V, p 166).

Albert Szent-Gyoergyi (reprinted from Synthesis, 1974, Vol 1, No 1, first printed in the Journal of Psychology)

Psychosynthesis

Chapter 2 Models of the Personality — Body, Feelings and Mind

The Body, Feelings and Mind (BFM) model is one of two core models of personality that we explore in the Fundamentals, the other being subpersonalities. Both embody a central principle in psychosynthesis which sees the person at the same time as both one and many. Within this context the Self is differentiated through different fields of consciousness – i.e. those of the physical, the emotional and the mental. Similarly the personality can also be seen as an expression of the whole and as comprising many parts. The purpose of exploring these models in terms of the parts is to help bring awareness and understanding where we are most identified with a part, whilst believing it to be the whole. As we develop the ability to reflect on our identifications we begin to step back – disidentify – and realise that we – the whole – are much more than the part. Through this process of identification and disidentification we begin to own both the parts with their attributes and limitations and the quality of the Self expressed through each part.

In this model we see that the body, the feelings and the mind follow a developmental process and as each develops, it adds to or limits the capacity for self-expression. This expansion of consciousness takes place through processes occurring over time, of identification and disidentification.

Ultimately the purposes of the Being are to make meaning of being in one's environment, and to develop the capacity for independent thought and action so that Being in the world has value.

A way of thinking about this process is as follows:

The Physical Body

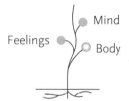

Psychosynthesis

In infancy comes the birth of the *sensate* being where the child experiences and begins to make meaning in the world, through its body, through touch, through its mouth, through physical closeness, physical experimentation and physical signals. As time goes on with the development of the emotions and the mind, we abstract from these experiences and come to understand the world through different levels of consciousness. However, we have increasingly understood how this deeper learning is profoundly affected by the ground that is laid during these early preverbal levels. The body as a vehicle of experience and expression develops to the degree that it is able to within the support and constraints of parenting and the environment within which it lives.

Given the independence of all parts, it is clear that although the development of the Feelings and the Mind are not foreground, resonances within these vehicles are set up so that the one impacts the other. These resonances either serve or limit development of consciousness as the Being seeks to expand the dimensions of its expression in and through the world.

The degree to which the physical world of the young child is responded to and celebrated, or rejected and denied, will often become suppressed or repressed by the person as they develop and will unconsciously control attitudes and behaviours later in life, thus limiting the full capacity for self-expression.

The Feelings

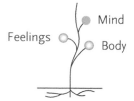

As the child develops, so their experience of the world begins to be gradually dominated by their emotional responses and reactions to their environment. Their feelings are initially very undifferentiated and crude, consisting of love or hate, anger or agreement, happiness or sadness. Frequently these crude feelings are very connected to physical actions and the body/feelings axis is strong. The remarkable step in most children when supported and allowed, is the way these extreme feelings differentiate over the middle and later childhood years. They can move from love, through liking, caring, acceptance, pleasantness to frustration, irritation, anger, rage and hate. This is a very sophisticated spectrum and some children, have difficulty acknowledging and allowing their own feelings, and fail adequately to develop the full range of their emotional life.

In order for there to be *emotional intelligence* in later life which deeply serves the meaning-making functions and the development of consciousness, it is vital for the extremes as well as the norms of the feeling range to be supported in order for the emotional vehicle not to be underdeveloped or repressed because surviving life as a child has been just too difficult. The child and the adult often therefore lose out on the colour and depth that access to these feelings will bring. Also the capacity for self-expression through the feelings is either enhanced or limited to the degree to which the person is able to acknowledge, allow and express their feelings.

The Mind

Parallel to the development of these two vehicles, is the development of the *incarnate being* in the world and its capacity for self-reflection. As a *sensate being* in the outer world it develops the capacity to sense or find its way in its environment, and through the *responsive being* it develops the capacity for appropriate reaction to its environment. The information received from these two vehicles is collated and made sense of through the development of cognition and during late childhood and early adolescence we see again the transition from one to another of these vehicles. At this stage the development of the mind and the mental faculties of the person begin to take much more prominence in the person's life.

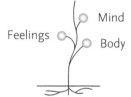

The faculty of analytical thought and reasoning, while beginning to develop earlier in childhood, now becomes a significant factor in the way that the young person experiences their world. Not only is the intellect being developed but more importantly the person is able to hold and return to consistent frames or mindsets that order their world. Many of these mindsets will have been in place via the superego much earlier

Psychosynthesis

but now we see the individual's own mental faculty is increasingly able either to feed these mindsets or reject them.

This is the time for rational and logical development of the ability to play with ideas and creativity. This can be a very significant time for most people in formulating their own ideas about their lives. It is also a time when the environment either supports this process or rejects it. The family or culture may be threatened by the mind of the young adolescent exploring new ideas and may only reward non-academic behaviour. Others may feel more threatened by strong emotional responses or by the adolescent culture breaking with the 'norm', and reward only academic responsiveness at the expense of these feelings.

How the young adolescent deals with these dynamics is crucial to the development not only of the intellect but also of the creative mind. The young person survives either by rejecting the parents' rejection and literally and metaphorically leaving home, or by repressing the mind. On the other hand they may be lovingly supported in this phase of development. Whichever route they choose will have a significant impact on their eventual capacity to abstract and contextualise meaning and creativity.

So the underlying principle to this model of Body, Feelings, Mind is a perspective on the extent to which these vehicles are broad enough and differentiated enough to serve the expression of the Self. To understand this we may need to understand where we are identified and why. For example:

▮ Am I identified with the body? Was by developing my body as a child e.g. by ballet dancing, the way that I received affirmation from my environment, or have I rejected and dismissed the body?

▮ Have I repressed my feelings because strong feelings were not acceptable in my family? Or have I identified with my feelings as a way to get recognition/love rather than getting rejected for using my mind?

▮ Am I identified with the logical rational mind? As a way of avoiding feeling the pain of a terrible split or separation as a child, was using my mind to work things out the only way to survive? Or have I rejected the mind I have because it was not ok to be bright and smart in our house?

Psychosynthesis

In each of these scenarios we see the impact of identification and repression of body or feelings or mind, in one way or another limiting the ability of the Self to express itself.

By beginning to recognise our relationship to these three dimensions we begin to see where we may be over-identified. We can also perhaps see where we need to be identified in order either to reclaim parts of ourselves so that they can be developed over time to serve the Self, or where we need to disidentify so that we can access much more of our own beauty and richness.

Creativity

Ultimately, it is not enough to know that we experience the world, but through the processes of disidentification described so far, we come to know what is causal to our existence. This is dependent on the development of the capacity for Self-reflection and the consequent capacity for independent thought and action. We then become more than sensing responding Beings serving no more than our own independent survival, but active cooperative Beings serving and advancing the processes of evolution.

Further Reading

Ferrucci, Piero, *What We May Be*, Thorsons, 1995 (Chapter 2)

Psychosynthesis

Psychosynthesis
Research
Foundation

The Balancing and Synthesis of Opposites

Polarity is a universal fact; it is inherent in cosmic manifestation. It is true that the Ultimate and Supreme Reality is the One, the Absolute, the Transcendent; but it can only be defined by what it is not.

From the very moment that cosmic manifestation begins to unfold, duality is born. The first fundamental duality is precisely that between manifestation and the Unmanifest. In the *Bhagavad Gita* this is expressed in the words "Having pervaded the whole Universe with a fragment of myself, I remain." In the process of manifestation the fundamental polarity is that of Spirit and Matter.

It is at once necessary to state that all polarity is a relationship between two elements, and that, as such, it is never absolute, but relative even to a particular pair of opposites: the same element can be positive in its relation to a certain 'pole' and negative in its relation to another. An instance of the relativity of the 'polar relationships' exists in the fundamental polarity between Spirit and Matter. According to some, Spirit is the free and transcendent Reality which stands above the various pairs of opposites existing in manifested life. Such is the conception of Keyserling, contained in his book, *From Suffering to Fulfilment* (Selwyn and Blount) and *Das Buch vom Personlichen Leben*, Deutsche Verlag-Anstalt, 1936, pp 505, 510, 515) by the same writer). According to others, Spirit corresponds to the positive pole, to the dynamic and creative element in all duality. Such is Jung's idea. In other words, Keyserling regards the 'tension' between Spirit and the various manifestations of life as existing in a 'vertical' direction, which he refers to as the 'dimension of intensity', while Jung conceives polarity more as a horizontal relationship.

Physical Polarity

In the physical world, the most commonly recognised polarity is that between the positive and negative poles in electricity. This polarity is the basis of the constitution

Psychosynthesis

of matter since, as is well known, each atom contains charges of electricity differentiated into a positive nucleus and a varying number of negative electrons. Electric polarity manifests itself in various ways which have many practical applications, as in induced and alternating currents, etc. Interesting analogies can be found in various polarities in the field of psychology, such as emotional attraction and repulsion, ambivalence and the 'compensatory' function.

Within living organisms, such as the human body, there are various polarities. One of the most important is that between the sympathetic and the parasympathetic nervous systems: the former stimulates catabolism, the latter assimilation or anabolism. Other polarities exist between the different endocrine glands.

One of the most important and general polarities in the three kingdoms of organic life (vegetable, animal and human) is the sexual. The positive pole is represented by the masculine element, the negative by the feminine element. This does not mean that the former is active and the latter passive. Both are active, but in a different way, the masculine element being the dynamic, initiating pole, while the feminine element is the receptive, 'gestative', elaborative pole. This type of polarity extends far beyond the man-woman relationship to innumerable manifestations in life. It has been particularly and deeply emphasised by the Chinese who regard these two principles as the foundation both of cosmic evolution and of every aspect of human life. The creative aspect, symbolised by the father and Heaven, they call Yang, while Yin is the receptive and elaborative aspect, symbolised by the mother and the Earth. The well-being of Man depends, in the view of Chinese philosophy, on the harmonious accord between Man and the cyclic evolution of the Universe, woven from the innumerable relationships and interactions of Yang and Yin (numerous Chinese texts deal with this point. One of the most interesting is the *I Ching or The Book of Transformations* (RKP, 1951), which, disguised under the form of a method of divination, contains treasures of wisdom. Jung in *The Secret of the Golden Flower* (1962), and also Keyserling, expressed great appreciation of it).

Emotional Polarity

In the field of the emotions and feelings we find those dualities which are familiar to all: pleasure-pain, excitement-depression, confidence-fear, attraction-repulsion, love-hate. Such is their extent that one might say that the life of the average human being is based on his emotional reactions to things, to events and to persons. These reactions

---

have a definite function and purpose, provided they are maintained within appropriate bounds. But if we allow them to take over – as too often is the case – we are apt to become their slaves. Later we shall consider how the limitations of these opposites can be overcome.

Mental Polarity

In the mental realm there is the polarity between the analytical activity of the concrete mind and the synthetic operation of the abstract intelligence; between the inductive process (from the particular to the general) and the deductive process (from the general to the particular).

Consideration of the human personality in its totality discloses various fundamental polarities which have been extensively investigated by modern psychology. The knowledge about the human being acquired in this process has stimulated the development of important psychological, educational and psychotherapeutic techniques. The principal polarities here are: Body-Psyche, Consciousness-the Unconscious, the lower Unconscious-the Superconscious, Pathos (Receptivity, Sensitivity, Reactivity)-Ethos (Activity, Dynamism, Will), Eros (Feeling)-Logos (Reason).

Spiritual Polarity

The fundamental duality in the spiritual realm is that existing between the personality and the Transpersonal Self, a polarity which is the cause of many inner conflicts, until harmonious relationships and an increasing blending or unification (spiritual psychosynthesis) are achieved.

Interindividual Polarity

There are also many 'inter-individual' polarities which are of the utmost importance. The first and fundamental one is that existing, on all levels, between Man and Woman. Then there is that between adults and young people, particularly in the interaction between parents and their children. There are, further, the various relationships between individuals and the different groups to which they belong.

Among them we find the family considered as a unit, as a 'psychic entity', which is made up not only of members who are alive, but also of ancestral influences and family traditions. Such influences are sometimes a help to the individual, offering him an ideal and a way of life which he may be encouraged to live by. Other times, and perhaps more often, they may hem him in and even oppress him.

Then come the social groups of different kinds (social and professional classes, cultural and religious groups, nations) with which the individual may find himself associated, in a condition of passive subordination or of cooperation, as leader and directing agent or in conflict. Similar relationships exist among groups; both among those of the same kind and size (i.e. between families and families, classes and classes, nations and nations, etc.) and the 'hierarchical' ones (i.e. between the family and the state, classes and nations, between a state and a federation of states).

Two kinds of polarities which are of great importance are that between the northern and southern individuals and groups in each nation and continent and that between Western and Eastern peoples.

Balancing Opposite Poles

Each of these numerous polarities confronts us with the problem of their interplay and balancing. The following is a brief survey of the general principles and methods of balancing opposite poles with the object of resolving 'polar tensions':

1 *Fusion of the two poles*, involving the neutralisation of their charges of energy.

2 *Creation of a new being*, of a new reality.

3 *Adjustment of the opposite poles*, by means of an 'intermediary centre' or of a principle higher than both. A regulating action of this kind can be brought about in two ways:

▮ By diminishing the amplitude of the oscillations between the two extremes, at times even to vanishing point, thus inducing a more or less complete neutralisation ('the happy medium'). An instance of this, of great actual interest, is the oscillation between excessive authority, and uncontrolled freedom in education and the search for a balanced attitude

▮ By consciously and wisely directing the alternations so that the result is harmonious and constructive, and in accord with the cyclic alternations of both individual and general, human and cosmic, conditions (this is the method taught by Chinese philosophy and particularly by the *I Ching*)

Psychosynthesis

4 *Synthesis*, brought about by a higher element or principle which transforms, sublimates and reabsorbs the two poles into a higher reality

The different types of polarity require correspondingly appropriate solutions. Man often has the freedom – and consequently the responsibility – of choosing between different methods of balancing. It should, however, be pointed out that the indicated solutions are not always as clear-cut as the above enumeration might lead one to believe. Sometimes, as the following examples will show, they can overlap or be combined in various ways.

In the field of electricity, the most simple outcome is neutralisation through the fusion of the positive and negative charges. However, the conditions in which this fusion is effected determine the results, which are thus subject to considerable variation. When, for instance, the poles are brought towards each other, and the voltage with which they are charged overcomes the resistance of the medium which separates them, a discharge is produced which manifests as a spark. Lightning is an instance of this phenomenon. When, on the other hand, the poles are kept apart but connected by a conducting wire, with some 'resistance' introduced at a point along the conducting wire, the electrical energy becomes susceptible to various transformations. This latter process is being utilised with increasing ingenuity in the transformation of electricity into light, into heat, or into movement. In these cases the process of neutralisation produces various useful effects.

In the biological realm, health can be defined as a dynamic equilibrium ever threatened and ever restored between a series of polarities, such as exist between the divisions of the nervous system, between various endocrine glands, and in general between the anabolic and catabolic functions. In the same way, *psychological life can be regarded as a continual polarisation and tension between differing tendencies and functions, and as a continual effort, conscious or not, to establish equilibrium.* Among the most important psychological polarities are: impulse-inhibition, feeling-reason, extroversion-introversion.

In sexual polarity, the union of the two physical elements has a creative effect. The dynamism of their fusion brings about the birth of a new organism similar to that of the parents. In humanity this wonderful physical creative function is closely associated with the *psychological* polarities, and this often produces very complex situations and difficult problems.

Psychosynthesis

In the fields of drives, emotions and feelings, the balancing of opposite qualities requires the intervention of a higher regulating principle of a mental or transpersonal nature. The first task is to prevent the drives and the emotions from overwhelming and submerging the reason and the will. The best way to achieve this is to learn how to disidentify oneself from them at will, in order to be free at any time to maintain the 'I' as the centre of consciousness, on a higher level above them, in order to be able to observe and evaluate them, and to wisely regulate them as needed.

Let us make it clear that to regulate does not mean to 'suppress', and that this does not in any way lead to aridity or a lack of sensitivity. Let us, for example, consider a fundamental polarity, pleasure-pain. As long as we remain slaves of this duality, always actively seeking pleasure and fearfully fleeing from pain, we shall not find lasting peace or permanent satisfaction. On the other hand, a forced inhibition, an artificial impassivity, certainly does not constitute a satisfactory solution. This can only be arrived at by means of that clear insight which enables us to understand the causes, the nature and the functions of both pleasure and pain. This insight carries the recognition that, in accepting pleasure without craving for it and attachment to it, and in accepting pain, when unavoidable, without fearing it and rebelling against it, one can learn much from both pleasure and pain, and 'distil the essence' which they contain. Moreover, one can gradually raise the quality and level of these 'opposites'; one passes by degrees from the physical pleasures in and of themselves to the joys of feeling and of the mind, finally experiencing spiritual joy. One makes one's way from physical suffering to emotional troubles, to intellectual turmoils; then to compassion for the sufferings of others and then of the whole human race. From all these experiences one gathers the fruits of wisdom, and learns to keep the centre of consciousness stabilised more and more at a level above the alternations of personal pleasure and pain. Finally we can acquire the ability to identify ourselves with the Universal Life, with the Supraindividual Self, with the Supreme, which transcends all 'opposites' in ineffable bliss.

If we examine more closely the specific polarities of the emotional field, we can clearly distinguish two main types of solutions. One is realised on the same level; it can be called 'the middle way' of compromise, the blending of the two poles. The other solution is achieved at a higher level: it is the fusion of the poles into a higher *synthesis*.

The method of synthesis which is analogous in a certain sense to a chemical combination, includes and absorbs the two elements into a higher unity endowed with quali-

---

Psychosynthesis

ties differing from those of either of them. The difference between the solutions achieved through compromise and those brought about through synthesis can be clearly indicated by a triangular diagram. Here are a few examples:

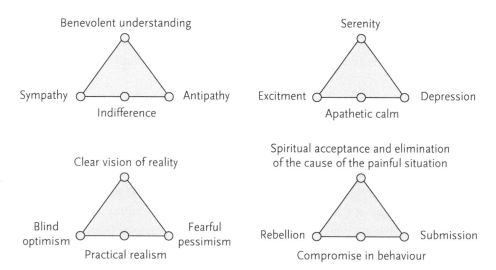

The polarity between 'mind' and 'heart', between reason and feeling (*logos* and *eros*), is regulated in the first place by the recognition of their respective functions and of the legitimate field of action of each of the two functions, so that neither dominates the other. This can be followed by a mutual and increasing cooperation and interpenetration between the two, finally arriving at the synthesis so well expressed by Dante in the words 'Intellectual light full of love'.

The polarity between sensitivity and receptivity (*pathos*) and dynamism or Will (*ethos*) which, in a wider sense, corresponds to psychosexual polarity – for the former pole is the 'feminine' and the latter the 'masculine' modality – can also at first be controlled by a balanced adjustment, to be superseded by a creative synthesis.

The fundamental polarity between the human personality as a whole and the spiritual Self can also be resolved into a unity. This is the aim of the process of harmonisation and transmutation involving a protracted series of conflicts, approaches, and contacts, each producing partial, increasingly expanded fusions. In short, this is the process of spiritual psychosynthesis. It constitutes the noble effort, the central drama of Man who, either consciously or unconsciously, aspires to this high goal, or is pushed

Psychosynthesis

towards it by his inability to find lasting satisfaction or a true peace until he has attained it.

The interaction between the Self and the personality creates a series of 'triangular' relationships similar to those previously indicated. Here are some of them:

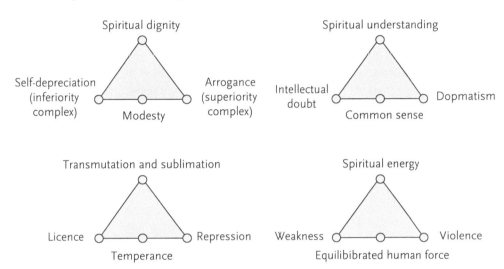

The various equilibrations, adjustments and syntheses can be produced in different ways. At times, they are preceded by intense crises and conflicts. In other cases they are reached in a more gradual and harmonious way by means of a progressive decrease in the oscillations of the 'pendulum'. A clear understanding of this process of synthesis enables one to achieve it more easily and rapidly. The essential requirement, as previously mentioned, is to avoid identifying oneself with either of the two opposite poles, and to control, transmute, and direct their energies from a higher centre of awareness and power.

Roberto Assagioli (reprinted from the Psychosynthesis Research Foundation, 1972)

Psychosynthesis

Chapter 3 Models of the Personality – Subpersonalities

The One and the Many

Psychosynthesis describes an evolutionary process whereby entities come together and higher order patterns come into expression. Working with the personality works with the vehicle which brings the Self into expression. This process of evolution is towards Synthesis whereby parts become wholes. We look at the diverse parts, in order to move towards harmony and unity. There is then conscious cooperation with the process.

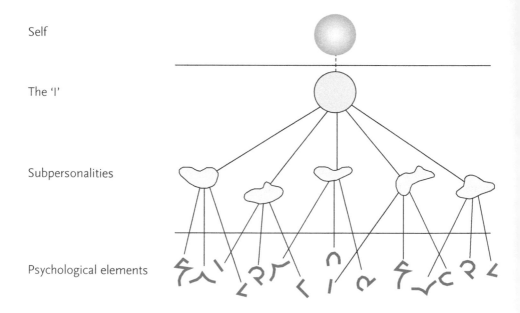

Self

The 'I'

Subpersonalities

Psychological elements

The multiplicity which makes up the many parts of the personality organises around a higher order centre – the 'I' – which integrates the elements into a coherent whole. The centre attracts psychological elements around an inner drive to create what can be considered to be its own body – its vehicle of expression, the subpersonalities. The outer core of this drive is expressed as a want and connects to social programming. At a deeper level this want manifests as a need which is transpersonal in nature, through which the personality is a vehicle for expression of the Self. The 'want' is learned from

the environment to satisfy the deeper need, and the form – the subpersonality – limits the quality of the Self.

A subpersonality can be seen as a synthesis of traits, habit patterns, complexes and other psychological elements which become organised around a centre, an inner drive or urge which strives to be expressed or realised.

Overview of the Model

The subpersonality model offers a systems view of the personality; the one and the many. We only have to reflect a little upon our behaviour in the world to see that it is often different in different situations; that in taking on certain roles or in entering particular types of situation (say, where there are new people, or where we come up against authority figures, or people at work or at a party) our behaviours and our characteristics tend to be of a certain type. In reflecting on this, we may begin to recognise that we have different sets of characteristics and behaviours which may dominate at particular times. In this way we can begin to distinguish subpersonalities, named characters who appear on the stage of our lives, seemingly, at will.

There may, for instance, be a Rebel-type who tends to emerge when we come into contact with authority. We may find that a gregarious Entertainer takes over when we are in a crowd or that a shy and self-effacing Wallflower keeps us out of contact with others. We may find we are repeatedly surprised by the strength of a subpersonality – maybe a Critic or a Victim – who tends to take over in close personal relationships, sabotaging our conscious intention to create harmony.

In any of these cases, there will be certain strengths and weaknesses inherent in the subpersonality; qualities which have the potential, if released and directed appropriately, to bring positive benefits in our lives, or habitual ways of behaving which cause us trouble and unhappiness. The degree to which the different subpersonalities which coexist within each of us can be brought under our control and conscious direction determines the degree to which we can build harmony in our inner world and in our outer relationships.

We may think of the subpersonalities as the instruments in an orchestra. Each has a part to play, has its own unique voice to sound; but the orchestra must be under the control and direction of the conductor – the 'I' – who decides which instrument plays when, how loud and for how long. Operating in this way means not only that we can reduce the amount of internal conflict which we may feel, but also that we can begin to express ourselves more fully in the world, in all our potential.

The difficulty is that our subpersonalities are often not under the control and direction of the central coordinating function in the personality. This may be because history has taught us to suppress certain of their characteristics (whether these be 'positive' or 'negative') or because really to acknowledge the existence of the subpersonality would be to open to a deep level of pain, or need, or vulnerability; because each subpersonality has formed itself partly as a defensive structure, it carries history and wounding, and it has developed a pattern of behaviour and response designed to protect us from further wounding.

Because the nature and design of the subpersonality tend to remain unconscious, the behaviours remain outside our control and the potential strengths and capabilities of that part of ourselves remain unavailable to us.

Suppressing or ignoring the subpersonality does not make it go away. We should remember that each subpersonality is a vehicle for Self, that each part contains a fragment of the whole which is bound to seek to express its true nature, though this may be in a form which has become distorted or degraded. Thus it contains, at the core, and beyond its outer behaviour, its demands and its deeper needs, a transpersonal quality seeking expression.

The Five-Stage Model of Harmonisation

This model offers a means of bringing a subpersonality fully into our awareness and, through a process of acceptance and understanding, beginning to harness its potential and direct its energy so that it can operate in harmony with other subpersonalities and, ultimately, in relationship to others and in the world.

The key is, who chooses the roles we play? Often it is not the 'I' but the semi-autonomous individual subpersonalities with the resultant inner conflict. When any succeed, others are cut off. They are still very much present and demanding attention. The more integrated the personality, the more the 'I' has the capacity to choose.

Psychosynthesis

■ Recognition: subpersonalities develop unconsciously. Initially during this stage we develop awareness as to how they operate, and see how they shape our view of ourselves and the world. The more the individual becomes conscious of the parts, the more a sense of 'I-ness' – the one who chooses – develops. Within the complexity of 'I am this, that and the other', comes 'I am all of this – I am me'

■ Acceptance: this stage is devoted to seeing 'what is' without value judgement. This is often difficult because the process of limitation described above may cause the subpersonality to be viewed in a negative light. The more a part is suppressed, the more it asserts itself. This requires time to work through

■ Coordination: this is the stage of inner refinement. Exploring the deeper need aids the evolution of the subpersonality as well as increases the capacity to choose how to 'Be' in the world. Initially, when recognised, the need seems to take over as if the subpersonality is starving, but time and space allowed for this need to be expressed brings maturity and cooperation

■ Integration: this brings the subpersonality into relationship with other parts and through a process of time-sharing brings deeper needs into expression. Initially, there may be conflict between the parts; this is followed by cooperation and harmony with more nourishment and space for the personality as a whole to develop

■ Synthesis: this final stage is mediated by the self, or 'I', which brings the personality into relationship with the world, and by the Higher Self, allowing values and altruism to emerge

Exercise Following This Section

The following exercise on the Evening Review serves to build awareness of these subpersonalities and the ways in which our freedom to choose how to be in our lives is limited.

Further Reading

Assagioli, Roberto, *Psychosynthesis: A Manual of Principles and Techniques*, Harper Collins, 1993 (Chapter 3)

Ferrucci, Piero, *What We May Be*, Thorsons, 1995 (Chapter 4)

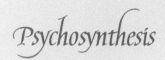

The Evening Review Exercise

What is happening in your life? Do you allow yourself the time to really look? Many of us keep a close watch over how we spend our money, but have only a vague awareness of how we are using our time. Modern psychology has demonstrated that we live our lives more unconsciously than we think. Yet consciousness can be increased. As we become more aware of how we are living our lives, we can also become more aware of other possibilities and options. Through increased awareness, we increase our ability to live our lives the way we choose, unhindered by our habits, by our fears, by our past.

The Evening Review is a technique for increasing this awareness. It is deceptively simple, and even obvious – yet it is very powerful. It cuts through all kinds of vague impressions about how your life is going so that you can encounter and understand more fully what is actually happening. The basic technique is as follows:

1 At the end of the day, preferably just before going to sleep, find a quiet place free from outer distractions.

2 Close your eyes, give attention to relaxing your body, quieting your feelings, and as much as possible stilling the activity of your thoughts. Your mind should be quiet and receptive, but remain alert.

3 Now review your day in your mind, playing it back like a movie, but backwards, beginning with where you are right now, then the time of late evening, then early evening, then the dinner hour, and the late afternoon and so on until morning when you awakened.

4 Throughout the experience it is important to maintain as much as possible the attitude of an objective, detached, non-critical observer, calmly and clearly registering the events of the day, neither becoming elated at a success, nor depressed and unhappy about a failure. The aim is not to relive the experience, but to register non-critically in consciousness the patterns and meaning of the day.

5 Finally, write down your general impressions of what happened and anything particular that you have learned.

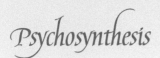

Variations

There are many variations of the Evening Review. In the form just described, it is very effective for gaining a greater sense of the whole of our lives. It can also be modified to focus on a particular aspect that is currently in need of special attention. Some of these aspects are as follows:

Subpersonalities

An important application of the Evening Review is in the work with subpersonalities. During the review, you can focus on such questions as:
▌ Which subpersonalities were dominant during the day?
▌ What circumstances (inner or outer) made them emerge or withdraw?
▌ Did any of your subpersonalities come into conflict with each other?
▌ How much did the subpersonalities help or hinder what you wanted to do? Who was in the driver's seat?

The Evening Review can be used for getting in touch with a multitude of subpersonalities, or it can be used for focusing on one or two that are in need of special attention.

Often, as we begin to work with subpersonalities, we have an inaccurate impression of which ones are truly the most dominant. One client, a middle-aged businessman, discovered (in a guided day-dream) a subpersonality, which he called 'The Spiritual Seeker'. The Seeker was very upset because, he claimed, another subpersonality, 'The Materialist', was dominant and in control, and was not allowing him any space. During the discussion afterwards, the client said he could not understand why the Seeker was so upset. Perhaps the Seeker was too critical or demanding. The client did not feel that the Materialist was excessively dominant at all, so the counsellor suggested that he do an Evening Review, focusing on which subpersonalities were the most active during his day. Two weeks later he returned, overwhelmed with the discovery that the Materialist was indeed his most dominant subpersonality, taking tremendous amounts of his time and energy and generally interfering with any activity the Materialist did not approve of. Having recognised the amount of control which the Materialist exerted, the client was motivated to do what was needed to change the situation and was then able to allow time and space in his life for the Spiritual Seeker. (Note to professionals – As can be seen by this client's discovery, the Evening Review is of real usefulness in helping a client recognise, on his own, some pattern of his behaviour he may be ignoring or resisting. A client may show resistance to a therapist's suggestion that a problem area may exist and is worth exploring. But frequently, by means of an Evening Review, the client will discover the problem by himself, and will thus become motivated to work on it.)

Managing Your Time

An area that frequently needs attention is that of time management. How many people feel their lives are not what they could be, simply because 'there isn't enough time'. Certainly much of our time is spent in activities that are important or necessary – that we can't, or don't want to eliminate – working, caring for home and family, sleeping and eating. But many minutes and even hours of our day are spent, without our quite being aware of it, in less important or outright trivial activities that we would not consciously *choose* to do, but that we allow to slip in almost automatically, due to external pressure or routine habits. It is useful to realise that beginning from this moment, we always have an unlimited amount of time before us. The question – and the source of the difficulty – is how we choose to use it. The Evening Review is an ideal technique for becoming more aware of how you are choosing to use your time.

A young woman who was in a great deal of conflict around the fact that she 'did not have enough time', felt that she had to exclude one of the two major activities in her life, and was in considerable conflict over which it should be. She tried the Evening Review, focusing on precisely how much time she devoted to each area of activity. It was not long before she discovered, to her genuine surprise, that activities which were of very little importance to her were consuming vast amounts of her time. She found she did not have to exclude either one of her favourite activities. She simply had to become more aware of herself, so she would no longer be distracted by unimportant activities.

Other Applications

The Evening Review can be used to expand our awareness of nearly any issue that is at the forefront of our growth. Someone who tends to ignore or repress feelings can review the day looking for emotional experiences and thereby bring them into greater awareness. Someone who excessively withholds his energy can watch for times he was withholding, and what feelings caused him to do it – *when* does he withhold, *what*

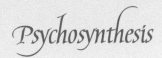

does he withhold? By increasing awareness he increases the number of his alternatives, his options to try out new behaviour.

The Evening Review can also be helpful for developing desired qualities, such as serenity, openness, or courage. Reviewing the times during the day when we were able to express these qualities will help us understand and appreciate them more, and will help us also discover which circumstances and situations make it difficult for us to express them.

Patterns to Watch For

The most common pattern to guard against in using the Evening Review is the tendency we all have to react emotionally to a review of our day. As we said, during this exercise we need to avoid becoming elated at a success, or depressed and unhappy at what we see as failure. Such an emotional involvement in the exercise gets in the way of its purpose – the calm and objective registering in consciousness of the day's pattern and meaning. When these feelings emerge, we can remind ourselves once again to shift our focus, gently, to the position of the objective observer.

If maintaining the position of the observer is very hard or impossible for you, it is best to postpone using this exercise and to practise instead taking the position of the observer at various times during the day. After you gain facility in doing so, you can try the exercise again.

Some people have such a strong inner critic that they find it impossible to review their day without constantly judging and evaluating their actions. In this case it may be best to suspend the Evening Review and work with their critical subpersonality. After a while, the Evening Review may be useful in this work. For example, when working with a critical subpersonality who only sees failure, one can do an Evening Review, in writing, to look for successes. In this way, the Evening Review can be used to break down the perceptual distortions created by subpersonalities.

People who are excessively introverted, who spend much of their time in their own inner world, would do well not to give further attention to subjective experiences. For this reason, the Evening Review in general may not be as desirable for them. At times, however, it may be helpful if a strong emphasis is placed on recording the external

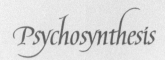
activities of the day. In this way, the person can increase his awareness of an interest in the 'outer' world.

Questions Frequently Asked

How Often Should I do the Evening Review?

Once a day, in the evening, preferably for at least one week. When you do the Evening Review over a number of weeks you will create a continuity so that you can observe larger patterns and long-term trends not otherwise apparent.

How Long does it Normally Take?

This depends on how deeply you want to explore. The basic review – quickly rerunning the day's events to increase your general awareness – usually takes less than five minutes. You may also use it as a daily 'workshop', where you can do some in-depth exploration of a particular pattern or subpersonality, in which case it may take longer.

What Shall I Write Down in My Workbook Afterwards?

Besides taking notes on the area you are currently exploring, you may want to write down general impressions and especially anything which came into your awareness that was new or surprising, that you hadn't clearly seen during the day. The purpose of the exercise is to increase your awareness. And as you gain new awareness, it is helpful to strengthen and solidify it through writing.

Why is the Day Run Backwards Rather Than Forwards?

Experience has shown that reviewing the day from evening to morning, although not essential, is more effective. It also seems that this is how the mind more easily plays back stored experience and is therefore the most natural route for us to follow. People who come close to dying have reported that they saw their whole life 'pass before their eyes', moving backwards through the years. This movement backwards as a means of exploration is also a major element in psychotherapy. We begin with our present condition and, as we explore the underlying dynamics, move backwards to earlier time periods.

Psychosynthesis

Chapter 4 Identity and Personal Freedom

Disidentification and the 'I-Self'

"We are dominated by everything with which our self becomes identified. We can dominate and control everything from which we disidentify ourselves."
(Assagioli, Roberto, 1965)

As we have seen from Assagioli's Egg Diagram, the 'I-Self' is central to psychosynthesis thinking where the Self is held to be both individual and universal, and the 'I' is the reflection of that Self within the personality. We can think of the 'I' as that much of Self that we can be aware of and express at any point in time.

What this means is that the Self is present at all times, dimly experienced and perceived in the depths of our unconsciousness and increasingly experienced as we awake to greater levels of awareness of our authentic identity and historical identifications. With this awakening comes the possibility of conscious choice as to whether it is appropriate to be identified or to act differently. In this way we become more 'I' conscious and release the personal will to take responsibility for our spiritual Being. This process of increasing awareness of identification and gradual dis-identification, as a practice, is also a central contribution of psychosynthesis to psychology.

In effect the latter exercise is a deep spiritual practice which acknowledges the power and importance of identification and also acknowledges, when we are ready to let go of an identification, that 'I' (the 'I-Self') am not that identification; that 'I' exist beyond this identification and that 'I' am a centre of awareness and Will.

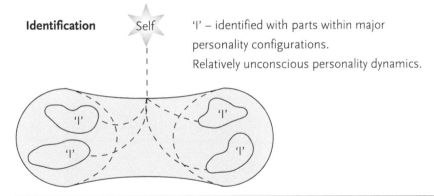

Identification   Self   'I' – identified with parts within major personality configurations.
Relatively unconscious personality dynamics.

Psychosynthesis

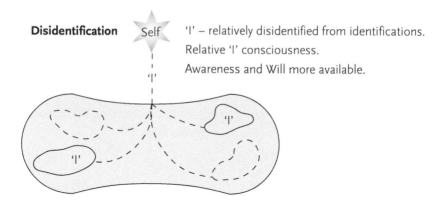

Disidentification   Self   'I' – relatively disidentified from identifications.
Relative 'I' consciousness.
Awareness and Will more available.

Exercises Following This Section

The following exercises on Disidentification and Self-identification' and Who Am I?
deal in some depth with these core elements of psychosynthesis and we encourage
readers to use them on a regular basis.

Further Reading

Assagioli, Roberto, *Psychosynthesis: A Manual of Principles and Techniques*, Harper
Collins, 1993 (pp 111-125)

Assagioli, Roberto, *The Act of Will*, David Platt, 1999 (Chapters 2, 3 and 4)

Ferrucci, Piero, *What We May Be*, Thorsons, 1995 (Chapter 5)

De Vries, Marco, *The Redemption of the Intangible in Medicine*, Institute of
Psychosynthesis, 1981 (Chapter 3)

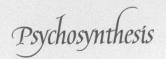

Disidentification and Self-Identification Exercise

The central, fundamental experience of self-consciousness, the discovery of the 'I', is implicit in our human consciousness ('self-consciousness' is used here in the purely psychological sense of being aware of oneself as a distinct individual and not in the customary sense of egocentric and even neurotic 'self-centeredness'). It is that which distinguishes our consciousness from that of the animals, which are conscious but not self-conscious. But generally this self consciousness is indeed 'implicit' rather than explicit. It is experienced in a nebulous and distorted way because it is usually mixed with and veiled by the *contents* of consciousness.

This constant input of influences veils the clarity of consciousness and produces spurious identifications of the self with the content of consciousness, rather than with consciousness *itself*. If we are to make self-consciousness explicit, clear, and vivid, we must first *dis*identify ourselves from the contents of our consciousness.

More specifically, the habitual state for most of us is to be identified with that which seems, at any one time, to give us the greatest sense of aliveness, which seems to us to be most real, or most intense.

This identification with a *part* of ourselves is usually related to the predominant function or focus of our awareness, to the predominant role we play in life. It can take many forms. Some people are identified with their bodies. They experience themselves, and often talk about themselves, mainly in terms of sensation; in other words they function as if they *were* their bodies. Others are identified with their feelings; they experience and describe their state of being in affective terms, and believe their feelings to be the central and most intimate part of themselves, while thoughts and sensations are perceived as more distant, perhaps somewhat separate. Those who are identified with their minds are likely to describe themselves with intellectual constructs, even when asked how they *feel*. They often consider feelings and sensations as peripheral, or are largely unaware of them. Many are identified with a role, and live, function, and experience themselves *in terms of that role*, such as mother, husband, wife, student, businessman, teacher, etc.

This identification with only a *part* of our personality may be temporarily satisfactory, but it has serious drawbacks. It prevents us from realising the experience of the 'I', the

Psychosynthesis

deep sense of self-identification, of knowing who we are. It excludes, or greatly decreases, the ability to identify with all the other parts of our personality, to enjoy them and utilise them to their full extent. Thus our 'normal' expression in the world is limited at any one time to only a fraction of what it can be. The conscious – or even unconscious – realisation that we somehow do not have access to much that is in us can cause frustration and painful feelings of inadequacy and failure.

Finally, a continuing identification with either a role or a predominant function leads often, and almost inevitably, to a precarious life situation resulting sooner or later in a sense of loss, even despair, such as in the case of an athlete who grows old and loses his physical strength; an actress whose physical beauty is fading; a mother whose children have grown up and left her; or a student who has to leave school and face a new set of responsibilities. Such situations can produce serious and often very painful crises. They can be considered as more or less partial psychological 'deaths'. No frantic clinging to the waning old 'identity' can avail. The true solution can be only a 'rebirth' that is, entering into a new and broader identification. This sometimes involves the whole personality and requires and leads to an awakening or 'birth' into a new and higher state of *being*. The process of death and rebirth was symbolically enacted in various mystery rites and has been lived and described in religious terms by many mystics. At present it is being rediscovered in terms of transpersonal experiences and realisations.

This process often occurs without a clear understanding of its meaning and often against the wish and will of the individual involved in it. But a conscious, purposeful, willing cooperation can greatly facilitate, foster, and hasten it.

It can be best done by a deliberate exercise of *disidentification* and *self-identification*. Through it we gain the *freedom* and the *power of choice* to be identified with, or disidentified from, any aspect of our personality, according to what seems to us most appropriate in each situation. Thus we can learn to master, direct, and utilise all the elements and aspects of our personality, in an inclusive and harmonious synthesis. Therefore this exercise is considered as basic in psychosynthesis.

Identification Exercise

This exercise is intended as a tool for achieving the consciousness of the self, and the ability to focus our attention sequentially on each of our main personality aspects, roles, etc. We then become clearly aware of and can examine their qualities while maintaining the point of view of the observer, and recognising that *the observer is not that which he observes*.

In the form which follows, the first phase of the exercise – the disidentification – consists of three parts dealing with the physical, emotional, and mental aspects of awareness. This leads to the self-identification phase. Once some experience is gained with it, the exercise can be expanded or modified according to need, as will be indicated further on.

Procedure

Put your body in a comfortable and relaxed position, and slowly take a few deep breaths (preliminary exercises of relaxation can be useful). Then make the following affirmation, slowly and thoughtfully:

▍ **I have** a body but **I am not** my body. My body may find itself in different conditions of health or sickness, it may be rested or tired, but that has nothing to do with my self, my real 'I'. I value my body as my precious instrument of experience and of action in the outer world, but it is only an instrument. I treat it well, I seek to keep it in good health but it is not myself. I have a body but I am not my body

Now close your eyes, recall briefly in your consciousness the general substance of this affirmation, and then gradually focus your attention on the central concept: '**I have** a body, but **I am not** my body'. Attempt, as much as you can, to realise this as an experienced fact in your consciousness. Then open your eyes and proceed the same way with the next two stages:

▍ **I have** emotions, but **I am not** my emotions. My emotions are diversified, changing, sometimes contradictory. They may swing from love to hatred, from calm to anger, from joy to sorrow, and yet my essence – my true nature – does not change. 'I' remain. Though a wave of anger may temporarily submerge me, I know that it will pass in time; therefore **I am not** this anger. Since I can observe and understand my emotions, and then gradually learn to direct, utilise, and integrate them harmoniously, it is clear that they are not my self. **I have** emotions, but **I am not** my emotions

▍ **I have** a mind but **I am not** my mind. My mind is a valuable tool of discovery and expression, but **it is not** the essence of my being. Its contents are constantly changing as it embraces new ideas, knowledge, and experience. *Often it refuses to obey me! Therefore, it cannot be me, my self.* It is an *organ of knowledge* in regard to both the

Psychosynthesis

outer and the inner worlds, but it is **not my self**. **I have** a mind, but **I am not** my mind

Next comes the phase of *identification*. Affirm slowly and thoughtfully:

▌ After the disidentification of *myself*, the 'I', from the contents of consciousness, such as sensations, emotions, thoughts, *I recognise and affirm that I am a centre of pure self-consciousness. I am a centre of will*, capable of observing, directing, and using all my psychological processes and my physical body

Focus your attention on the central realisation: 'I am a centre of pure self-consciousness and of will.' Attempt, as much as you can, to realise this as an *experienced* fact in your awareness.

As the purpose of the exercise is to achieve a specific state of consciousness, once that purpose is grasped much of the procedural detail can be dispensed with. Thus, after having practised it for some time – and some might do this from the very beginning – one can modify the exercise by going swiftly and dynamically through each of the stages of disidentification, using only the central affirmation of each stage and concentrating on its *experiential* realisation:

▌ **I have** a body, but **I am not** my body

▌ **I have** emotions, but **I am not** my emotions

▌ **I have** a mind, but **I am not** my mind

At this point it is valuable to make a deeper consideration of the stage of self-identification along the following lines:

▌ What am I then? What remains after having disidentified myself from my body, my sensations, my feelings, my desires, my mind, my actions? It is the essence of myself – *a centre of pure self-consciousness*. It is the permanent factor in the ever-varying flow of my personal life. It is that which gives me a sense of being, of permanence, of inner balance. *I affirm my identity with this centre* and realise its permanency and its energy

[pause]

▌ I recognise and affirm myself as a centre of pure self-awareness and of creative, dynamic energy. I realise that from this centre of true identity I can learn to observe, direct, and harmonise all the psychological processes and the physical body. I will to achieve a constant awareness of this fact in the midst of my everyday life, and to use it to help me and give increasing meaning and direction to my life

As the attention is shifted increasingly to the *state of consciousness*, the identification stage also can be abridged. The goal is to gain enough facility with the exercise so that one can go through each stage of disidentification swiftly and dynamically in a short time, and then remain in the 'I' consciousness for as long as desired. One can then – at will and at any moment – disidentify from any over-powering emotion, annoying thought, inappropriate role, etc., and from the vantage point of the detached observer gain a clearer understanding of the situation, its meaning, its causes, and the most effective way to deal with it.

This exercise has been found most effective if practised daily, preferably during the first hours of the day. Whenever possible, it is to be done shortly after waking up and considered as a symbolic second awakening. It is also of great value to repeat it in its brief form several times during the day, returning to the state of disidentified 'I' consciousness.

The exercise may be modified appropriately, according to one's own purpose and existential needs, by adding stages of disidentification to include other functions besides the three fundamental ones (physical, emotional, mental), as well as subpersonalities, roles, etc. It can also begin with disidentification from material possessions. Some examples follow:

▌ **I have** desires, but **I am not** my desires. Desires are aroused by drives, physical and emotional, and by other influences. They are often changeable and contradictory, with alterations of attraction and repulsion; therefore they are not my self. **I have** desires, but **I am not** my desires. (This is best placed between the emotional and mental stage)

▌ I engage in various activities and play many roles in life. I must play these roles and I willingly play them as well as possible, be it the role of son or father, wife or husband, teacher or student, artist or executive. But I am more than the son, the father, the artist. These are roles, specific but partial roles, which I, myself, am playing, agree to play, can watch and observe myself playing. Therefore I am not any of them. I am self-identified, and I am not only the actor, but the director of the acting

Psychosynthesis

This exercise can be and is being performed very effectively in groups. The group leader voices the affirmations and the members listen with eyes closed, letting the significance of the words penetrate deeply.

Roberto Assagioli (extract from The Act of Will, Turnstone Press, 1974, Appendix 1)

Psychosynthesis

Who am I? Exercise

This exercise is designed to help one develop self-awareness and reach toward one's true self. It is based on the assumption that in each one of us there are various layers surrounding the central core. These layers of self-perceptions, which may be positive or negative, represent different aspects of our personality and of our relationship to the world. Some of the layers may be like a facade or mask hiding those aspects of ourselves we do not like. Others may function as protective layers or shells, but somewhere within each of us lies a deep centre which is positive and creative – the true self, the innermost essence of our being. The Who Am I? exercise, repeated at frequent intervals, leads one to look deeper and deeper within oneself with successive attempts to answer the question. Thus one reaches progressively toward the source of one's being, toward one's true centre of identity. This exercise may be used also as an indicator of change, and utilised over a period of time, can provide valuable insight into the direction of one's own growth.

Procedure

Step 1

Select a place where you are quiet and undisturbed. Take a sheet of paper from your loose-leaf workbook, write the date at the top, and give your page the title 'Who Am I?' Then write your answer to this question as freely and as honestly as possible.

Step 2

Sit in a relaxed position. Close your eyes. Clear your mind. Ask yourself again 'Who Am I?' and this time look for the answer in the form of an image on the screen of your mind. Do not try to reason or interpret at this point. Simply look for an image and write down whatever you saw, giving as much detail as possible. Write down any feelings you had about this image and what it meant to you.

Step 3

Now stand up and close your eyes. Ask yourself, once again, 'Who Am I?' and this time let your body answer the question. Let it move, spontaneously, in whatever way it wants, to tell you who you are. If a movement begins, go with it. Really experience this movement and be aware of your feelings as you move. Then write down any feelings or insights that this movement may have given you.

It is recommended that you continue to use this method as a means of furthering your own growth and self-knowledge. It has been found that continuing gains are made with its repeated use.

(Adapted from 'Approaches to the Self: the 'Who am I?' Techniques in Psychotherapy' by Martha Crampton and G Taylor, Psychosynthesis Research Foundation, 1968)

Psychosynthesis

SYNTHESIS

Identity and Personal Freedom

Lisa is a woman in her mid-thirties who is vital, outgoing, loving and creative. She's a wife and mother who has written two books and has a third in progress. Her own paintings hang on the walls of her home, and although there is always something going on she is calm and cheerful, rarely losing her sense of humour.

She wasn't always like this. When I first knew her, she was quite depressed and withdrawn. The change over the past six years, although gradual, has been remarkable. I asked her to describe this process of change as she experienced it:

'I know that the change in me has taken years to work out and become real, but there was a central moment – one point in time – when something happened to me. I saw something about myself, really understood it, and from then on I had something that couldn't be lost. It has never been the same since.

My relationship with my husband had been really bad. He was not a kind man, and had troubles of his own. He felt embarrassed and ashamed of me, and was always putting me down. My father, too, had been excessively critical of me in my childhood, and I guess I was trying to make up for not having won his love and approval by winning Ralph's, instead. As the years went by I felt more and more that I was a terrible, inadequate, wrong person. This hurt me deeply – I was always hurting so much during those years. I had to deaden myself, so I wouldn't feel the pain and could cope.

But I kept sinking into the pain and depression anyway. One day I began to think about suicide. That shocked me – like an electric shock. I remember that I sort of jumped back from myself and said, 'My God, what am I doing? Where am I?' It was as if a veil had been lifted from my eyes. I could think clearly. I felt like I was waking up from a sleep. And then I had a sudden, striking realisation: 'I don't *have* to be like this. I can *choose* not to be this way!' *That was it*. That was the moment.

Psychosynthesis

I saw that the problem wasn't that Ralph or my father or anyone else was causing me all this pain. *I was allowing it to happen,* playing right along, acting my role of 'victim' perfectly. Oh yes, I was very good at it. I was sunk in this pattern of behaviour, submerged in it. It was as if I were trapped. I truly believed that I *was* this 'Victim'.

But in that instant I realised that I was not a Victim – it was only a role, and *I could choose to play any role I wanted.* I understood that I, myself, was in some very profound way, distinct from all my roles and all my characteristics and possessions. It was as if I were stripped of everything that I had thought was 'me'. This was what I had imagined dying would be like, yet there I was, more alive and more awake than I had ever been in my life. I don't really know how to describe it. I was just 'I', solid, whole, *there.*

So that was how all these changes began. Now I have a deep sense of wholeness and OK-ness inside, and even when I feel hurt and confused I know that I'm really not these feelings – I am *me!*

Of course I still have to work at remembering all this, that I am not a put-upon, put-down Victim. And it isn't always easy. At times, I get caught up in it again. But every time it is quicker and easier for me to come out from under. Since I've begun working on this, I've discovered all sorts of good things about myself, and it's exciting just to be alive, to be me.'

Experiences like Lisa's, experiences of liberation or *disidentification* from a specific, restrictive state of consciousness, are not uncommon. Yet they often go unrecognised. Many people have had similar experiences, though they are usually less dramatic, and so less easy to understand for what they are. Because of this lack of understanding, many miss the opportunity of applying them and making such lasting changes in their lives as Lisa did.

Furthermore, when these experiences are not understood, they may be disturbing. When we are completely identified with any one thing, we think, we feel, and act accordingly. We then believe that we are for example, 'rational', or we *are* a 'victim' or we *are* 'strong', and we begin to feel that we are this *to the exclusion of all else.* The prospect of letting go of what we are so strongly identified with can then become frightening, even inconceivable. We feel as if it is our very self that will be lost.

Psychosynthesis

For our sense of self, of 'I-ness', of personal identity, is perhaps the most precious thing we have. So we often fight against ourselves and against our urge to grow in order to preserve this sense of self untouched, even if it is restricted by specific identifications.

Years ago, if someone had told Lisa that she was not really a victim, but had become identified with playing that role, she would have felt extremely threatened. Her identification with being a victim was so total and so complete that she could not see beyond it. She was submerged in 'victim-hood'. She related to other people, to situations, to objects, as a victim. She felt and thought as a victim. One could say that, for all practical purposes, she was a victim – down-trodden, unfairly wounded, persecuted. Even her posture reflected it. And to a large extent her identity was self-perpetuating: because she looked and acted like a victim, people tended to treat her like one. This reinforced her self-image, maintaining the status quo.

Her perception of other people and of her environment was also limited by her identification. She gazed out at the world through 'victim-coloured' glasses, and all the data she gathered from her environment had to pass through this filter of victim-hood. So the happenings around her became distorted and misinterpreted to fit with her identity as a victim, reinforcing that identity. And because Lisa's perception of the environment was distorted by her self-image, so too were her responses. She was not responding to what was really happening, but to the 'victim's' perception of it.

While Lisa's situation was rather extreme, it applies to some extent to most people. One is often identified with something, and tends to respond to his or her own filtered perceptions, rather than to what is actually there. But we can become aware of our identifications. And the more we are aware of what we are identified with, the clearer our perceptions of the world become. *Awareness of an identification is the first step to becoming free from its restrictions and distortions*. With this awareness, we can learn to choose at will, and according to our need, to identify with, or disidentify from the many inner and outer elements and qualities that surround our 'I', or personal self. This is the basis of real freedom, and of realising our true identity.

Varieties of Identifications

Identification with a variety of diverse elements occurs in everyone. It is a natural psychological process. According to June, "One or another basic instinct, or complex of

Psychosynthesis

ideas, will invariably concentrate upon itself the greatest sum of psychic energy and thus force the ego into its service. As a rule the ego[1] is drawn into this focus of energy so powerfully that it identifies with it..." (CG Jung, 'Two Essays on Analytical Psychology', RFC Hull (trans), World, Cleveland, 1969, p 82). In other words, we experience a variety of pulls on our awareness, originating from many different sources. And in general, as long as we are not aware of our identifications *we tend to identify with whatever has the greatest 'pull' on our consciousness*: whatever we perceive as most interesting, most important, most central. This could be whatever makes us feel more alive, more ourselves – whatever best allows our energy to flow, or whatever fulfils our strongest desire, need or urge. Thus we can identify with objects, such as our house; with roles, such as being a mother; with specific psychological formations, such as the victim; or with one of our basic personality functions, such as the mind, or feelings.

Because these identifications are usually unconscious, we may identify with something that, if we thought about it objectively, we would *know* is not really us. For instance, I know a man in his late forties who almost seems *to be* his car. It's a very expensive foreign model, and he spends most of his free time with it. He talks to it, tunes it, waxes and polishes it. Then he drives around town and shows it off.

One Sunday afternoon he came out of a friend's house to find his parked car scratched on the outside front fender. He was very disturbed, and felt physically uncomfortable driving his car all that day. Not until he could take it into the body shop the next day did he feel at ease. And one time when the muffler became too noisy he was mortified. He felt ashamed, awkward and unpresentable. He felt that he couldn't 'go out this way', he didn't 'look right'. He drove on the side streets to avoid being seen and took a taxi to a cocktail party. If the car is insulted, *he* feels insulted. And if the car is praised, *he* feels praised. It's not clear to him where its boundaries end and his begin (a conscious experience of change in boundaries as a result of a new identification is described in 'Fat Self, Thin Self', *Synthesis*, Vol 1, No 1, 1974). He once said, only half jokingly, 'If

---

1   Although Jung's use of the term 'ego' is here synonymous with the term 'I' as used in psychosynthesis, this is not the case in most psychological systems. Insufficient understanding of the phenomenon of identification has caused most of the confusion surrounding these various terms, for few Western psychological thinkers have seen through the identifications of the 'I' to the 'I' itself. So one often finds that the word 'ego', or 'self' is used to indicate a variety of theoretical constructs, and to it are attributed characteristics, needs, and qualities that actually belong to the personality which is organised around the self. Sometimes the world 'self' is even used to refer to the specific personality elements that one is identified with.

Psychosynthesis

anything were to happen to this car I think I'd be thrown into a full-blown identity crisis.'

Similarly, homemakers can become identified with their homes, collectors with their collections, artists with their creations, and so forth. Such identifications with material objects are often masquerading as 'self-expression'. True self-expression is valuable, of course. But when we invest much of ourselves in objects, when we feel in some way threatened at their loss or change, then there is something other than self-expression happening. When we seem to have an *inappropriate* amount of ourselves at stake concerning some object, we are likely to be identifying with it. Our boundaries may have begun to include it. And instead of expressing ourselves, we begin to express it – we become the servant of the object with which we identify.

Besides identifying with material objects, we can identify ourselves with the groups we belong to – whether cultural, racial, religious, ideological or political. We frequently identify ourselves with our functions and careers in life, such as being a parent or a doctor, a son or an accountant, and so on.

Lisa gave us an example of a more subtle kind of identification. For Lisa was identified with a developed, powerful, and highly energised *subpersonality* (a full description of subpersonalities, including techniques to work with them, is the central topic of the Workbook in *Synthesis*, Vol 1, No 1, 1974 – reprinted in this book). She was consistently identified with this subpersonality, to the exclusion of all else. Like Lisa, people can be 'stuck' in such an identification with a specific subpersonality. Depending on what that subpersonality is like, they can be dissatisfied and hurting, like Lisa was, or relatively content and free from conflict, although limited to only a part of what they can be.

Other people *shift their identification* among a number of subpersonalities. We all have experienced how, for example, 'we are different when we are with our children than when we are with our parents' or how we have been in some stressful situation where 'we are not ourselves'. When people shift their identification in this way, they often do so *reacting to the demands of the situation they are in*. They are drawn – largely unaware – into the subpersonality that is 'suitable', that can best act 'as is expected of them'. Increasingly, they feel boxed in, powerless, controlled by the expectations of their environment and the demands of their personality, and caught in the ambivalence, confusion, and conflict that exist among their many subpersonalities

Psychosynthesis

(see 'Subpersonalities', *Synthesis*, Vol 1, No 1, 1974, pp 12-13 and 18-19 – reprinted in this book). So the mere reactive shifting of identification can be just as restricting as a single identification – *until we learn to choose and shift our identifications at will.*

The Process of Identification

We have seen that identification occurs as a largely unconscious response to the pull of a variety of needs and urges. And that any identification with only one aspect of our personality is restrictive and possibly distorting. So an identification can be a source of difficulty; but depending on the circumstances, there can also be a useful aspect to it.

Because of the very fact that it is restrictive, *identification is specialised.* So it can help us stay focused in a particular direction, increasing our awareness and effectiveness. When we identify with any one part of ourselves, we are able to experience it fully, without being distracted. We feel the way it feels, see the way it sees, for it represents a particular, specialised state of consciousness. Our outlook on life changes, our perceptions and sensations alter. Our energy flows through it and this 'feeds' it and makes it grow. It is thus that – often without our awareness – specific facets of ourselves are nurtured and developed, as imagination through an artist subpersonality, or determination through a leader subpersonality.

Through specific identifications we can develop and refine a quality, or an attitude, we can learn when a certain behaviour or response is useful, and when it is inappropriate. Each one of our identifications provides therefore, in some way, a learning and growing experience. In fact, a great deal of our early learning and growing takes place primarily through a*n unconscious process of successive identifications.* For many people this unconscious or unplanned mode may remain the central means of growth throughout their lives.

But as long as this process is unconscious, it has a great drawback. For while the development of a new quality can *complement* the qualities we already have, leading to a more well-rounded, more inclusive and effective personality, it can become *exaggerated* if we are caught for too long in a particular identification. Personality development is then lopsided, causing conflict, imbalance, and the inhibition of other important and useful qualities. So, depending on the circumstances and on its duration, any identification can be beneficial or harmful, growth-producing or restricting. Or, more precisely, at different times each identification helps and hinders personal growth in different ways and in various proportions.

For example, being identified with a 'Conscientious Worker' subpersonality may help a person develop competence and efficiency, but could prevent him or her from developing playfulness and humour, compassion and sensitivity to fellow workers, calmness or the ability to relax when appropriate. On the other hand, being identified even with something as painful and restrictive as the Victim can eventually bring about positive results – such as greater understanding and empathy for the sufferings of others. So we need to learn first to become aware of our identifications, and then to choose, consciously and in the moment, which identification we believe to be most in line with our purpose and most useful to our growth. Once we have gained whatever is to be gained from a particular identification, it is time to move on: we must release ourselves from it in order to continue growing. Otherwise our identification will become restrictive and control us, limiting our further growth.

But releasing ourselves from an identification does not mean abandoning or rejecting it. For once we disidentify from something that we have fully experienced and mastered, it can be a most effective tool of awareness, expression and action, always available to us whenever we need it.

What we have said up to now implies *three stages* of growing awareness and skill in dealing with the aspects and elements of our personality.

In the first stage, the process of identification is unconscious, and largely beyond our control. Our identification is with one or another personality element (such as a feeling, a subpersonality, a role) and will change responding to the pressure and demands of inner and outer conditions much more than to our desires and aims.

As we become aware of our identifications, we reach the second stage. We can now consciously *choose* to shift our identification from one personality element to another. As we have seen, this mode gives us a greater range of expression, and a more balanced development.

There is, however, yet a third stage that is possible. Lisa alludes to this stage when she speaks of her experience of a gradually emergent 'sense of wholeness'. For, we don't always have to be identified with a subpersonality or other personality element. On the contrary, as will become clear further on, we can learn to disidentify from all of these, and to identify as the 'I', the personal self, our true centre of identity and awareness. We now have an even greater range of expression available: we can choose when it is more appropriate to identify with any personality element, and when to be identified as the 'I'. As the 'I', we not only have experience of personal identity and individuality, we can also be most objectively aware of our psychological life and our interactions in the world, and can therefore guide our actions and development with the greatest effectiveness.

In actual practice – as is usually the case for psychological processes – the three stages are not discretely separate in time. For example, we can learn to disidentify from personality elements and also to identify with our 'I' gradually and simultaneously. Progress in one stage reinforces further progress in the other. The following case study of 'Mike' more extensively illustrates progress along these three stages, through Mike's increasing understanding of the process of identification.

The Striver Subpersonality

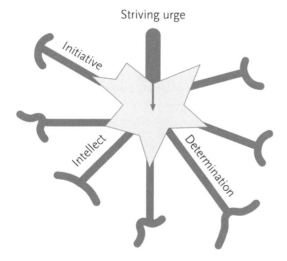

Mike had been identified with a dominant subpersonality, the 'Striver', for most of his life. He was the only child of older parents who had great expectations of him. High achievement was presented to him as a prerequisite for parental love and acceptance, and his childhood was characterised by efforts to win their approval. He got good marks in school and became an award-winning boy scout. A youthful businessman, he was diligently earning money at age seven with a lemonade stand and a paper-route, and later with snow shovelling and gardening jobs. His parents' attitude was that his efforts were good – but 'could be better'. Their approval was promised as a reward for his future achievements, and became like the carrot that entices the donkey to move forward. So Mike's striving pattern was firmly set early in life.

In adolescence, Mike strove for a high grade average and athletic leadership, which were considered by his peer group to be signs of success. He achieved both, and graduated from high school as valedictorian. He continued striving through college, and although the goals he set himself were reached one by one, they seemed to lose their meaning as soon as he attained them. He never felt satisfied. Eventually, this dissatisfaction and continued striving landed him in serious medical trouble (a difficult ulcer).

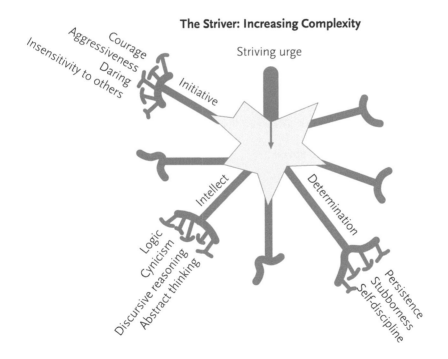

The Striver: Increasing Complexity

Striving urge

Insensitivity to others · Aggressiveness · Courage · Daring · Initiative

Logic · Cynicism · Discursive reasoning · Abstract thinking · Intellect

Determination · Persistence · Stubborness · Self-discipline

But there was a positive side to it too. From the time he was small, Mike's urge to strive stimulated the differentiation and development of many useful functions, traits and abilities. He had to learn to be trustworthy and dependable, how to make himself get up on cold mornings, how to handle money, how to take initiative, and so forth. He exercised his intellect and his will, and learned early about choice and values. He taught himself how to harness and direct his energy and how to persist in what he chose to do. Through his skill at evaluating situations, making decisions, and carrying them out, he earned the respect and trust of many people.

Early in his life, the striving urge became the nucleus, the *partial unifying centre*, around which these many important elements of Mike's personality came together, developed, and were integrated. And the Striver subpersonality was born. As Mike grew, the complexity of organisation around the Striver kept increasing. Eventually it evolved into a complex psychological structure, which included a large number of personality elements and systems.

But although the Striver had helped Mike develop many valuable and useful abilities which he otherwise might never have learned, we have already seen that Mike was at its mercy. He could not control the Striver. In fact, the Striver was in control of Mike and was limiting him.

Where were Mike's feelings, for example? Where were his receptivity and gentleness? Humour was only present as cynicism, and his higher values were being ignored. Such functions as imagination and intuition were stunted, and his inner life was altogether barren. Mike knew little of beauty, love, serenity or peace.

Mike Identified with the Striver

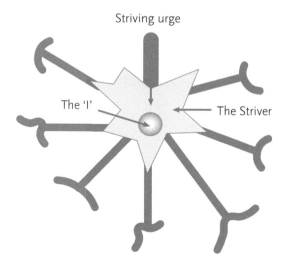

Striving urge

The 'I'

The Striver

Psychosynthesis

Mike's identification with the Striver began to be restrictive during his mid-twenties. He ceased to grow and fell into stasis. He was unaware of his gradually increasing crystallisation at the time, and was at a loss to understand the anxiety and sense of futility which he began to feel. He had reached the limits of the Striver, which instead of being a vehicle of growth, was now becoming a trap.

The core of the Striver, as of all subpersonalities, was a drive, urge or need – in this case, the urge to strive. Mike was aware of this urge, but he assumed it was an intrinsic personality trait, an unchangeable part of his nature. And he was not at all displeased with this 'trait' because, as the Striver, he felt in control of himself, capable, and with a strong sense of personal identity.

But behind the Striver subpersonality, pushing to be recognised, was a deeper, earlier need that Mike had lost touch with. This was the need for acceptance and approval – a vitally important need which had not been sufficiently met in his childhood.

The Rejected Child

Need for acceptance

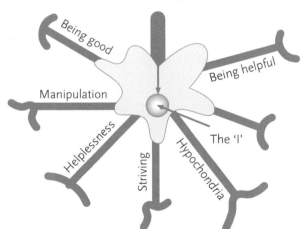

Long before the Striver subpersonality came into being, this need controlled Mike's life. It had itself become the core of an even earlier subpersonality with which Mike had been identified. This subpersonality Mike later – in the course of therapy – came to call the 'Rejected Child'. As the Rejected Child, Mike had tried many different ways to be accepted and win love, attention and approval – such as being good, being helpful, manipulating, pretending to be sick, to need help, as well as striving for various

---

achievements. Because of his family environment and his own specific talents, striving turned out to be by far the most effective way of being accepted. So it was striving that became his habitual behaviour. And it was in this way that Mike's striving urge, in turn, became the core of the Striver.

The Rejected Child and The Striver

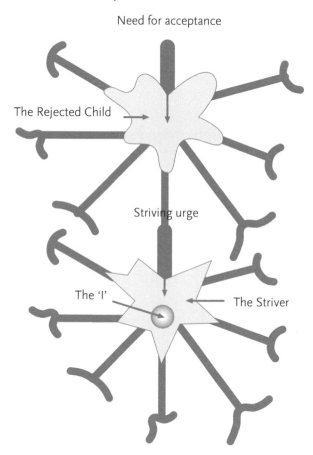

After its formation, the Striver became Mike's major channel of expression in the world, his main subpersonality. And Mike became more and more identified with it. The earlier subpersonality, the Rejected Child, soon was repressed, as its qualities, particularly the need for acceptance, were quite incompatible with the strong, self-sufficient style of the Striver.

From then on, although Mike was given a great deal of approval for striving, it never reached him. For it was given to him while he was identified with the Striver, who could not receive it. Because ironically, the Striver, which was originally formed to fulfil the need for acceptance and approval, now obscured that very basic need and actually prevented its satisfaction. The Striver subpersonality was organised and unified around the urge to strive, and its very identity depended on striving. So its deepest fear was that if it ever reached the original goal of its striving – to have Mike feel accepted and approved of – its very reason for being would be threatened (but in reality if the goal could have been reached, the Striver would not have disappeared nor have been destroyed. Mike would have simply disidentified from it. To the limited awareness of the Striver this was seen as tantamount to death). Speaking with the voice of Mike's parents, the Striver would say, 'You can do better', and with this it invalidated all approval from the environment and any lasting gratification for having achieved a goal – forcing Mike to turn immediately toward the next goal to be reached. It became impossible for Mike to feel anything but constant dissatisfaction while he was identified with the Striver. And not only did the Striver shut *itself* off from approval, more importantly, it prevented any approval from reaching the Rejected Child, who was now in a worse situation than before the Striver came into being. Not only did it feel rejected by the environment, but it was rejected by the Striver as well.

This created a double-bind situation for Mike: he couldn't stop but he couldn't win. The only way he knew to get approval was through striving, but the more he strove the more approval became distant and empty. What Mike really needed was to accept the Rejected Child within himself, whether successful or unsuccessful, irrespective of any achievement.

Though his personal growth had largely ceased in his twenties, and though anxiety troubled him, Mike had continued striving. Or, more accurately, the Striver had kept Mike diligently moving forward. By the time Mike reached his early thirties he was a highly promising junior vice-president in a large corporation – with an ulcer that refused to heal. He strongly resisted slowing down, feeling that if he took any pressure off himself, he'd collapse. His invalidating of all approval, combined with the constant fear of lack of inner worth, gnawed away at his achievements.

Mike had not been consciously aware of the deep conflicts within him – though he experienced the resultant pain. The situation was becoming critical. If he had continued in the same way, he probably would have brought a serious crisis on himself – a major crisis of identity, with the likelihood of severe physical side effects.

Psychosynthesis

Integration

Instead, Mike decided to seek help. In the course of therapy, he learned about disidentification. Gradually he was able to disidentify from the Striver, and uncover and temporarily identify with the Rejected Child. He became aware of the deep pain, sadness and anger at having felt rejected, and was able then to let himself express these feelings within the therapeutic setting. He was also able to recognise his need for acceptance, and to understand what had happened to him. At the suggestion of the guide, he began practising self-identification (exercises). While doing so, he disidentified from the Rejected Child as well. Like Lisa, he began to cultivate the sense of his personal existence, unhampered by any activity, any desire, any identification. As he put it in those first days of discovery: 'I was just myself, a person, Mike'. In this way, he gradually freed himself from his overwhelming need for acceptance from others, realising that while it was an important and deep part of his personality, *he was not it*. It still needed to be satisfied, of course, and now he was in a more effective position to do this. So Mike *himself* learned to give to the Rejected Child within him the full and unconditional acceptance that it needed and had been unable to find in the world.

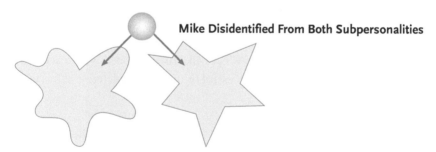

Mike Disidentified From Both Subpersonalities

As Mike was increasingly able to direct his own growth process, the deep need for acceptance was becoming satisfied and the Child began to grow and transform. Its latent traits and qualities blossomed, and it became an adult subpersonality, complementary of the Striver – creative, relaxed, playful, funny, with a great deal of empathy, affection and warmth toward other people. Mike called it 'Mellow Mike'.

Mike saw that it was important not only to express the newly available qualities of Mellow Mike, but also to combine them with those of the Striver by fusing the two subpersonalities (on the fusion of two subpersonalities, see 'Subpersonalities', *Synthesis*, Vol 1, No 1, 1974, pp 41-46 – reprinted in this book). This would bring him far greater personality integration. And he wanted his life to reflect and facilitate this synthetic process. At this point he began to feel that his job held him back and was no longer satisfying. After considering the issue for several months, he left his firm and returned to school. He is now working toward a doctorate in education, relying often on the considerable talents of the Striver in his studies, while teaching in a creative environment where Mellow Mike can find ample opportunities for expression. The fusion process is well on its way. He said recently that his long-term goal is to contribute innovations and improvements to the educational system.

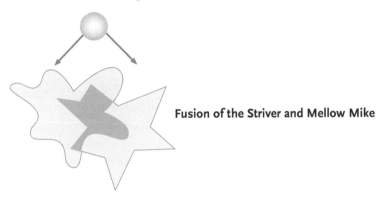

Fusion of the Striver and Mellow Mike

Through Mike's experience we have seen the process by which we can move toward a more inclusive state by freeing ourselves from restrictive identifications. But this experience also suggests an internal mechanism which pushes aside experiences and aspects that are not compatible with such restrictive identifications. This mechanism can be described as *disowning*.

Disowning

When we are strongly identified with something, such as a major subpersonality, most of our energy flows through it. And our energy is filtered by it as well. In other words, only energy of a quality compatible with the basic quality of that subpersonality will be allowed to flow. This means that whatever we are identified with controls the acceptance and rejection of our experiences. For instance, suppose a businessman is identified with a 'Loser' subpersonality – one which has acted as a unifying centre for negative experiences, feelings of inadequacy, and so forth. And let us say that something positive happens – the boss congratulates him on a project he's just completed. Does he hear him and believe him? No. He distorts ('He was being sarcastic'), or invalidates ('He was just trying to build my morale'). Or he immediately 'forgets' it happened, and blocks it out of consciousness.

Psychosynthesis

A positive experience is simply not acceptable to the 'Loser' because its quality is different from, and inconsistent with, that of his self-image. But it goes even further: a positive experience is actually threatening. What if he were not really a Loser? Who would he be then? As we saw earlier, this fear of loss of identity, of a deep void or inner emptiness, if not correctly understood is often too overwhelming to be faced. In such a situation it frequently seems less painful to have a negative sense of self than no sense of self at all. So as in the case of the man identified with his Loser, positive experiences are excluded from consciousness and become invalidated, distorted, or repressed. More precisely, the energy content of a positive experience is of an *opposite quality* to the energy that makes up the core of the Loser subpersonality. So if the experience were accepted by the Loser, the incoming energy would neutralise an equal amount of energy in the subpersonality core, thus *reducing its intensity*. This would be experienced by the Loser as a diminished sense of self, as something directly threatening to its own identity and existence. Therefore it is unacceptable.

But when energy that is opposite to the dominant subpersonality develops within ourselves, and is repressed, where does it go? What happened, originally, to Mike's emotions, humour and intuition? What became of Lisa's inner strength, self-assertion, and ability to nourish herself? These qualities, as well as many others, being incompatible with the qualities of the identifications – the Striver, the Victim – were disowned. By disowned we mean *unconsciously repressed, consciously suppressed, ignored or otherwise discounted*. And to the extent that there is disowning, personality development and integration will be held back.

But we cannot really get rid of portions of ourselves. Whether repressed or suppressed, they do not go away; they remain with us at some level. Their energy accumulates in the unconscious and emerges in various forms – often disguised – such as dreams, symbolisations, sudden urges and desires, various 'neurotic' manifestations, and so forth. As Abraham Maslow writes, in accordance with Freud's formulation, "those portions of ourselves that we reject or repress...do not go out of existence. They do not die, but rather go underground. Whatever effects these underground portions of our human nature have...tend to be unnoticed by ourselves or else felt to be as if they were not a part of us, e.g. 'I don't know what made me say such a thing.' 'I don't know what came over me.'" (A Maslow, *The Farther Reaches of Human Nature*, Viking Press, 1971, p 158).

Psychosynthesis

As time goes on, disowning takes ever-increasing energy to maintain. Eventually this becomes a vicious circle: the more one is troubled by unwanted parts of oneself the more forcefully will they be rejected, and the more forcefully one rejects them the more trouble they will be.

Frequently these disowned qualities and experiences 'feed' a subpersonality that is opposite to the dominant one – or, if such a one does not exist, they create it (see for example 'Subpersonalities', *Synthesis*, Vol 1, No 1, 1974, p 42 – reprinted in this book). And as this opposite subpersonality grows and develops, it gains access to more and more energy. Eventually it may come into real conflict with the dominant one. Usually the conflict is unconscious at the beginning, and the emerging subpersonality expresses itself indirectly – perhaps even somatically, as in the example of Mike's ulcer.

But such a conflicting subpersonality is not a hindrance, something undesirable, to be avoided – although it may appear so at first (this is explained in 'Subpersonalities', *Synthesis*, Vol 1, No 1, 1974, pp 35-36 –reprinted in this book). Because it is opposite, it is also *complementary*, and through it we gain access to a broad range of valuable qualities not before available.

In other words, the disowned emotions, thoughts, desires and experiences which make up such a subpersonality are not necessarily harmful or 'bad'. On the contrary, many of these disowned ideas or urges can be towards growth, or towards altruism and 'sublime' qualities. Maslow describes our 'unconscious fear and hatred of the true, good and beautiful' in his theory of our defence against our own growth, which he terms the "Jonah complex". (*The Farther Reaches of Human Nature*, Viking Press, 1971). Frank Haronian, in his article 'The Repression of the Sublime' (*Synthesis*, Vol 1, No 1, 1974, p 51, also reprinted in this book) discusses the tendency to repress the goodness, nobility and beauty of human nature as well as the sexual and aggressive drives. Thus, contents of our consciousness are usually disowned not on the basis of their actual value, but because whatever that content is, it is incompatible with our – often unconscious – sense of who we are. And, as we have seen, the sense of who we are is determined, in each moment, by whatever we are identified with.

Release

When we are identified with something that has become restrictive, how do we manage to release ourselves? Mike's identification with the Striver was only broken after the resulting inner conflicts and tensions caused much pain, anxiety, and even an ulcer. And it was only after considerable suffering that Lisa spontaneously 'stepped back' from her identification, experienced her 'I', and became aware of the Victim.

People often maintain an identification until it becomes too difficult, too painful, or impossible to do so. But a *permanent* identification with any function, subpersonality, or other personality element is jeopardised sooner or later by the simple process of life and time. Eventually it will be impossible to maintain, and the individual's life situation may become precarious. He or she may experience a sense of loss, futility and despair, as might a student who must leave school, a businessman who must face retirement, or a spouse whose partner grows steadily beyond where he or she was when they married

The same crisis also comes to people whose identifications have become too restrictive because of inner growth, even though their external life conditions remain the same. We have seen examples of this in Mike and Lisa.

Although this crisis is quite common, its real nature is seldom understood. Many go through it blindly and powerlessly, while with a clearer understanding they could deal with it less painfully, and use it as an opportunity for growth. For a crisis is a message that says: 'Let go! You are identified with something that is now too small for you.' So the first step to surmount a crisis is to look for the restricting identification that one needs to let go of. In this way the crisis is seen suddenly as an *opportunity* rather than a setback. And this crucial insight points the way to the resolution, showing the means to reach it with greater effectiveness and far less struggle.

Yet disidentification need not be precipitated by crisis. It can be achieved through a conscious, deliberate act of will. Nor must one fear that achieving disidentification will lead to a crisis. If the need for it is recognised in time, disidentification can be calm, smooth, painless, and will bring about increased harmony and freedom.

However, recognition of our restrictive identifications can be difficult because we often do not realise that we are identified with anything. An exploration of our personality can bring to light many of our identifications. Another – and complementary – approach is to disidentify 'en masse' from the three main aspects of the personality: body, feelings and mind. This will eventually release us from our more specific identifications, and give us the freedom to identify with our true centre, the 'I'. This latter approach is the basis for the Identification Exercise. (While identifications with objects, roles or even subpersonalities are often not difficult to recognise and deal with, the identification with a basic personality function – such as the mind, or the feelings – is deeper, and can be more elusive. It is often expressed through identifications with one or more corresponding subpersonalities, such as those which are primarily of an intellectual or emotional nature. Examples might be respectively, 'the scholar' or 'the frightened child'.)

But recognising an identification is only the first step. For we may recognise an identification but not the need to let go of it. For instance, we may be identified with a strong and evolved subpersonality which helps us to be very one-pointed, focused and effective in some particular purpose. To others and to ourselves, we may seem 'centred', actualised and integrated. There is little conflict in us; we seem calm and strong. And we are centred, but only around a *partial* unifying centre. As we have seen, such a centre is partial because only the parts of our personality which are consistent and compatible with the basic quality of that centre can be integrated around it.

If, after freeing himself from the Striver, Mike had not proceeded to identify with his 'I', he might have been drawn instead into a permanent identification with Mellow Mike, and eventually would have become restricted again. He would have owned what he had previously disowned as the Striver, and developed whole new areas of his personality – and this would have been good and valuable for a while. But, in turn, as Mellow Mike *he would have disowned the Striver* and all that made it up. He would have disowned much of himself that was skilled, capable and effective. Instead, by accepting that he had *both* the Striver and Mellow Mike within him, that he had many different qualities which were not mutually exclusive but rather complementary, he prevented another crisis in the future. And not only was this preventive, it was also constructive and integrative. For he laid the foundation of a higher order subpersonality, one that will include both the Striver and Mellow Mike.

Disidentification

What did Mike do to bring this about? First of all, he deliberately practised disidentification. Disidentification is an experience which most people have had at one time or another; it is an empirical fact which you can probably recall or observe in your own experience. Have you ever been alone in a thunderstorm and felt a little frightened, and found that fear 'disappeared' and courage took its place when one of your children ran in to seek reassurance from you? Your identification *shifted* from frightened-child part of you to a protective-parent part. Or you may have had the experience of talking to one person and feeling that you are – indeed, have always been – confident and sure of yourself. Then you talk to another person and you feel that you are – and have always been – inadequate and unsure. Again, your identification shifted between two parts of your personality.

So we all know something about disidentification, yet many of us have never thought of it as a deliberate practice, as something we can consciously *decide* to do. As we have seen earlier, many people – perhaps most – shift their identifications in this way, unconsciously; it just seems to happen to them. They go through the day shifting from one identification to the next, in response to outer conditions and inner processes, like a boat adrift on a stormy sea. They are not in control of the shifting, and often not even aware of it. But they can learn to be; they can train themselves to choose, to *direct* their identification at will.

A person who has – and uses – this directing ability takes increasing responsibility for him or herself in actions, words, thoughts and feelings. Such a person will begin to truly live in accordance with his or her values. Choosing our identification in this way is *an act of will*, just as it is where to turn our eyes, what sound to listen to, or what to think about. We can exercise this power of choice, or we can let our awareness – and then our 'I' – wander toward what attracts it most. This choice is extremely simple in principle, although in practice we are limited by how developed and strong our will is, and by our skill in using it. (As we said earlier, each content of our consciousness – anything that we are aware of – exerts a pull, a 'magnetic attraction'. And we tend to identify with whatever has the greatest pull. To prevent this automatic identification from happening, we need to use our will to neutralise that attraction. Let us say that a certain subpersonality has the greatest pull. If our will is strong enough – stronger than the subpersonality – we can apply it directly, freeing our self from the subpersonality's influence, and remaining identified with the 'I' or choosing any other identification. But if our will is not strong enough to do this, we can still disidentify, by using the *technique of substitution* (this technique is described in Assagioli, *The Act of Will*, Viking Press, 1973, pp 57, 67-68 and 75). In other words, we choose another subpersonality that has a fairly strong pull, and is more in line with our needs than the first subpersonality. Then we use our will to identify with it. This is possible provided that the pull of this second subpersonality and the strength of our will *combined* are stronger than the pull of the first subpersonality. It is this combined strength that

Psychosynthesis

makes shifting identification between our main subpersonalities easier than identifying with the 'I'.)

While the core of a subpersonality is an urge, desire, or drive, that has a specific quality, or colour, the 'I' – which is the core of the whole personality – is a spark of pure being, without qualities in the ordinary sense. But though it has no qualities, it has functions, and its two main functions are *consciousness* and *will*. Through *self-identification* – or identification as the 'I' – we gain the greatest freedom to use that consciousness and that will – or more exactly, we re-own what are in fact our consciousness and our will. When we use our consciousness while remaining identified as the 'I', we take the attitude of *observer*. Similarly, when we use our will, we take the attitude of *director*.

The observer and director are not subpersonalities, and as such they are not coloured, but clear. They are limited in how far they reach, but, in their pure form, they are not biased and do not distort. They are attitudes we take, or functions we use when we are identified as the 'I'. Accordingly, they can be distinguished from subpersonalities such as the 'Dictator' or the 'Critic', which at first can be confused with them. As observer, we are disidentified from all elements of our personality, and are simply looking at them. From this position, we are able to see ourselves, and our environment objectively, without distortions or 'coloured glasses'. This is the stable place from which we can look at ourselves without self-criticism, with full acceptance and clear perception. As director, drawing on our awareness as observer, we can use our will to express ourselves according to our values and our purpose, and to effectively harmonise and bring together the many elements of our personality into one coherent unit.

It was as observer that Mike became aware that the Striver was only a subpersonality and not his real self. And it was as director that, later, he was able to begin to bring the Striver and Mellow Mike together as parts of a larger whole.

The following report of 'Jane' is a good illustration of a person who disidentifies from personality elements and acts both as observer and director at the same time.

Jane is a middle-aged wife and mother who recently returned to college to work towards a Master's Degree in Art History. She reports here the results of her use of the Identification exercise:

Psychosynthesis

Let me tell you about an experience I had that will perhaps best illustrate how I use disidentification. I had been practising the exercise for several months, even though I didn't really understand it at first. When this incident occurred, I felt that I finally knew what it was all about.

It is a hot summer night and I am at the airport checking in for one of those cheap mid-night flights to New York where I will make a connection with my long-awaited charter flight to Europe. I have arranged my entire summer so I can have three weeks to visit museums and cathedrals.

There is only one airline clerk on duty and a long line ahead of me. Time is running out. The clerk is tired and irritable. When I reach him, he tells me that the airline has no record of my reservation and that the flight is full. He already had to turn a few people away.

He says there are no other flights to New York until the morning. I check those out but they will arrive too late. All those months of anticipation, saving money, plans and charter club dues are about to be lost. The fate of my entire trip appears to rest with this irritable clerk.

Now I have many subpersonalities which have conflicting ideas about what I should do. The strongest subpersonality at this point is 'Queen Jane', who wants to imperiously demand her rights and tell the clerk off. Next strongest is 'Baby Jane', a helpless feminine girl-child who manipulates through fluttery weakness.

Recognising the familiar pull of these subpersonalities, I try to disidentify from them as much as I can, and take the attitude of observer. From this angle I survey the situation and I can imagine the consequences of expressing either of those subpersonalities. As observer, I can also keep the most important aspect of the whole situation clearly in mind: how can I get to New York in time?

I know that Queen Jane would probably only further irritate the clerk, who then won't be disposed to help me at all. In fact he might even pass over possible alternatives just to get rid of me. Baby Jane might work, but I am not sure. The clerk is so grouchy he might well be disgusted by a show of helplessness, and there may have been so much of this sort of thing in his career in dealing with people that he can see right through it. And even if it worked, I would be making 'bad vibes' and manipulating, which I don't

Psychosynthesis

want to do. In the past, I would have automatically become Queen Jane first, and if that didn't work I would have fallen into Baby Jane. This would all have been unconscious; I used to think it was 'just me' and that I was simply responding to a situation. These subpersonalities used to control me so completely that I didn't even realise I was being controlled.

So I decide to steer away from an emotional appeal, as the clerk seems to be so identified himself with his negative feelings. I decide instead to appeal to his best nature as objectively as possible.

I tell the clerk in a calm way that I am sad and upset, that the trip to Europe had been planned for many months, and if I miss my charter flight I will not be able to go. I made reservations a long time ago for this flight to New York, and perhaps in the space of months in between my reservation was misplaced. I understand he is not personally responsible, but the trip really means a great deal to me, and I would very much appreciate any alternative the clerk can suggest.

The clerk, listening to me, has spontaneously disidentified a bit from his grouchiness. There is still irritation in him, of course, but now he is paying attention to another part of himself, the reasonable and good-willed part I appealed to. Now he and I are working together toward a common goal. Eventually, he manages to reroute me through Chicago in time to make my connection.

This incident showed me something important. When I disidentified from my panicked subpersonalities, I was able to calm down and get some perspective. I saw that I had a choice between two things; venting my frustration and pique at the clerk, or honing in on getting myself to New York. Venting my feelings probably wouldn't have worked and wouldn't have been fair. I feel really good about the way I dealt with this.

Jane's account illustrates how effective and practical disidentification can be. It also illustrates the valuable ability to disidentify from *feelings* and *moods* such as hurt, frustration or impatience, and purposefully identify as observer. This can refresh us, enabling us to gain a clear perspective. It can also enhance our creativity. 'Shelley', a research scientist in her mid-thirties, writes: 'I believe I have been disidentifying most of my life. It's become automatic, like focusing my eyes. When I experience myself as confused, troubled or hurt, or when I have been analysing a problem to death, I step back, and from this quiet place I can begin to see what's going on. I find access to deeper and broader awareness, and there is a different kind of creativity or problem-solving ability which becomes available. Afterwards I feel both serene and energised.'

Many people use the same approach as Jane and Shelley. They have learned to disidentify from troublesome or confusing subpersonalities, identify as observer, then, as director, carry out the most appropriate course of action. They can shift identification and express various subpersonalities at will. They know how to step out of painful, destructive or overpowering moods and feelings so that other, more positive states become available. They have attained a sense of perspective, and can act in the most effective and rewarding fashion. This is possible because identification as the 'I' brings freedom. It gives us the freedom to choose at any moment to become fully identified with any part of ourselves – an emotion or habit pattern or subpersonality – to be involved in it and experience it deeply. Or, on the other hand, it gives us the freedom to observe and to act while remaining fully disidentified from it – or to choose any intermediate degree of identification between these two extremes.

The 'I' is not Repressive

Sometimes people resist the idea of identifying as the 'I' because they fear that with such 'detachment' the richness of life will fade away and be lost. They fear that both strong and subtle emotions, such as passion and aesthetic appreciation, will give way to a dry and impersonal attitude; that spontaneity and merriment, harmless mischief and pleasure will be eliminated. But the loss of these would be signs of a repressive, critical subpersonality at work. The 'I' within is never moralistic. Therefore, it does not eliminate. As observer it accepts, as director it regulates, transforms and harmonises.

It is important that the 'I' not be confused with any kind of repressive agent. As the 'I', we are able to accept ourselves, including all our faults and limitations, all our negative and immature subpersonalities (accepting our limitations does not mean accepting the status quo. On the contrary, recognising and accepting what is in us is a necessary prerequisite to changing it. The function of acceptance as a stage of personality development is presented in 'Subpersonalities', *Synthesis*, Vol 1, No 1, 1974, pp 35-38 – reprinted in this book). The following report by 'Ron', a graduate student in Eastern Philosophy, illustrates the difference between the activity of the 'I' and that of a critical, repressive subpersonality:

Psychosynthesis

For many years I thought I was centred when I was able to achieve a spiritual, flowing, idealistic state of consciousness. I thought I had identified with my personal self and even my Transpersonal Self. When I was into this state, I felt a gap between the usual, daily me, and this higher me. And I was very critical of what I believed to be my short-comings towards attaining enlightenment. For instance, I wasn't meditating regularly, or keeping a pure diet. In fact – and you may laugh at this – I really loved hot fudge sundaes. I had to be very hard on myself to prevent myself from 'slipping' and eating one. When I did slip, I berated myself for it for weeks afterwards.

Doing the Identification exercise the first time amazed me. I moved fairly easily to what I had believed was 'my centre' and then found I could disidentify even from that. What I had thought was my centre turned out to be a spiritually oriented subpersonality. I saw this subpersonality clearly for the first time in my life.

Now I use disidentification frequently, especially when I feel that spiritual subpersonality telling me that I should live up to its demands. I disidentify from it and for me that means realising that I have a choice to follow its urgings or not. That I'm free to choose and won't necessarily be struck by lightning or denied grace if I decide not to do what it says at any given moment. So, I'm eating those hot fudge sundaes now – not just eating, but enjoying – though I don't seem to want them so much any more. My 'centre' used to tell me I was too attached to sundaes. But now I know that what I was too attached to was my 'centre'. Anyway, the effect of all this on me has been a lessening of anxiety and the beginning of a more clear-headed and, I think, more genuinely spiritual life.

Often, as in Ron's case, once we take the attitude of observer, we recognise that many tendencies we had considered to be undesirable are in fact harmless, or even valuable, and can be freely expressed. But what about impulses that are truly harmful, danger-ous, or otherwise inappropriate? As observer, we do accept them, as we would accept any other element in us. This does not mean, of course, that we will freely act them out.

We know that often, strong urges and emotions which are deemed potentially hurtful and destructive (e.g. rage) are suppressed and repressed. As we have seen, repressed urges do not disappear but remain active in the unconscious, becoming a source of difficulty. Sooner or later they emerge in semi-disguised form, expressing themselves indirectly or becoming somaticised, and in general causing much conflict, discomfort and pain. There is a widespread belief that the only other alternative to repression is to

Psychosynthesis

'act out' these disowned elements. It is true that acting out may at first give substantial relief, particularly if the repression was a deep and severe one. But this is seldom enough to clear the problem, and may be unnecessary. When we act out a feeling, or urge, we usually identify with it. We are then dominated and controlled by this identification, and feed its new energy as we release the old. So it becomes very difficult, if not impossible to work the problem through completely. Rather than either blocking the energy of an inappropriate feeling, or acting it out, we can, from the vantage point of the 'I', regulate and guide that energy toward a more appropriate purpose, thus utilising it and, at the same time, transmuting and gradually refining it. The transmutation of energies is an important technique with a broad range of applications – another powerful tool that becomes available to us through disidentification and self-identification (the principles and practice of transmutation of psychological energies are described extensively by Assagioli, *Psychosynthesis: A Manual of Principles and Techniques*, Viking Press, 1971, pp 267-277, and by Crampton, 'Psychological Energies and Transformations', *Journal of Transpersonal Psychology*, No 1, 1974, pp 39-56).

The 'I' as the Unifying Centre of the Personality

As we learn more and more to identify as the 'I' and to act as observer and director, we become increasingly able to coordinate and integrate our subpersonalities. We can use the clarity of our awareness and the power of our will to effectively harmonise the many elements within our personality into one coherent whole: the *integrated personality*. So the 'I' has a synthetic effect upon the personality, and becomes its unifying centre: the focal point around which a new, all-inclusive organisation is created. This process is not merely the formation of a 'bigger and better' subpersonality, but is a major step forward in personal unfoldment. It is a *higher order* process because the 'I' is of a different nature than the partial unifying centres which are the core of each of our subpersonalities.

Let us look at this in terms of energies. We have seen that in a subpersonality the urge or drive that constitutes its core has a certain quality, or 'colour'. Therefore it will attract, and act as a unifying centre for, all that is compatible with that quality, but it will repel anything that is not. The Striver for example attracts diligence, power, efficiency, and repels sensitivity, compassion and so forth. The 'I', on the other hand, has no quality as such: its 'colour' can be compared to white light, which contains all colours and is the *synthesis* of all colours. Therefore it can act as a unifying centre for the *whole* personality. There are no elements of the personality which are of a quality

Psychosynthesis

incompatible with the 'I'. For the 'I' is not of the personality, rather it *transcends* the personality, just as it transcends the limitations of specific qualities. Thus all personality elements, all functions and all qualities can be brought into integration around it. Once we are able to identify as the 'I', we can express ourselves through a personality composed of many interrelated elements, and any inner sense of limitation and fragmentation is increasingly replaced by variety, richness and wholeness.

It would be unrealistic to expect, however, that identifying with the 'I' will produce 'instant integration' of the personality, or even 'instant harmony' between any conflicting parts of ourselves. It is true that no element of the personality is incompatible with the 'I'. Yet a personality element may well be incompatible with another such element, or with that portion of the personality already integrated around the 'I'. We have seen this incompatibility between two personality elements in the case of Mike, where the Rejected Child was, at first, incompatible with the Striver. From the vantage point of the 'I', however, we can understand the causes of such incompatibility within ourselves, see what changes are needed to resolve it, and then guide our inner processes toward a fruitful resolution. But the actual integration of that particular element will be possible only after the necessary changes have taken place.

In many cases, this may take relatively little time and energy. But occasionally considerable work or time may be required before a particular element can find its place within the integrating personality. We may need to transform that element so that it will fit the existing personality pattern, (this is the essence of *coordination*. See 'Subpersonalities', *Synthesis*, Vol 1, No 1, 1974, pp 39-41 – reprinted in this book) or we may need to wait until the personality itself is transformed so as to be 'ripe' for it – until other needed elements have been added and are themselves sufficiently integrated. So we see that *personality integration, like any other form of synthesis, proceeds according to a specific pattern and a specific sequence. Therefore the needed elements must come together according to a specific order, or 'plan', which is unique for each individual.* (Note to professionals: This explains why, at times, unusually high resistance on the part of a client is best dealt with by the guide's 'backing off', rather than by trying to have the client achieve a breakthrough. Resistance of this kind may be an indication that things are not yet 'ripe' in that particular area, and that the best course of action is for the guide to allow life experience and the client's higher nature to continue fostering the process at their own pace, trusting that the opportunity for resolution will come at the appropriate time. In the meantime, the guide can be just as effective assisting the client's growth in other, more open areas. In general, the basic

Psychosynthesis

dichotomy between 'directive' and 'non-directive' forms of guidance can thus be bridged through an approach that is directive, but which follows the direction and patterns of growth and integration produced by the influence of the client's own higher nature. As we understand more and more that this higher nature is the fundamental agent – the prime mover – of growth and integration, it will become increasingly clear that the most effective guidance is done by paying attention to the natural process of growth and to the higher emerging trends of the individual, by fostering this process and cooperating with those trends, rather than by attempting to impose an external model of what the individual should become.) This is a fundamental principle of synthesis. It can be seen not only in the integration of the individual personality, but also within groups of individuals, within the many organisations and structures of our society, within the nations of our planet and within humanity as a whole.

Furthermore as a synthesis proceeds, and more and more elements are integrated, there will be some elements that create much conflict, and seem most at odds with the emerging pattern. In some cases considerable time needs to elapse, and much energy needs to be spent to produce the changes that are needed before these elements can be allowed to become a part of the emerging entity. But it is often these most difficult elements that contain some of the qualities that are most valuable to, and needed by the organised whole.

The Experience of Identity

When we identify as the 'I' and take the attitude of observer, we can gain much useful awareness about our personality. Taking the attitude of director enables us to bring our personality into harmony. But, even more important, *the 'I' is self-conscious*: it can 'look at itself'. And it is then that we can realise our true personal identity – our individuality.

This experience of identity is not cognitive in the sense of grasping a concept or understanding a principle. It is an immediate, direct, *supra-rational* knowing.

So the nature of the 'I' cannot be fully described, but must be experienced. Sri Aurobindo writes: 'There is something beyond to be known, and it is when the knower of the field [the 'I' in its observer function] turns from the field itself to learn of himself within it...that real knowledge begins, the true knowledge of the field no less than the

Psychosynthesis

knower." (Sri Aurobindo, 'Essays on the Gita', *Sri Aurobindo Ashram*, Pondicherry, India, 1970, p 400).

What follows is a transcript of a young housewife being guided to turn her attention inward from the contents of her awareness, the experience of the 'I' itself:

Guide Close your eyes...Relax...Take some deep breaths...[pause]...What are you aware of right now, Natalie?

Natalie I'm aware of my whole body, especially my back, and my breathing. I'm aware of my feet and how they feel...my legs...all the parts touching the chair. I'm aware of my face and some tension around my eyes. I'm aware of my hands.

Guide Okay. Focus on all these awarenesses...[pause]...now tell me, who is aware?

Natalie The middle of my head.

Guide Tell me more about that.

Natalie It's a big space. I think it's empty. [laughs]

Guide Can you tell me more about that space?

Natalie Yes... it's white. The main thing about it is that it seems empty.

Guide Okay. Now, who is aware of that space?

Natalie The part that notices everything.

Guide What is that part like?

Natalie I don't know. It's not like anything else.

Guide How do you know it's there?

Natalie When I'm aware, there's always something that is the same. And it's the something that is perceiving – knowing.

Guide And who is that?

Natalie [pause] Wow, [laughs] I can't say.

Guide You are aware of it, though...Can you get in touch with it now?

Natalie Yes...I like just accepting that it's there. It's hard for me to understand – just intellectually, it's hard for me to believe.

Psychosynthesis

Guide What the mind says is important, but now it gets in the way of your awareness. Let's come back to it later. Now just go back to your awareness of the one that notices everything.

Natalie [pause] Yes...

Guide Who is aware?

Natalie I...I can't describe it...it's just awareness...It's...It's me. I am this. I am aware.

Guide Stay with this awareness...Have you experienced yourself this way before?

Natalie Yes, it's familiar. But I didn't realise it was me...and that I could make it happen.

Guide You can always come back here.

Natalie Yes, and I will. I just need to remember to come back here...[pause]...That was beautiful.

The process of 'turning inward' described by Aurobindo can be clearly recognised in Natalie's experience. It is realised in two phases. The first is to take the attitude of observer. A simple way to begin is to observe objectively what we are aware of in the moment [observing what we are aware of is different than 'thinking about it' – although it can include the observation of one's thoughts. How to take the attitude of observer is explained in detail in the exercise 'The Observer and the Consciousness of 'I', *Synthesis*, 1975, Vol 1, No 2 – reprinted in this series]. It is useful to try this with eyes open and with eyes closed, to see which way is easier. We then ask ourselves, 'Who is observing?' and, avoiding any intellectual construct but rather focusing on direct experience, we can become aware of being the observer. Then we can distinguish the *observer* from the *contents of consciousness*, the 'Knower' from 'Field of Knowledge'.

At times, it may take several steps to do this. In Natalie's experience, the first 'observer' was the 'space in the middle of her head'. But it was the observer of that 'observer' who turned out to actually be the 'I'. We can conceive of this sequence of observers as stepping stones, by means of which we can travel 'upstream', along the river of our awareness, toward its source – the 'I' – where the second phase of this process occurs. This is the *reorientation of our awareness toward its source; it is consciousness turning back on itself and becoming self-aware*. It is when consciousness is reflected back on its source – thus becoming true self-consciousness that we can finally realise our individual identity – 'It's me...I am this...I am aware' – and become one with it.

This fundamental reorientation of our awareness becomes perfectly normal, and also extremely simple – once we realise how to do it and practise it. Some people have found out gradually, on their own, how to achieve it. Others are able to do it, but don't practise it because they do not know it *can* be practised, or do not recognise the value of doing so. Others still – probably a majority – can learn after a certain amount of practice with appropriate exercises. In actuality, it often turns out that learning how to identify with the 'I' is more elusive than difficult. In other words, for many people it is a matter of understanding *what* to do rather than *developing the capacity* to do it. It is true that focusing our awareness toward the 'I' requires an act of concentration – an effort of will – and if one's will is not sufficiently strong, it needs to be developed. (A broad range of techniques and exercises for developing the will can be found throughout Assagioli, *The Act of Will*, Viking Press, 1973.) But for many people the will is already capable of the task, and all that is lacking is knowing how to use it. This is because from birth we are impelled to turn our awareness away from our centre toward the *contents* of consciousness – inner as well as outer – and we have become used to this, accepting it as the only possible mode of awareness. (With rare exceptions, this is in fact the only mode of awareness we are capable of up to the time of adolescence. After age 15 or 16, self-identification becomes increasingly possible, and can be practised advantageously. Until then, children and adolescents can learn to shift their identification at will among their subpersonalities and other personality elements.) To experience the 'I', however, we must reverse direction. So it is not surprising that this re-orientation may seem strange at first, even unnatural, and that we may not know quite how to proceed. Using the metaphor of the river of our awareness, when we first begin travelling toward its source, we do so while looking backwards. We face downstream while we paddle ourselves upstream. We perceive our movement as *away from* where we are, from the familiar, and don't yet see where we are really going.

This usually happens because we do not know what the source – our 'I' – is like, how to recognise it, in what direction it lies, or even, sometimes, that it exists at all. And understandably so. Because the 'I', being transcendent to the personality, cannot be fully or accurately described. So it can only be truly known when it is experienced. That is why reading about it, for example, is no substitute for actively and steadfastly seeking to reach it by means of such methods as we have indicated here.

Psychosynthesis

The 'I' and Beyond

If, as we travel towards the 'I', we try to imagine it, we are likely to be led astray. Yet enough can be said about the 'I' and how people have experienced it to help us recognise what it is not. With this knowledge, we are able to step back from anything that is not the 'I', and thus proceed towards it, so to speak, 'backwards'. Eventually, by this process, when we reach the 'I' we will be able to recognise it for what it truly is.

One of the first things people say about their experience of the 'I' is that it is permanent and unchanging. Natalie said, 'When I'm aware, there's always something that is the same.' This is very much in contrast to the constant state of change and flux of our personality elements, and of the contents of our consciousness. While the life of the personality – the myriad thoughts, emotions and sensations – go on, the 'I' is changeless: it is experienced as 'a stable point', 'always there', 'immutable', 'permanent'. (Although the experience of the 'I' can change in intensity – from strong to very faint – at different times, this is a change of our awareness, not of the 'I' itself.) Some people have been able to identify with the 'I' simply when asked to 'be aware of whatever within you is always the same'. In the words of Clark Moustakas: "The individual self, or being, is an ultimate core of reality which remains unchanged throughout changes of personality qualities or states." (Clark Moustakas (ed), *The Self*, Harper & Row, 1956, p 272). The 'I' is like the hinge of a door: the door opens and closes or swings back and forth, while the hinge remains stable – and, at the same time it sustains the door itself.

There is another aspect to the experience of the 'I' that many people find remarkable. The 'I' is self-conscious, aware of itself, and in this awareness *there is no duality*. In normal consciousness, one is aware of something which is other than oneself. In other words, there are three elements to normal awareness: the one who is conscious; the object or content of consciousness; the consciousness itself, which is the bridge that links the two. But in the experience of pure self-awareness there is no object, or content. There is no observer-observed duality. There is only *undifferentiated consciousness* – consciousness which is not restricted to the awareness of any specific feeling, sensation, process, pattern or quality of any kind. So people who have fully identified with the 'I' often try to describe its nature through paradox: 'empty but full', 'nothing but everything', 'one moment but eternity'.

Psychosynthesis

Perhaps one of the most beautiful portrayals of both the permanent nature and the transcendence of duality that are characteristic of the 'I' is given by TS Eliot in his poem, 'Burnt Norton' (*Four Quartets*, Faber & Faber, London, 1972, pp.15-16): "At the still point of the turning world. Neither flesh nor fleshless; Neither from nor towards; at the still point, there the dance is, But neither arrest nor movement. And do not call it fixity, Where past and future are gathered. Neither movement from nor towards, Neither ascent nor decline. Except for the point, the still point, There would be no dance, and there is only the dance."

The initial experience of the 'I' may come as an intense flash lasting only an instant, or it may be a slow change, so gradual that we do not recognise it for quite a while. Occasionally, it comes as a spontaneous realisation, as was the case with Lisa. This occurs most often when a deep and long-standing identification is suddenly released.

However, one does not need to wait for a spontaneous experience. Many people have discovered the 'I' as the result of deliberate introspection, or by practising appropriate techniques of self-development. The Identification exercise is a modern presentation of a technique which has proven fruitful through the ages.

The discovery of the 'I', and even a very brief moment of identification with it, can have a profound effect. In the realisation that *we are* that 'permanent core of reality within' lies our true humanness, our sense of identity, of individuality, our power to become masters of our lives. While we are identified with the 'I', we are no longer immersed in a current of emotions, a stream of thoughts, or the loud clamouring of subpersonalities. The sense of inner conflict and fragmentation ceases. Feelings and moods which many had to learn to live with, such as guilt, fear or semi-conscious anxiety, are dissipated the way frightening figures in a wax museum lose their power when the lights are turned on – for we realise that we have been seeing things out of proportion.

So the 'I' becomes a source of perspective, of peace, of absolute security – the unshakable ground that underlies our existence. A writer tells the story of his experience in the Los Angeles earthquake several years ago which illustrates this quality literally. In his life he had difficulty trusting people and his environment. But somehow, he had experienced a certain reliable grounding in the earth itself. He always 'trusted' the earth to be there underfoot – reliably solid and real and safe. But he was on the sixth floor of a large hotel in downtown Los Angeles the morning of the 1970 earthquake, and was shaken to the core by the realisation that not even the earth was 'real and safe'. What could he trust? Was there nothing, then, to rely on? That experience led to an extended crisis. And then a year and a half later, while meditating, he experienced 'that there is something inside me which can't be touched, maimed or destroyed. There is no exact way that I can give voice to this experience because it was at once perfectly soundless and yet it implied all sound. It can be described – in an imperfect way – as an experience of endless restfulness combined with vast dynamic power. Thus a profound dynamism, coexistent with perfect calm. One seeks for poetry, for a language beyond the precision of language. It was the experience of my absolute being and, at the same time, of the absolute being of everything. Like a funnel which we enter from below: inside is outside; thou art that. It was this realisation of my own absolute being that made me realise the absolute being of everything else. And it gave me a kind of serenity, and a confidence that things will work out. And, at a deeper level, a confidence of eternal being.'

In this experience, he reached the 'I' and went beyond it. For identifying with the 'I' is not the final goal: like every culmination, it is a new beginning. It is like awakening from a dream and opening our eyes for the first time. With our eyes open, we see the world in a new and clearer light, and can begin to live our lives accordingly.

Eventually this fuller life, lived as the 'I', leads to a greater culmination: the experience of the Transpersonal Self. Assagioli refers to "...the direct awareness of the Self, which culminates in the unification of the consciousness of the personal self, or 'I,' with that of the Transpersonal Self." (*The Act of Will*, Viking Press, 1973, pp 121-122). The Transpersonal Self can be reached from the 'I' because the 'I' is in fact a projection, a spark, an intrinsic part of the Transpersonal Self. It is as much of the Transpersonal Self as we are able to experience at the time.

Reaching towards the 'I' gives us a true sense of our identity, uniqueness, and *individuality*. As we reach toward the Transpersonal Self we experience *universality* – yet at the same time, paradoxically, the sense of 'I-ness' – of identity and individuality – is enhanced. Eventually, individuality and universality blend, into the true experience of Being.

While maintaining such a state at will is a very very distant goal for the great majority of people, a first glimpse of the Transpersonal Self – as can be seen in 'Burnt Norton' and more clearly, in the writer's earthquake experience – may occur at times sponta-

Psychosynthesis

neously, or while following certain types of meditation, and especially as the result of practising self-identification.

The experience of the self – whether personal or Transpersonal – has been often compared to returning to our true home. It is, as Assagioli has noted, a joyous experience: "...the realisation of the self, or more exactly of *being a self*...gives a sense of freedom, of power, of mastery which is profoundly joyous." (*The Act of Will*, Viking Press, 1973, p 201).

Such a realisation may be lasting or it may remain for only an instant, but the knowledge of it always stays with us at some level. In the course of daily living, we may be drawn away from it and may even 'forget' that it exists; yet if we were to sit down to recollect the experience and even to relive it, we would find it present, fresh, real. But how often do we remember to do so?

For this reason, the *practice* of self-identification is of the greatest value. Through practice, we learn to disidentify from the field of our awareness and identify more and more with our true nature. It is a gradual, sometimes slow process. Yet it is through this gradually increasing self-identification that we can fully actualise ourselves in everyday living.

And here is the paradox again. For it is only by realising our unique individuality that we can begin to take our places as fully functioning, effective *parts of the greater whole* – be that our family, a group, a community, a nation, or the larger life and destiny of the planet itself.

Betsie Carter-Haar (reprinted from Synthesis, 1975, Vol 1, No 2)

Psychosynthesis

Chapter 5 Self-Realisation and Spiritual Awakening

Self and Duality

Inherent in psychosynthesis and in the reality of the Self is the paradox that we are both human (personal) and divine (spiritual). That is, the Self as a spiritual being lives within the lower and middle unconscious, and also in the superconscious. We take on in life the masks of Being-in-the-World and the cloaks of belonging to the cultures in which we live. The journey of self-realisation or spiritual awakening is the journey of remembering who we most authentically are and learning to express that.

Thus in psychosynthesis theory and practice we attempt to hold this paradox as we look at ourselves in relationship to others. This is often difficult because the elements of this paradox – the spiritual and the personal – appear to be polarised into a basic duality in our lives. The majority of psychologies emphasise the personal and discount the spiritual as a flight from or denial of a personal reality. The rational nature of society during the past 300 years has tended to confirm this split or duality and has compartmentalised the personal, placing the spiritual within a religious or supernatural context. The consequences have been severe, in that the Being tends to be seen as the personality rather than as the spiritual Being who has this personality.

Within a psychosynthesis framework, therefore, we believe it important to begin to create an environment within which we are able to listen to the language and promptings of the Self and to experience our spiritual nature – not as something alien to us – through opening to the energy of the superconscious.

For many this happens spontaneously, and we have the peak experience of something 'other', 'bigger', 'more than', that comes from the incredible beauty of a sunset, the wonder of seeing a child being born, the joy in a child or a friend's face, the intense feelings of interdependence when love is directly experienced; that small, still, inner voice that tells us we are not alone. For many of us these experiences and dimensions are so filled with wonder and so precious that we want to protect them and ourselves because of the fear that they will be denied and so trampled upon. In extreme cases we repress them, i.e. we repress the sublime – and split them off from our normal everyday personal issues, living out the duality. Like any splitting off or repression, the

Psychosynthesis

experience goes underground and controls us, either causing us to react to that in others or to project these qualities on to something or some person.

In psychosynthesis we are attempting to hold the paradox and thereby normalise the coexistence of the spiritual and the mystical with the personal, in that both are inherent in who we are, that is the Self. It is important however, for us to distinguish between the nature of the field of the Superconscious and its relation to the Self.

The Superconscious and the Self

Perhaps the greatest confusion in dealing with the higher realms of human nature is the lack of a clear understanding of the distinction between the superconscious and the Self.

Such a distinction can be made. It will be of much practical help to those who want to understand their own experiences, and who seek a clear direction, with stable and recognisable landmarks, along the transpersonal dimension.

Let us begin with the superconscious. Strictly speaking 'superconscious' is just a term to designate the higher, spiritual, or transpersonal region of the psyche. In it various psychological functions, processes, and energies are to be found, just as in the personality, although in the superconscious they can display much greater activity and diversity. So the *difference between the superconscious and the personality is one of level, not of nature*. And superconscious experiences consist fundamentally *in becoming aware of the activity* which is going on in the higher levels of the human consciousness. For example states of ecstasy, of joy, of love for all living creatures, reported by many mystics, impulses to self-sacrifice of the herd, creative flashes of the artist, all belong to the higher levels of the superconscious.

Instead the Transpersonal Self is basically 'ontological'. Onthos means *being* – which is *not process*, which is something standing in itself.

To make a very simple analogy, the Self is like the pivot point, or hinge of a door; the door swings, but the hinge remains steady. Yet, the Self is not only the focal point around which the many superconscious processes occur; it is also the *cause* of those processes, and the *source* of the energy that makes them possible. So the Self is the

Psychosynthesis

unchanging, enduring reality; a stable centre of life on its own level, which *has* functions but is *not* a function.

The key thought is in the Gita: "Having pervaded with one part of myself the whole universe, I remain." What 'remains' is *the Self on its own level*. Yet while it remains there, it can pervade and is pervading the whole universe of the personality, and this it does *through* the superconscious.

We can get a feeling for this apparent paradox if we consider the analogy of the electric power system in our large cities. At the source – the generator, situated in a remote location – there is electricity of a certain *intensity*, or voltage. This electricity *pervades* the whole amazingly complex and intricate power network of the city and is suitably stepped down in voltage along the way by means of transformers, but the intensity (voltage) at the source remains stable and unchanging. And an unchanging voltage is found also at all power outlets in every home. Yet the current, the stream of electric energy, which flows along the wires to energise a multitude of machines, appliances, light sources, etc. constitutes a *vast and continually changing process* which pervades and animates the city.

In this same way the Self is unchanging in essence, yet it sends out its energies, which are stepped down in intensity and transmitted through the superconscious and received, absorbed and utilised by the personality. It is interesting to note that the German philosopher Herman Keyserling talks about intensity as the specific characteristic of the Self. And Jung (*Contributions to Analytical Psychology*, Harcourt, Brace, 1928, p 147) says that archetypes and symbols (which are important elements of the superconscious) are transmitters and transformers of energies.

From another point of view, it is as if the Self were the sun. The sun does not move relative to the earth. It is at the centre of the solar system, and remains there. But it pervades the whole solar system with its radiance, and at the same time sustains it and holds it together through its attractive force.

So the pure experience of the Self – of contact and eventually of identification with the Self – is very different from superconscious experiences or expanded states of awareness. We can begin to grasp this difference through a basic and most important analogy: the Self is to the superconscious as the 'I', or personal self, is to the elements

Psychosynthesis

and functions of the personality, with the difference that the 'I' is often identified with the personality elements, while the Self is not identified with the superconscious.

The experience of the Self might be reached in the measure in which the 'I' – which is a projection or emanation of the Self – ascends toward the Self, identifies with it, and is temporarily absorbed into it.

So the first step toward the experience of the Self is to achieve the experience of the 'I'. The 'I' is the personal centre of awareness and will. It is the *observer* and the *director*, and is distinct from the *contents* of consciousness. To reach it, one must first disidentify from feelings, thoughts, desires, drives, sensations, impulses – from the myriad contents of the personal consciousness. In other words one must relinquish the mistaken sense of being any of them. This of course does not mean in any way to abandon or suppress any of the personality functions. On the contrary, rather than being identified with, and therefore following, one or a few of them at a time, according to their whim, one can now direct and regulate them *at will*, and utilise any or all of them, at any moment, as means of expression in the world.

Achieving this condition of identification with the 'I' and of inner mastery and harmony is a major aim of personal psychosynthesis (see Roberto Assagioli, *Psychosynthesis: A Manual of Principles and Techniques*, Viking, 1971, particularly pp 116-125).

In the measure in which the 'I' succeeds in releasing itself from those mistaken identifications at the personal level, it becomes able to ascend, through the superconscious or transpersonal realm, toward the Self. During this process there can be an increased intensity of the sense of identity, of self-awareness, due to the closer proximity of the Self, *as well* as the awareness and experience of the superconscious process.

One of these two experiences will be prevalent, depending on the psychological type. For example, using the septenary classification mentioned in *The Act of Will* (Roberto Assagioli, Viking, 1973, Appendix V pp 250-1), the experience of the superconscious will be generally prevalent in the 'love/illuminative' type and the 'aesthetic/creative' type, while the increased sense of identity is likely to be the most salient in the 'will/power' type, the 'scientific/rational' type, and to some extent, in the 'active/practical' type.

Psychosynthesis

This is a basic, one could say 'constitutional' difference. But the relative prominence of the two experiences can also change in the same individual at different times depending on a number of factors, for example the particular stage of development, or as a result of deliberate activity undertaken for that purpose, such as specific meditation exercises.

If the experience of the superconscious is stronger than the sense of self-identity, there can be identification of the 'I' with the contents of the superconscious, just as on a previous turn of the spiral there was identification with the contents of the personal consciousness.

This identification with higher and higher aspects of the superconscious is useful, as it can constitute a ladder towards the Self, and thus it represents, for many people, the path of least resistance and the most appropriate path.

But to have a true experience, even a beginning one, of the Self, it is necessary to disidentify also from the superconscious. And that is very difficult, for transpersonal states of awareness are so joyous, so alluring, that one may become attached to them and enmeshed in them. Maslow has called this 'higher sidetracking'. These peak experiences are beautiful and often 'ecstatic', and if properly understood and assimilated can be of real value, but they are not the pure experience of the Self.

It is interesting to observe that the danger of over-attachment to the superconscious has been recognised more or less explicitly by many spiritual teachers of the past. In order to avoid the danger of 'higher side-tracking', a number of approaches to spiritual development adopted the strategy of completely and deliberately turning away from the superconscious. (In the language of the Christian mystics where the 'soul' is the emotional aspect of the personality, 'God' is the Transpersonal Self, and the 'Visions' relate to the superconscious, the emphasis against visions is well known. Similar attitudes exist in the East, for example in many forms of Zen Buddhism.)

I would like to stress the validity of a basic principle of psychosynthesis, that we can benefit from, and utilise, every function and element of our psyche, *provided we understand its nature and purpose, and place it in its right relation with the greater whole.*

Psychosynthesis

So provided we have an adequate roadmap and are aware of the pitfalls we can find along the way, then a balanced emphasis on the development of self-identity and on the awareness of superconscious processes will lead to our most harmonious, joyful, and effective development in the transpersonal realm. As we have said earlier, one or the other will normally be prevalent, depending on a number of factors. The point is to avoid a condition of excessive one-sidedness. This is often produced unwittingly by keeping our interest focused on the side that is more developed – and therefore richer and more interesting – thus developing it even further. But we can also 'feed' the less developed aspect, by deliberately focusing on it the energy of our interest and our attention.

In practice this is often easier to do in the case of the superconscious than of the Self. Because of the transcendent nature of the Self, which is quite beyond our normal range of experience – and therefore beyond the power of our imagination – we often form our concept of what the Self is like on the basis of superconscious experiences. Such a concept is necessarily erroneous and distorted. And later on it often happens that we will believe ourselves to be in touch with the Self while we are actually still experiencing some of the higher aspects of the superconscious.

Some indications can be given to avoid this confusion, but we must keep in mind that it is quite impossible to describe the experience of the Self in more than the most peripheral fashion. In the attempt to indicate what is ineffable, beyond words, various terms have been used: Atman, Tao (in its transcendent sense), The Void, Suchness, The Immovable Mover, The Omega Point.

The experience of the Self has a quality of perfect peace, serenity, calm stillness, and purity, and in it there is the paradoxical blending of individuality and universality.

The Self experiences universality but without 'losing' itself within the vast Universal Self. It remains at the centre, immovable. One way we can begin to realise this is by opening ourselves to the experience of infinity. For we can have the awareness of infinity, the perception of infinite space, without losing our sense of individuality. That is, it is the conscious 'I' who has the perception and the experience of infinity. Infinity IS...and man gropes to a feeble but increasingly profound realisation of its existence. The same can be said concerning eternity. And the experiences of eternity and of infinity – of transcending the limitations of time and space – combined, lead to their synthesis, the experience of universality.

Psychosynthesis

So the Self gradually extends its awareness and identification 'upward', into the vast realm of the Universal Self, yet remains fixed, aware of itself. The fundamental point is that *identification with the universal does not mean loss of identity*, rather its enhancement and intensification. This has been clearly stated by Sarvepalli Radhakrishnan "The peculiar privilege of the human self is that he can consciously join and work for the whole and embody in his own life the purpose of the whole...The two elements of selfhood: uniqueness (each-ness), and universality (all-ness), grow together until at last the most unique becomes the most universal." ('Human Personality' in *The Self*, Clark Moustakas (ed), Harper & Row, 1956, p 118)

In the East this is represented by the symbol of a lotus with a radiant jewel at the centre. The petals of the lotus represent whirlpools, or vortexes of energies of various quality, and as these vortexes develop, interact, and become highly organised, they symbolise the opening of the lotus. They correspond to the transpersonal, superconscious functions and processes. The radiant jewel at the centre represents the hub, the hinge, the Self...a spark of universality, the unmoved mover. Here we find again all processes sustained, and in a sense included, in an immutable reality. This is expressed in the Eastern formula 'Om Mane Padme Hum!'

The fact that all processes can be contained in an immutable, central core is another aspect of the paradoxical nature of the Self. Yet this has been realised experientially by many people. Here is one such account, reported with unusual clarity and detail at the culminating point of an inner exploration using a guided mental imagery technique: "...It's like a loop of white light...it's very bright without glaring...You can look directly at it...it's beautiful. (Guide: Let it slowly come nearer...let it become one with you.) Yes. Yes, I have. That's what I am! I can see it very much clearer now. It's spinning very very fast...That's a very important thing to me...it revolves around a point of white in the centre...Absolutely white...And I can go into the white dot, and if I do, it goes out, and it's like free-faring through the universe. I can go anywhere, the stars are all inside the white dot, everything is inside the white dot. It's hard to keep myself from going through it. (Guide: OK Go ahead...) I'm through. There I am, just shooting around and seeing, just space. The earth is there...I' m conscious of it, all of it. All of this is inside me, as well as outside me. It's the same thing...(long pause)...I'm very at home...There's nothing to say." (Susan Vargiu, 'Psychosynthesis Case Studies', *California Psychosynthesis Institute*, 1971).

Psychosynthesis

It is important to point out that although this subject was quite advanced, at the time of this experience he was quite naïve concerning the superconscious and had not yet been exposed in any way to the concept of the Self. Yet we can easily recognise the fast spinning loop of light as a symbol of the superconscious, and the central point as a symbol of the Self. As the experience progresses, first there is identification with the superconscious (note that it had already occurred spontaneously when the guide suggested it) and this in turn leads to the awareness of the Self, then contact with it, and the consequent simultaneous experience of individuality and universality.

I intentionally said *contact* rather than *identification* with the Self. Throughout this experience, the emphasis was on processes, movements, and forms. The 'point of white in the centre', although having no specific form or colour, was still an image. And the experience was of *going through it*. So this is not to be considered as a pure experience of the Self, rather as a superconscious experience which culminated in a *momentary contact* with the Self, and a glimpse – not in any way the full experience – of the synthesis of individuality and universality.

As I have said, many who have had even intense transpersonal experiences – experiences full of beautiful and ecstatic feelings, of light, of insight – believe that they have made contact with the Self, while in fact they only experienced the superconscious levels of awareness. In reaching toward the Self it is important to know how to recognise this difference. Anything that has movement, change, activity, direction, boundaries, dimensions, restrictions, limits, or specific qualities of any kind, in other words anything that is less than eternal and infinite, that seen from our normal point of view, contains or implies any kind of differentiation, is not the Self!

The reader may object at this point that I have not yet said what the Self is truly like. But the transcendent nature of the Self places it beyond the power of understanding of the concrete mind, and consequently beyond the possibility of describing it with words. The only recourse is to describe what the Self is not. This approach has been very popular in the East, where it is called 'the way of negation'. Its purpose is not so much to convey information about the Self as to gradually elevate the thinking processes beyond the level of dualities and of concrete thought. In the West this has been habitually misunderstood. Often, when we hear that the Self is changeless, we imagine it to be static; if it has no activity, we conclude that it must be passive; if it has no boundaries, it must be shapeless; if it has no qualities, it must be boring. So if it truly were to contain the whole universe, that universe could only be trivial and repugnant.

Psychosynthesis

Again, we have attempted to understand the Self in terms of our normal experiences, and arrived at a concept which has no relation whatsoever to the true nature of the Self. The 'way of negation' needs to be reinterpreted in its true sense. When we say that anything that has quality is not the Self, we mean anything that has specific quality. The Self has no quality yet at the same time it is the synthesis of all qualities, in the sense that all qualities are contained in it and harmoniously integrated. Both darkness and white light can be said to have no colour, yet white light contains all colours, and the right proportions. And the radiation of the Self can be experienced as blackness or as pure intense white light at different times. This has been reported by many mystics, the most famous of all being St. John of the Cross who used the term 'Dark Night of the Soul' to describe the state that *precedes*, and leads to the experience of the Self. Other mystics have talked about the cosmic 'voice of the silence', or 'music of the spheres' which can be heard when all normal sounds cease, and which yet contains all sounds. And the experience of the Void – the transcendence of bounded space and of all that is contained in space – has been described as terrifying or blissful in different circumstances (Karl Dürckheim, 'Horror Vacui – Benedictio Vacui', *Hermes*, 1969, p 63). This paradoxical nature of the Self is perhaps best stated by the Buddhist formula: 'Neither being, nor not-being, nor both being and not-being, nor neither being nor not-being'!

So we need to remember that any concept or picture of the experience of the Self that we may have before the actual experience, is likely to lead us astray if we take it as face value. What is important is not to try to understand beforehand what the experience will be like, but to actually have that experience, by first identifying with the 'I', and then as the 'I', by ascending toward the Self and becoming unified with it. To do so we need on one hand to recognise those aspects which are not the Self, thus becoming able to disidentify from them once they hold us back. On the other hand we can increasingly cultivate and develop the sense of self-identity – as the path which leads to the Self – at the same time as opening ourselves to, and realising as much as possible, the sense of eternity, infinity, and universality, as aspects which help us proceed along that path.

I said before that the experience of the Self has a quality of perfect peace, calm, serenity, etc., but these are not qualities in the normal sense, they are rather states that indicate synthesis, wholeness, unity. So the Self is in reality both the perfect, immutable, inexhaustible source, and the universal, all-encompassing point of convergence, of ultimate fulfilment. It is only in the identification with the Self that we can perma-

Psychosynthesis

nently overcome the innate sense of separateness and aloneness that we have almost come to accept as an inescapable aspect of being human.

To use Maslow's words, "...this is a special phenomenological state in which the person somehow perceives the whole cosmos or at least the unity and integration of it and of everything in it, including his Self. He then feels as if he belongs by right in the cosmos. He becomes one of the family rather than an orphan. He comes inside rather than being outside looking in. He feels simultaneously small because of the vastness of the universe, but also an important being because he is there in it by absolute right. He is part of the universe rather than a stranger to it or an intruder in it." (*The Farther Reaches of Human Nature*, Viking, 1971, p 277).

Identification with the Self gives freedom from all limitations and restrictions of the personal life, and provided the superconscious is adequately developed – freedom to act in the world at will and as a free agent, according to the perceived need, according to transpersonal purpose, and for the greatest good of all.

But this very high state is not in any way an ultimate one. It is the culmination of a cycle which leads to the beginning of a new one, just like the seed which germinates in the dark, pushes its way through the soil with great struggle, and emerges in the freedom of a new existence in the light and open space. Similarly by achieving identification with the Self, and the consciousness of universality, we find our rightful place in the greater whole, and in so doing enter a new cycle, that which Eastern sages have called 'the way of higher evolution'.

We said that in order to have the pure experience of the Transpersonal Self one has to disidentify from that which is not the Self; and that to be able to do so, one has first to have the experience of the personal self – the 'I'.

For this the will has to be used: first to acquire the awareness of the personal 'I', to identify with it, and second to reach up from it toward the Self. At the same time the Self, by means of the Transpersonal Will, attracts and reabsorbs the personal 'I' which it emanated. This indicates the coordinated action of the personal will and the Transpersonal Will (Roberto Assagioli, *The Act of Will*, Viking, 1973, Chapter 9).

As we can see, the 'I' is intimately related to the Transpersonal Self. More precisely, the 'I' is a projection or reflection of the Self, an outpost of the Self in the world of the

Psychosynthesis

personality. It is important to realise this, because the attempt to reach the Self by skipping the 'I' is an error, due to a misunderstanding. Many, with the best intentions, and at the cost of great pain, try to 'destroy' the personal 'I', the ego. Here we find an important difference between psychosynthesis and various other methods. In psychosynthesis we maintain that *nothing has to be condemned, or destroyed, or eliminated*. As I said before, 'we can benefit from and utilise every function and element of our psyche, provided we understand its nature and purpose, and place it in its right relation with the greater whole'.

So the 'I' is not to be destroyed. Personal self-identity is precious. It is the result of a long period of evolution, and cannot be thrown away. What we have to eliminate is our *attachment* to it, because the *personal self has to be brought back to its source!* And, as we have said, this is done through the coordination and alignment of the personal will with the Transpersonal Will, which leads to the reunification of the personal self with the Transpersonal Self.

A clear understanding of this process will show that attempts to 'kill the ego' not only will not help achieve this reunification, but actually lead in the opposite direction. This is clearly stated by Lama Anagarika Govinda (*The Way of the White Clouds*, *Shambhala*, 1970, pp 124-125): "Individuality is not only the necessary and complementary opposite of universality, but the focal point through which alone universality can be experienced. The suppression of individuality, the philosophical or religious denial of its value or importance, can only lead to a state of complete indifference and dissolution, which may be a liberation from suffering but a purely negative one, as it deprives us of the highest experience towards which the process of individuation seems to aim: the experience of perfect enlightenment, of Buddhahood in which the universality of our true being is realised. This is merely to 'merge into the whole' like the 'drop into the sea', without having realised that wholeness is only a poetical way of accepting annihilation and evading the problem that the fact of our individuality poses. Why should the universe evolve individualised forms of life and consciousness if this were not consistent with or inherent in the very spirit or nature of the universe?"

For the 'I' to freely align its will with the Will of the Transpersonal Self is a most difficult task and a culminating act, which only a strong 'I' with a fully developed will is capable of achieving, and for which all previous acts of will in the world of the personality can be considered, in a sense, as preparation and training.

Psychosynthesis

So the unification of the 'I' with the Self becomes possible only once the sense of the 'I', of personal identity, has reached a level of intensity – and the personal will a corresponding strength – such that it can freely and deliberately disidentify from the personality functions and elevate itself sufficiently to elicit a correspondingly attractive action by the Self.

The reader may rightly object at this point that some people have reported undoubtedly genuine experiences of the Self which occurred more or less unexpectedly, without any conscious effort of the individual. In this case it is the Transpersonal Self that initiates the process. (This issue of who initiates and who responds can be misleading. Here I talk from the point of view of experience at the level of the personality, which is necessarily limited and partial. From the view point of the Self – a view-point which is not limited by time and space, and is therefore much more true to reality – the reaching of the 'I' for the Self, and the attraction of the 'I' by the Self, are two aspects of one and the same rhythmic process, and therefore cannot be considered separately, rather they can be said to occur simultaneously.) Such true spontaneous experiences of the Self are extremely rare, and by their very nature, quite unpredictable. So the fact that they do occur is of profound psychological interest, but of little practical help for the person who is searching for an approach and a path he can follow for his own development in the transpersonal realm.

Furthermore such spontaneous experiences are usually of short duration, although their effects can be quite dramatic and beneficial. They typically leave the person with a most intense yearning to 'go back', to return to the state of consciousness. One is then likely to begin an active search for the 'way back'.

This phase is a crucial – and often a very painful one. It is perhaps during this period that one is most likely to get sidetracked, and to find himself repeatedly at a dead end. Spontaneous experiences are likely to occur with little or no effort, while the person is engaged in totally unrelated activities. But often one will assume unconsciously that it is this unrelated behaviour that caused the experience, and later in the attempt to replicate such experience, one may try to 'figure out what he did' that made it happen, and as a result waste much time and go to dangerous extremes, attempting to reproduce the conditions in which the experience occurred. Or remembering the state of peace, of serenity, of being, which he may have realised at the high point of the experience, he may decide to reduce to a minimum, or suspend, all personality activities, considering them a disturbing element, and antithetical to the state he is trying to reach. Such attempts are increasingly common today, and are the distortion of an attitude which is valid and appropriate *at its own level*.

This right attitude can perhaps be best illustrated by Wagner's symbolic epic of the Grail (Roberto Assagioli, *Psychosynthesis: A Manual of Principles and Techniques*, Viking, 1971, pp 208-211). Titurel, the knight, ascends the mountain, with much labour and courage. Then, after having reached the top, he spends the night in prayer, asking for inspiration, and waits in silence. In response to this prayer, a host of angels (symbol of the superconscious) appear, and bring him the Cup (the Grail, symbol of transpersonal Love) and the Sword (symbol of Spiritual Power and Will). We see here first the active phase, and then the *receptive* phase. This sequence is essential. The knight who leaves the world behind him and ascends the mountain with much labour is the symbol of the 'I' as it first disidentifies from all personality functions and aspects, and then, with an act of will, ascends as close as it can toward the Self. At the summit a receptive, contemplative attitude is taken, through the techniques of *meditation, contemplation*, and *silence* (Roberto Assagioli, *The Act of Will*, Viking, 1973, Appendix II).

This, if executed correctly, can lead to the inflow of the superconscious (which transmits to the personality the needed transpersonal qualities) and later to contact with the Self. So we must first 'reach the top', then assume the proper inner attitude, becoming silent at all levels of the personality, but from a *focused point of tension oriented upward*.

A common error is to try to suspend all activity before having reached the top, or even before having started to climb. This can make us open to undesirable or dangerous influences, and in any case is a state of passivity that leads to stagnation. The opposite error is to keep trying to climb, or to forget to turn the attention upward, after having reached the mountain top. Then the 'noise' of our physical, emotional, and mental activity prevents us from hearing, and turning ourselves to, the more subtle 'sounds' of the transpersonal realms.

Again, neither *activity* nor *receptivity* is to be rejected. Both are useful, even necessary, provided we understand their function and use each at the appropriate time and place.

Psychosynthesis

I said that the 'I' is a projection, an outpost of the Self. And there is a permanent connection between the two, through which energy can flow. When a good measure of genuine personal self-awareness is reached, then there are streams of energy which flow from the Transpersonal Self to the 'I'. This, again, is different from the energy which comes from the superconscious levels, for they bring no specific contents or intuitions.

They are intimations from the Transpersonal Self and are *experienced as intensification of self-awareness*. So this experience gives an acute sense of self-awareness accompanied by a sense of bliss. *Sat Chit Ananda*, 'Thou art that'.

For the Transpersonal Self is reality; it is of the same nature as the Universal Reality. Therefore its energy is charged with power and bliss, without any definite content. For this reason the ultimate reality to which it belongs has been described in terms of *purity*. This is the absence of specific quality, which is arrived at through the harmonious synthesis of *all* qualities (just as white light, the absence of colour, is the combination in right proportions of all colours). It is the void in a positive sense, the 'Suchness of the Void', a void which contains all life, to which everything belongs, and in which all is combined.

This is the true contact with the Self. All the rest is contact with the superconscious.

The Self is without dimensions; it is both a geometric point that occupies no space; it is both zero and infinity, the 'Laya Point', Aristotle's 'Unmoved Mover'. And it radiates beams of energy, emanates an energy field. An aspect of this energy reaches the superconscious. Another reaches the 'I'. The relationship between the Self and the 'I' is a direct one, in which the superconscious is not involved. One must learn to pass through the realm of the superconscious without looking right or left, so to speak, and that is very difficult, because it is so enticing, and understandably so. But one must remember that its charm can constitute the 'Higher Sidetrackings' of which Maslow talks about.

On the other hand the superconscious is of utmost importance in our development, and its vital place needs to be appreciated and understood, because parallel to the increasing intensity of the realisation of self-consciousness – which can be considered an ascent, or progress along a vertical dimension – there needs to be experience, expansion, and expression at all levels, along the horizontal dimension.

Psychosynthesis

Even at the personality level we don't, nor should we, live in the pure self-consciousness of the 'I'. The 'I' creates its personality. Personal psychosynthesis is just that – the creation of a fully harmonised and integrated personality by the 'I', the personal self. The 'I' must be able to express itself at all personality levels, must use all the energies and functions without forced identification with any of them, being free to be either *fully disidentified or partially identified* with any one function or group of functions, at any moment and *at will*, according to its own purpose. The personal self along the way of unfoldment and growth has to make use of its qualities, to express its power, its will, and to pervade the little universe of the personality while remaining at the centre.

In a similar way the Transpersonal Self on its own level must use the superconscious as its vehicle of experience and expression, as a means through which its energy is 'transformed' or 'stepped down' (such stepping down or transformations of energy are quite common, in nature and in man-made devices alike. Electric transformers, and the gear shift of automobiles and bicycles fulfil just such a function. In nature, when the powerful and lethal high energy radiation (gamma rays and x-rays) emitted by the Sun reaches the upper atmosphere of the Earth, it interacts with free electrons – a process called Compton Effect – and is stepped down into the visible light and heat which is vital to the biological world) into a form that can be utilised by the personality.

This is the normal course of evolution, a course that leads to increasing health and wholeness. Just as highly developed superconscious process without commensurate development of the sense of self can be overpowering, and lead one to be 'swept away', and in extreme cases to regress into the mass consciousness, so a premature inrush of energy directly from the Self, without the capacity to channel the energy into and through the superconscious, can produce imbalance and disorientation, and in extreme cases even psychosis. The intensity is too high, and the means to understand and assimilate the experience in relation to everyday awareness, and act accordingly, are not available. The experience of the Self remains unconnected. This can cause a most painful sense of split, and a lack of understanding, or lack of means of expression in the world – almost like being disabled. In extreme cases there can be rejection of the every-day world as non-real. (This is a basic experiential confusion: the world is real. What is non-real is our perception of it, as physicists proved at the beginning of the century. They have shown that what we perceive as solid matter is really almost completely empty space, in which atoms – themselves whirlpools of energy – interact at distances proportional to the stars in our galaxy.) At the opposite pole, there can be a confusion of levels where after the experience one believes that he is still identified with the Self when he has actually 'descended' once again to the level of the 'I'. This can cause 'ego inflation', feelings of omnipotence, and in extreme cases the individual, speaking from the personal self, says 'I am God', thus ascribing to the 'I' a spiritual nature that properly belongs to the Self.

However when parallel to the reaching upward toward the Self, the superconscious functions and processes are also developed, there is a safe, healthy, and immensely fruitful path through which the energy can flow. Then one can use compassion and wisdom, as well as strength, power and will: the strength and the power to express compassion according to wisdom; the wisdom and compassion to use power for the greatest good!

Exercises Following This Section

The following exercises on Evoking and Developing Desired Qualities and the Inner Dialogue serve to align the individual with the transpersonal self.

Further Reading

Assagioli, Roberto, *Psychosynthesis: A Manual of Principles and Techniques*, Harper Collins, 1993 (Chapters 2 and 4)

Assagioli, Roberto, *The Act of Will*, David Platt, 1999 (Chapter 9)

Ferrucci, Piero, *What We May Be*, Thorsons, 1995 (Chapters 12 and 14)

Hardy, Alistair, *Spiritual Nature of Man*, Alistair Hardy Research Centre, 1991 (Chapters 1, 4, 5, 6 and 8)

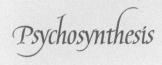
Psychosynthesis

Evoking and Developing Desired Qualities Exercise

The purpose of this exercise is to create inner and outer conditions through which one can foster and enhance a desired quality within oneself. It is suggested for daily practice. In the following outline, the quality of serenity will be used, but the exercise can be adapted for other qualities, such as courage, patience, joy, compassion, etc. It is important that the choice of such a quality and the decision to develop it come from within the individual himself, not as a 'should' but as something he has chosen purposely and freely as a further step in his growth.

Procedure

1 Assume a state of relaxation and take a few deep breaths. Then think about the idea of serenity: hold the concept 'serenity' in your mind, and reflect on it. What is its quality, its nature, its meaning, etc.? As you develop insights, ideas, or images associated with the concept, record them in your psychological workbook.

2 Open yourself to further ideas or images related to serenity that may emerge from your unconscious, and write down as above.

3 Realise the value of serenity, its purpose, its use, especially in our turbulent modern world. Praise serenity in your mind. Desire it.

4 Assume a physical attitude of serenity. Relax all muscular and nervous tension. Breathe slowly and rhythmically. Allow serenity to express itself on your face. It may help to visualise yourself with that expression.

5 Evoke serenity directly. Imagine you are in a place which makes you feel serene: a quiet beach, a temple, a cool green glade...perhaps a place where you have experienced serenity in the past. Try to feel it. Repeat the word 'serenity' several times. Let serenity permeate you to the point of identification with it, if possible.

6 Imagine yourself in circumstances common in your daily life which in the past would have tended to upset or irritate you; perhaps being with a hostile person – or facing a difficult problem – or obliged to do many things rapidly – or in danger – and

see and feel yourself calm and serene (this step may be postponed until you have gained some familiarity with the exercise).

7 Resolve as much as you can to remain serene through the day, to be a living example of serenity, to radiate serenity.

8 Make a sign with the word 'serenity', using the colour and lettering that best conveys this quality to you. Place this sign where you can see it daily and if possible at the time when you need serenity the most. Whenever you look at it recall within yourself the feeling of serenity.

This exercise to develop desired qualities can become the focus of a larger program. You can gather together poetry, symbols, music, drama, artwork, photography, dance, and biographical excerpts, all evoking or in some personal sense symbolising serenity, and use them for a total experience. By surrounding yourself with these materials, you can evoke and develop a deep sense of serenity – or of any other quality. You can use all that you find in your environment to foster a sense of serenity through your own creation of a synthesis of experiential forms.

A possible contraindication: in a minority of cases it is possible to experience a negative reaction to the exercise, i.e. attempting to evoke serenity may bring tension, restlessness, anxiety, etc. This is usually a sign that there is a core of negative emotions that block the development of the desired quality. Such a situation is most likely to be encountered during step 6 of the exercise. If the negative reaction is strong, it is best to suspend the use of the exercise, explore the negative feelings that emerged, and then release them through catharsis. After this the exercise can be resumed, and will then have particular value as a means of filling with a positive and desired quality the psychological space left vacant by the release of the negative feeling.

Transpersonal Qualities

▮ Beauty
▮ Compassion
▮ Courage
▮ Creativity
▮ Energy, power
▮ Enthusiasm

Psychosynthesis

- Eternity, infinity, universality
- Freedom, liberation, detachment
- Cooperation, friendship, brotherhood
- Generosity
- Goodness
- Goodwill
- Gratitude, appreciation, admiration, wonder
- Harmony
- Inclusiveness
- Joy, bliss
- Light
- Love
- Order
- Patience
- Positiveness
- Reality, truth
- Renewal
- Trust, faith
- Serenity, peace
- Service
- Silence, quiet, calm
- Simplicity
- Synthesis, wholeness
- Understanding
- Vitality
- Will
- Wisdom

Roberto Assagioli (adapted from 'Exercise for Evoking Serenity', in Psychosynthesis: a Manual of Principles and Techniques, Harper Collins, 1993, pp 166-175 and 223-227 and from 'The Technique of Evocative Words' Psychosynthesis Research Foundation, 1970)

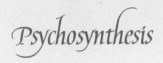
Psychosynthesis

The Inner Dialogue

Each of us has within a source of understanding and wisdom that knows who we are, where we have been, and where we are going. It is in tune with our unfolding purpose and senses clearly the next steps to be taken to fulfil this purpose. As we contact it, we can better recognise the difficulties we are having in our growth, and, with its help, can guide our awareness and will toward their resolution. Rightly used, it can help us direct our energies toward achieving increasing integration in our daily living, and toward unifying into one lived reality the personal and transpersonal dimensions of our lives.

Many images are associated with this source of inner guidance. Common ones are the sun, a diamond, a fountain, a star or point of light, an angel, an eagle, dove, or phoenix, the Christ or the Buddha. Different images emerge to meet different needs. However, the one most commonly associated with this source is that of a wise and loving old man or woman (these are two distinct archetypes, with many similarities but also specific differences. It is worthwhile to experiment with both so as to know each well, and know when to use one or the other according to the specific needs of the situation. In general, the wise old man is often encouraging, stimulating, inspiring; the wise old woman is more nurturing, supportive, allowing).

Procedure

This exercise is designed to facilitate contact with one's inner source of wisdom. The simplest procedure is to close one's eyes, take a few deep breaths, and then let appear in your imagination the face of a wise old man (or woman) whose eyes express great love for you. (If you have difficulty in getting an image, you can first imagine a candle flame, burning steadily and quietly, and then let his (or her) face appear at its very centre).

Engage him in dialogue and, in whatever way seems best, use his presence and guidance to help you understand better whatever questions, directions, choices, you are dealing with at the moment. (This dialogue may include words, but it may also take place on a non-verbal, visual level of communication and understanding). Spend as much time as you need in this dialogue, and when you are finished write down what

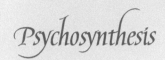

happened, if appropriate, amplifying and evaluating further whatever insights were gained.

After some practice the use of an image may become less necessary, for contact will become steadily more available, perhaps in the form of a inner voice (an example of this would be Socrates' daimon) or simply as direct knowing of what is the best thing for you to be doing in any given situation. Over time the contact with this inner source can grow, so that its love and wisdom increasingly can inform and guide our daily lives.

Afterword

In the use of this exercise, two further mental processes are necessary: discrimination and interpretation. We must learn to discriminate between those images which carry true wisdom and those which do not. For example, occasionally a critical and authoritarian figure appears, one who is not truly loving toward you. This can be the projection of a subpersonality or a known person on to the superconscious, and discrimination must be used to recognise it for what it is and 'unmask' it. Also, a positive projection on to the superconscious may result in hearing what you want to, not what is really being communicated.

Secondly, the message received is not always clear in its application and so must be interpreted correctly. A famous example of this is God's injunction to St. Francis to 'Go and rebuild my church'. At first Francis thought this meant to rebuild the little ruined church of San Damiano outside the walls of Assisi, and only later did he realise its true import – to rebuild the whole Catholic Church!

Finally, though this contact is important, it is also important not to over use it. The best procedure is to first explore as fully as possible the dimensions of the problem you are dealing with, and then, when and if you find no solution 'down here', then ask for guidance.

With these considerations in mind, the technique of the Inner Dialogue will prove effective and powerful as means to further the process of personal and spiritual psychosynthesis.

Psychosynthesis

Psychosynthesis
Research
Foundation

Symbols of Transpersonal Experiences

A discussion of what is transpersonal – and therefore, in a certain sense supernormal – should be prefaced by a clarification of what is meant by 'normal'. The current criterion of normality is generally considered to be represented by the average man who observes the social conventions of the environment in which he lives – in other words, one who is a conformist. But 'normality' understood in this way is a conception that offers little satisfaction; it is static and exclusive. This normality is a 'mediocrity' which either refuses to admit or condemns everything outside the conventionally accepted and thus considers it 'abnormal' without taking into account the fact that many so-called abnormalities in reality represent the first steps or endeavours to rise above mediocrity.

Now, however, a reaction against this narrow-minded cult of 'normal' has set in; thinkers and scientists of our time are opposing it vigorously. Among the most outspoken one may mention Jung (*Modern Man in Search of a Soul*, Harcourt Brace, 1933), who has not hesitated to state: "To be 'normal' is a splendid ideal for the unsuccessful, for all those who have not yet found an adaptation. But for people who have far more ability than the average, for whom it was never hard to gain successes and to accomplish their share of the world's work – for them restriction to the normal signifies the bed of Procrustes, unbearable boredom, infernal sterility and hopelessness. As a consequence there are many people who become neurotic because they are only normal, as there are people who are neurotic because they cannot become normal."

Another writer, Professor Gattegno of London University, has gone even further, stating that he regards the ordinary average man as a pre-human being and reserves the word 'Man', with a capital M, only for those who have transcended the common level or stage of development and are, in this respect, supernormal.

Psychosynthesis

In the past, the veneration of superior beings was widespread. The genius, the sage, the saint, the hero and the initiate were recognised as the vanguard of humanity, as the grand promise of what each man could become. These superior beings, while in no way disdaining ordinary humanity, sought to arouse in it the urge and the longing to transcend the 'normality' and mediocrity in which it existed, and develop the transpersonal possibilities latent in every human being.

In speaking of the transpersonal we are faced with a serious difficulty and that is the inadequacy of human language, particularly of modern language, which is rational and objective. All words designating psychological or spiritual conditions or realities are in origin metaphors or symbols based on concrete things. For instance, soul (*anima*) is derived from '*anemos*', meaning wind; spirit from '*spiritus*', meaning breath. But the difficulty is not insurmountable if we remember and keep constantly in mind the symbolic nature of every expression, be it verbal or other kinds. Symbols properly recognised and understood possess great value: they are 'evocative' and induce direct intuitive understanding. Indeed, the fact that the words indicating higher realities have their roots in sensuous experience serves to emphasise the essential analogical correspondences between the external and the inner worlds.

Yet symbols have their dangers. In fact, he who takes them literally and does not pass beyond the symbol to reality, but halts before it, does not arrive at the underlying truth. Moreover, symbols are unilateral. No symbol can express more than an aspect, a quality, a partial conception of a given reality. This qualification can, however, be obviated by the employment of different symbols to indicate the same truth. Thus the sum, the convergence, the synthesis of many points of view can provide a greater and more integrated understanding of the reality they symbolise.

So, to designate the transpersonal experiences and achievements open to man, we find that there are fourteen categories or groups of symbols:
1 Introversion
2 Deepening – Descent
3 Elevation – Ascent
4 Broadening – Expansion
5 Awakening
6 Light – Illumination
7 Fire
8 Development

Psychosynthesis

9 Strengthening – Intensification
10 Love
11 Way – Path – Pilgrimage
12 Transmutation – Sublimation
13 Rebirth – Regeneration
14 Liberation

These symbols are not only suggestive and illuminating; they can be used as subjects of meditation, indeed of 'psychospiritual exercises'. This has already been done for anagogic and psychotherapeutic purposes. These meditations and exercises have proved themselves very effective, sometimes producing surprising transformations ('The Exercise of the Rose', a description of which is given at the end of this article, provides an example of such use).

1 *To the first group belong the symbols of introversion, of inner orientation.* Introversion is an urgent necessity for modern man; our present civilisation is exaggeratedly extraverted and man is caught up in a frenetic vortex of activities that become ends in themselves. 'Normal' man today may be said to live, psychologically and spiritually, outside himself. This expression – which in the past was applied to the mentally ill – is well-fitted to describe modern man! He has now reached the point of living everywhere except within himself; he is in reality 'ex-centric', that is to say, he lives outside his own inner centre (in French there is another apt expression: désaxé, off one's axis).

The external life must, therefore, be counterbalanced by an adequate inner life. We must turn back into ourselves. The individual must renounce his many and continuous escapist expedients and address himself to the discovery of what has recently been termed 'inner space'. Recognition must be given to the existence not only of the external world, but of different inner worlds, and to the fact that it is possible, and indeed man's duty, to know them, explore them and conquer them.

Modern man has learned to control nature and exploit her energies, but generally is not aware that, in reality, all that he accomplishes externally has its origin in him, in his mind, and is the result of desires, drives, impulses, programmes and plans. These are psychological, that is, inner activities; every external action has its source in inner causes. First of all, therefore, these causes should be known, examined and regulated. Goethe, a genius who well knew how to play the part of the 'normal man' when he

Psychosynthesis

wanted, said: "When we have done our part within, the exterior will unfold itself automatically." .

Interiorisation, besides giving balance and nervous and psychic health, is the way to experiences of a transpersonal character. Turning within ourselves, we discover our Centre, our true Being, the most intimate part of ourselves. Here belong the 'peak experiences' so ably described by Maslow (*Toward a Psychology of Being*, Van Nostrand, 1962).

2 *The second group of symbols is composed of those associated with deepening, with the descent to the 'ground' of our being.* The exploration of the unconscious is symbolically regarded as the descent into the abysses of the human being, as the investigation of the 'underworld of the psyche'. This symbol has come into use particularly since the development of psychoanalysis – although not discovered by it. Its origin is remote and, indeed, in antiquity it carried a deeper meaning. Let us recall the descent of Aeneas into Hades in Virgil's Aeneid and Dante's description of hell. Furthermore, many mystics have spoken of the 'abysses of the soul'. Beside psychoanalysis in the strict sense, there is the 'depth psychology', represented by Jung and others. Its fundamental principle is that man must courageously become aware of all the discreditable and obscure aspects of his being, those which have been called 'the shadow', and then incorporate them into his conscious personality. This recognition and this inclusion are acts of humility and, at the same time, of power. The man who is willing and courageous enough to recognise the lower sides of his personality, without allowing this knowledge to overwhelm him, achieves a true spiritual victory. But this carries its own dangers: the allegory of *The Sorcerer's Apprentice* contains a warning of how easy it is to make the 'waters' gush out, but how difficult then to control them and command them to retreat.

In this connection the practice of Robert Desoille (*Le Rêve Éveillé en Psychothérapie*, Presses Universitaires de France, 1945), with his method of the '*rêve éveillé*', is valuable. He makes use of the symbol of the descent, but puts greater emphasis on that of the ascent. Of the descent he observes that it is to be used prudently and 'fractionatedly', i.e. commencing by seeking to activate the higher realisation and then, as the subject becomes stronger, cautiously exploring the zone of the lower unconscious. The aim is the elimination of the dissociation between the consciousness and the lower unconscious, which has been produced by repression and condemnation on the part of the conscious ego and his unwillingness to admit, from pride or fear, that there exists this aspect of the personality. To repress it serves no useful purpose; far from eradicating it, it exacerbates it, while it is man's task to redeem it. But to accord it recognition does not mean surrendering oneself to its demands; it is preparing the way for its transformation.

3 *The third group of symbols is of widespread use; it includes elevation, ascent, the conquest of 'inner space' in an upward direction.* There is a series of inner worlds, each of which has its specific characteristics, and its higher and lower levels. Thus the first, the world of emotions and feelings, exhibits a marked difference of level between blind passions and the loftiest sentiments. Then there is the world of the intelligence, of the mind; and here also are found different levels: those of the concrete, analytical mind and of higher, philosophical reason (*nous*). There are, moreover, the world of the imagination; the world of the intuition; the world of the will and – higher still – the ineffable world which can only be indicated with the designation, world of transcendence.

The symbolism of elevation has been used in every age. Every religion had temples erected in high places, on mountain tops; and in antiquity many mountains were considered sacred. Moreover, there are symbolic legends, such as that of Titurel's ascent of the mountain to build on its summit the Castle of the Holy Grail. The symbol of the sky, or heaven as a superior realm, the habitation of the gods and the goal of human aspiration, is universal.

4 *The symbols of the fourth group are those of expansion, or broadening, of the consciousness.* It is well to note that, although the different symbols may appear to be contradictory, in reality they are not so, but indeed are integrative. In the same way that the descent does not exclude ascent – it is in fact advisable, as we have said, to ascend first in order to be able to descend without danger – so the ability to expand the consciousness without losing oneself in its vastness, requires the taking up of a firm, stable position at the centre of one's being. Those two realisations complement and do not exclude each other.

The psychiatrist Urban speaks of the 'spectrum of consciousness', and maintains that we are only conscious within a limited area corresponding to the band of the light spectrum between red and violet, while there are other psychospiritual areas corresponding to the infra-red and ultra-violet bands. Our consciousness can be enlarged or broadened, to include increasingly large zones of impressions and contents. This

Psychosynthesis

expansion must be conceived spherically, that is, in all directions, vertical as well as horizontal, that is from the individual to the group, to society, to the whole of humanity. But it is necessary to maintain one's self-awareness within the whole and not 'lose' oneself therein.

Another series of symbols of magnitude and breadth is based on the Sanskrit root *'mah'*, which means 'great', and from which are derived *'magister'* (master), magician, mahatma, etc. One generally speaks of 'great' men in distinction to 'little', ordinary men. The expansion that leads to the inclusion of other beings in oneself is associated with the symbolism of love (see Group 10).

Time provides another direction in which expansion takes place. Man generally lives in the present, absorbed in the interest of the moment; but he can expand his consciousness to include ever wider cycles, a temporal continuum of varying dimensions. This leads to comprehension that the meaning and value of a human life do not lie in any one isolated moment, but in a process which unfolds, at the very least, between physical birth and death. This expansion in time, this inclusion of ever-widening cycles, serves as a preparation for the passage – one might say the leap – from time to the eternal, understood not as unlimited duration, but as an extra-temporal transcendental dimension, in which our inner centre, the Self, exists and persists above the flow of the temporal current.

5   *We come now to the fifth group of symbols, which are among the most suggestive and effective: the symbols of awakening.* The state of consciousness of the average man can be termed a dream state in a world of illusions: the illusion of the 'reality' of the external world as our senses perceive it, and the many illusions created by the imagination, the emotions and mental concepts. As far as the external world is concerned, modern physics has demonstrated that what appears to our senses as concrete, stable and inert is, on the contrary, constituted of congeries of infinitesimal elements in extremely rapid motion, of energy charges animated by a powerful dynamism. Thus matter, as our senses perceive it and as it was conceived by materialistic philosophy, does not exist. Modern science has thus arrived at the fundamental Indian conception, according to which all that 'appears' is maya, illusion.

Then there are the emotional and mental illusions, which concern us more closely, conditioning our life and continuously producing errors of evaluation and conduct, and sufferings of every kind. In this field also, modern psychological science has

Psychosynthesis

reached the same conclusions as the ancient wisdom, that is, that man sees every thing and every being through a thick veil of colouring and distortions deriving from his emotional reactions, the effect of past psychic traumas, external influences, etc. The effects of this are mental illusions which lead him to believe that he is thinking objectively, while instead he is being affected by what Bacon called 'idols', by preconceptions and by collective influences.

All this creates a veritable dream state from which one can and should wake up. This awakening demands first of all an act of courage and the confrontation with reality. We have to reach the recognition of our psychological multiplicity, of the various sub-personalities co-existing within us, to the extent that every human being can be said to be a Pirandello character. The first step consists, therefore, in becoming aware of all that exists and stirs restlessly within us; the second, in discovering what we really are: a centre of self-awareness, the Self, the spectator of the human tragi-comedy.

The doctrine and practice of the awakening are of ancient date. The Buddha laid particular insistence upon it in his teachings, so that he became known as the 'Perfectly Awakened One'. An effective exercise for promoting the awakening can be performed after the normal waking up from sleep in the morning, by passing from this state to a true second awakening in the world of transpersonal awareness. The relationship between the two states might be expressed in the form of an equation: sleep is to ordinary waking state as this state is to transpersonal wakefulness.

6 *In the sixth group of symbols are found those of light, of illumination.* Just as ordinary waking marks the passage from darkness of the night to the light of the sun, so the awakening transpersonal awareness marks the transition that has been designated 'illumination'. The first step – which corresponds to the first stage of the waking state – is a simple (but not on that account easy) ability to see clearly within ourselves; the second, of illumination, is the solution of problems hitherto appearing insoluble, and this by means of the specific instrument of inner vision, the intuition. Thus intuitive awareness comes to replace intellectual, logical and rational consciousness, or better, to integrate and transcend it. The *intuition* in fact leads to identification with what is seen and contemplated, and to the recognition of the intrinsic unity between object and subject.

There is a further degree or kind of illumination: it is the perception of the light immanent in the human soul and in the whole of creation. We have numerous evidences of this; many mystics have described their inner illuminations. In Buddhism, and particularly in Zen, special disciplines aim at producing a sudden illumination with its accompanying revelation of reality.

7 *The seventh group – the symbols of fire – is one of the most comprehensive and at the same time most essential.* The worship and veneration of fire are found in all religions. Everywhere, on altars, in torches and in lamps, the sacred fire burns – the flames glitter. The flame of the Olympic torch is a symbol of contests in which athletes strive to give proof of exceptional physical prowess. The inner experience of fire has been lived through by many mystics: it is sufficient to mention St. Catherine of Sienna and Blaise Pascal. The function of fire is primarily one of purification, and it is employed with this intent in 'spiritual alchemy'.

8 *The symbols of the eighth group are among the most closely associated with human experience, and are indicated by the words evolution and development. In a certain sense these words might be said to be synonymous.* Development signifies release from encumbrances and denotes the passage from the potential to the actual. The two principal symbols of development are the seed and the flower: the seed which enfolds within itself the potentiality of the tree; the flower which opens from the closed bud and is the precursor of the fruit.

Familiarity has bred in us indifference to the miracle by which the acorn develops into the oak, and the child into the adult. Where, in reality, is the tree in the seed, where the oak in the acorn? Aristotle speaks of 'entelechy', others of 'model' and 'archetype'. An immanent Intelligence must be admitted which directs the various phases of the development of the seed from the tree, from the cell or germinal cells to the complete organism.

The other symbol, widely used since ancient times, is the flower: the Golden Flower (in China), the lotus (in India) and the rose (in Persia and Europe). The symbolism of the lotus is closely associated with what happens in man. The lotus has its roots in the earth, its stalk grows in the water, and its flower opens in the air in response to the action of the rays of the sun. It is an apt symbol of man, who has a physical body as a terrestrial base and develops psychologically in the sphere of the emotions ('water') and of the mind ('air'). The realisation of the Self, the inner centre, corresponds to the opening of the flower brought about by the vivifying action of the sun, the symbol of the spirit. Some Eastern methods of development and meditation are based on this symbolism of the lotus.

The same applies to a great extent to the rose, whose symbolism originated in Persia, where the mystic poets speak of the rose in this sense. In Europe we find *Le Roman de la Rose*, Dante's 'mystic rose', and certain more or less secret movements, in particular those of the Rosicrucians. I have used the symbol of the rose in a special exercise which has proved very effective in stimulating and promoting the opening, or blossoming, of the transpersonal consciousness.

The symbol of development is applicable to two different stages: the first, extending from childhood to adulthood; the second, from the state of 'normal' man to that of the 'awakened' individual. Maria Montessori, who devoted herself to the education of children and revolutionised preceding educational systems, is justified in saying: "Development of the child into the man takes place actively within, and the child pursues this task joyously when the adult does not interfere by dispensing the treasures of his wisdom. The child is the human seed: as the oak tree subsists in the acorn, so the adult subsists in embryo in the child."

We may recall that Plutarch had already said: "Man is not a vessel to be filled, but a fire to kindle. "To educate, in fact, should be – as its etymology indicates – (to) 'e-ducere', to draw forth (from within), that is, to *develop*.

Of the second phase of man's development, it may be said to be truly representative of the passage to a transpersonal stage.

9 *The ninth series of symbols includes those of strengthening, or intensification.* Transpersonal experiences may be regarded as a reinforcement or intensification of the life consciousness, a tension or psychological 'voltage' higher than that in which the average man lives. Keyserling (*From Suffering to Fulfilment*, Brandon & Son, 1938) speaks of a "dimension of intensity", associating the symbolism of intensification with that of proceeding along a different dimension which he terms 'vertical' (the other dimension being horizontal). In using this term 'vertical dimension', he refers to a 'verticality' that rises from the world of becoming, or flux, towards the world of being and of transcendence. He applies this symbol also to time, a 'vertical passing' from time to the extra-temporal eternal. Strengthening also has two stages or degrees. The first consists in the reinforcement of all man's latent, underdeveloped energies and functions. In his essay, The 'Energies of Men', William James draws attention to a number of energy-potentialities existing in man, waiting to be brought into manifestation when he wills to discover, activate and use them. The second degree of reinforcement permits the passage from the personal to the transpersonal level referred to above, in which also the manifestation of various parapsychological powers may occur. At times. such powers, when associated with the higher ethical and spiritual endowments, have been ascribed to illuminates, to the 'awakened', to 'initiates' from Moses to Pythagoras, from Buddha to Christ and various mystics. Some have employed them deliberately and consciously; in others they manifested spontaneously, even against the will of the subject. One might say that these powers are sometimes a consequence, a by-product as it were, of transpersonal experiences.

10 *The symbols of the tenth group are those of love.* Human love itself is, in a certain respect, a desire and an attempt – more or less conscious – to 'come out' of oneself, to transcend the limits of separate existence and enter into communion, to fuse oneself, with another being, with a 'thou'. The devout and mystics of every age have spoken of their experience of communion with God or with Higher Beings, employing the symbolism of human love. One may recall the 'Song of Songs' in the Bible and the expressions – sometimes of a surprising audacity – used by St. Catherine of Sienna and St. John of the Cross.

11 *The symbols of the eleventh group include those of the Way, the Path and of pilgrimage.* These two have been, and are, universally used. The religious employ the term 'mystic way'. The symbol of 'pilgrimage' has often been, and still is, used in a physical and external manner in connection with the pilgrimage to various sacred places. Dante's passing through the Inferno, Purgatory and Paradise has been called a pilgrimage. Bunyan's Pilgrim's Progress will also be recalled in this connection.

12 *We now come to the twelfth group, the symbols of transmutation.* The body and psyche can be transmuted by means of a regenerative transformation. This produces an organic and harmonious unification of all man's aspects, a 'biopsychosynthesis'. A 'psychospiritual alchemy' is achieved. When one speaks of alchemy, one thinks of the attempts to make gold (something which used to appear incredible, but now seems less fantastic since man has learned to transform one element into another by the manipulation of atoms). But in reality the Arabian and medieval alchemical books often veiled in chemical terms the psychospiritual alchemy, that is, the transmutation of man. This has been recognised by some modern writers, notably Jung (*Psychologie*

Psychosynthesis

und Religion, Rascher Verlag, 1940), who devoted much time during the last years of his life to the study of, and to writing about, alchemical symbolism. In his book *Psychology and Religion*, he discusses it extensively and relates how he discovered this symbolism in the dreams of his patients and in the drawings of both the ill and the healthy.

Transmutation and transformation occur in two different ways, in two opposite directions, but ways which are not in opposition; they alternate and complete each other. The first is transmutation through sublimation; the second is the transformation produced by the descent, the irruption of superconscious energies into the personality, including the body. Their combined action brings about a complete biopsychosynthesis.

13 *The thirteenth group comprises the symbols of regeneration, of the 'new birth'.* It is related to the preceding group, since a complete transmutation prepares or opens the way to regeneration, which, in its most profound and essential meaning, constitutes a 'new birth', the birth of the 'new man', of the spiritual man within the personality. In India, Brahmins are called Dwigis, that is, twice-born. This symbol has been much used in Christianity, and mystics have spoken of the 'birth of the Christ in the heart'.

14 *The symbols of the fourteenth group are those of liberation and have a relationship with those of development.* They mean the elimination of the encumbrances, a process of liberation from our complexes, our illusions and from identification with the various 'parts' we play in life, the 'masks' we assume, with our 'idols', etc. It is a release in the etymological sense of the term, a freeing and activation of latent potentialities.

The symbolism of liberation has pervaded all the great world religions. In India, the Buddha said: "As the water of the sea is all pervaded by salt, so my whole teaching is pervaded by liberation." In Christianity, Paul affirms the 'liberty of the Sons of God'.

In our times, during the second World War, Franklin D Roosevelt proclaimed the Four Great Freedoms: freedom of expression, religious freedom, freedom from need and freedom from fear. The last, the freedom from fear, is fundamental, since only he who is free from fear is truly free.

Here, however, we find ourselves confronted by a paradox. In contrast with his spontaneous yearning for freedom, man fears it at the same time. This can be explained by the fact that freedom implies commitment, self control, courage, and other qualities. It has been justly said, 'The price of freedom is eternal vigilance'. Freedom must be won again and safeguarded every day, one might say every moment. Man, even if unaware of this, but feeling it intuitively, fears this 'burden of freedom' and, in consequence, recoils from it. This fear is one of the motives of the wish to remain at the pre-adult level, or even to regress into infancy and take refuge therein. This is a general tendency, and if we look with sincerity within ourselves, we can find a number of infantile and regressive elements. The nostalgically minded of all ages, who lament 'the good old times' are examples of this. But it is a useless and dangerous tendency – useless, because every attempt to arrest the irresistible forward course of life in us and around us is doomed to failure; and dangerous, because it is apt to create serious neuropsychic conflicts and disturbances.

All these symbols can be utilised in psychological exercises for fostering the corresponding transpersonal experiences and to bring about an increasing synthesis between the personal and the transpersonal aspects or levels, the manifestation of the Whole Man.

Exercise on the Blossoming of a Rose

Let us imagine looking at a rose. Let us visualise its stem and leaves with a bud closed. This appears green because the sepals are closed, but at the very top a rose-coloured point can be seen. Let us visualise this vividly, holding the image in the centre of our consciousness...Now begins a slow movement; the sepals start to separate little by little, turning their points outward and revealing the rose-hued petals, which are still closed...The sepals continue to open...We can see the whole bud of a delicate rose colour...The petals also slowly separate...until a perfect fully-opened rose is seen.

At this stage let us try to smell the perfume of the rose, inhaling its characteristic well-known scent...so delicate, sweet, pleasant...Let us smell it with delight.

Let us identify ourselves with the rose itself, let us 'introject' it into ourselves... Symbolically, we are a flower, a rose...The same life that animates the Universe and has created the miracle of the rose is producing in us a like, even greater miracle...the awakening and development of our spiritual being and that which radiates from it.

Through this exercise, we can effectively foster the inner flowering.

Psychosynthesis

Supplement: Notes on Symbols

The subject of symbolism is vast and manifold, and requires a corresponding extensive treatment and discussion. The following notes aim only at indicating some fields for further study, research and experimentation.

Paradoxical nature and function of symbols: this has been clearly expressed by Carlyle: "In a symbol lies concealment or revelation." The solution of this apparent contradiction lies in the realisation that the difference depends not on the symbols themselves, but on our attitude towards the symbol. If we stop at its appearance, at its form, then it veils and hides. If we try to understand its meaning and succeed in grasping what it signifies, then it is a means of revelation.

Plurality of meanings of a symbol: this multiplicity, which corresponds to the various levels of reality, has been well described by Dante in his Convito. According to him, symbols have or can have four meanings: Literal, Allegorical, Moral and Mystical (the full text of Dante's discussion is reported in Appendix A). It is important to keep clearly in mind this plurality of meanings of symbols, in order to avoid errors in their interpretation. An historical example of such a misinterpretation is that of St. Francis. After his conversion one day, while he was praying, he heard an inner voice, which he thought was the voice of God, saying: "Go and restore my church." There was in the neighbourhood a small church half-ruined. St. Francis thought he had been ordered to rebuild it, and he set himself to work. But later he realised that the inner command was to work at the restoration of the Catholic Church, which in his times was decaying, and all his subsequent activity was courageously directed towards that great mission.

Various kinds and classes of symbols: they are many and various and may serve or be used for different purposes. There are Nature Symbols, Animal Symbols, Human Symbols, Man-Made Symbols, Religious and Mythological Symbols, Abstract Symbols and Individual or Spontaneous Symbols (a list of the principal symbols of each category is given in Appendix B).

A special class of symbols is that which is expressive of transpersonal experiences:
1 Introversion
2 Deepening-Descent
3 Elevation-Ascent

Psychosynthesis

These symbols are not only indicative, but if used as subjects of meditation can be helpful for inducing or fostering the corresponding inner experiences and realisation.

Universality of symbolism: owing to the fundamental oneness of Reality and the synthetic correlation of all its parts and aspects, each of its manifestations has a symbol, character and meaning, and can be a means of perceiving under or behind the multiplicity of the appearances which overlie that unity. This has been beautifully expressed by Shakespeare (As You Like It, 1599, 2.i.12): "...Finds tongues in trees, books in the running brooks, sermons in stones and good in everything." Goethe has summed up the same truth in a synthetic way at the end of Faust: "Alles Vergängliche ist nur ein Gleichnis." (All that is transitory is only a symbol.)

Humanitas, Vol 8, No 2, 1972

Appendix A

Since I, the servant, with preliminary discourse in the preceding treatise, have with all due care prepared my bread, the time now summons, and requires my ship to leave the port: wherefore, having trimmed the mizen-mast of reason to the wind of my desire, I enter the ocean with the hope of an easy voyage, and a healthful happy haven to be reached at the end of my supper. But in order that my food may be more profitable, before the first dish comes on the table I wish to show how it ought to be eaten. I say then as is narrated in the first chapter, that this exposition must be Literal and Allegorical and to make this explicit one should know that it is possible to understand

Psychosynthesis

a book in four different ways, and that it ought to be explained chiefly in this manner.

The one is termed Literal, and this is that which does not extend beyond the text itself, such as is the fit narration of that thing whereof you are discoursing, an appropriate example of which is the third Song, which discourses of Nobility.

Another is termed Allegorical, and it is that which is concealed under the veil of fables, and is a Truth concealed under a beautiful Untruth, as when Ovid says that Orpheus with his lute made the wild beasts tame, and made the trees and the stones to follow him, which signifies that the wise man with the instrument of his voice makes cruel hearts gentle and humble, and makes those follow his will who have not the living force of knowledge and of art, who, having not the reasoning life of any knowledge whatever, are as the stones. And in order that this hidden thing should be discovered by the wise, it will be demonstrated in the last Treatise. Verily the theologians take this meaning otherwise than do the poets: but, because my intention here is to follow the way of the poets, I shall take the Allegorical sense according as it is used by the poets.

The third sense is termed Moral, and this is that which the readers ought intently to search for in books, for their own advantage and for that of their descendants; as one can espy in the Gospel, when Christ ascended the Mount for the Transfiguration, that, of the twelve Apostles, he took with Him only three. From which one can understand in the Moral sense that in the most secret things we ought to have but little company.

The fourth sense is termed Mystical, that is, above sense, supernatural; and this it is, when spiritually one expounds a writing which even the Literal sense by the things signified bears express reference to the Divine things of Eternal Glory; as one can see in that Song of the Prophet which says that by the exodus of the people of Israel from Egypt Judea is made holy and free. That this happens to be true according to the letter is evident. Not less true is that which it means spiritually, that in the Soul's liberation from Sin (or in the exodus of the Soul from Sin) it is made holy and free in its powers.

But in demonstrating these, the Literal must always go first, as that in whose sense the others are included, and without which it would be impossible and irrational to understand the others. Especially is it impossible in the Allegorical, because, in each thing

Psychosynthesis

which has a within and a without, it is impossible to come to the within if you do not first come to the without. Wherefore, since in books the Literal meaning is always external, it is impossible to reach the others, especially the Allegorical, without first coming to the Literal. Again, it is impossible, because in each thing, natural and artificial, it is impossible to proceed to the form without having first laid down the matter upon which the form should be. Thus, it is impossible for the form of the gold to come, if the matter, that is, its subject, is not first laid down and prepared; or for the form of the ark to come, if the material, that is, the wood, be not first laid down and prepared. Therefore, since the Literal meaning is always the subject and the matter of the others, especially the Allegorical, it is impossible to come first to the meaning of the others before coming to it. Again, it is impossible, because in each thing, natural and artificial, it is impossible to proceed unless the foundation be first laid, as in the house, so also in the mind. Therefore, since demonstration must be the building up of Knowledge, and Literal demonstration must be the foundation of the other methods of interpreting, especially of the Allegorical, it is impossible to come first to the others before coming to that. Again, if it were possible that it could be so ordered, it would be irrational, that is, out of order; and, therefore, one would proceed with much fatigue and with much error. Hence, as the Philosopher says in the first book of the Physics, Nature desires that we proceed in due order in our search for knowledge, that is, by proceeding from that which we know well to that which we know not so well; so I say that Nature desires it, inasmuch as this way to knowledge is innate in us; and therefore, if the other meanings, apart from the Literal, are less understood – which they are, as evidently appears – it would be irrational to demonstrate them if the Literal had not first been demonstrated.

I, then, for these reasons will discourse in due order of each song, firstly upon its Literal meaning, and after that I will discourse of its Allegory, that is, the hidden Truth, and sometimes I will touch incidentally on the other meanings as may be convenient to place and time.

Dante Alighieri, The Banquet (Il Convito), translated by EP Sayer, Routledge, 1887, Chapter 1, pp 47-50

Appendix B

Nature symbols: these include air, earth, fire, water; sky, stars, sun, moon. Among the chief nature symbols are the mountain (with its correlated technique of 'ascent'), sea,

---

Psychosynthesis

stream, river, lake, pond, wind, cloud, rain, fog; cave, tree, flames and fire, wheat, seed, flowers (rose, lotus, sunflower, etc.); jewel, diamond and various symbols related to light (including sunrise, sunset, rays of light, etc.) amid darkness including shadow), etc.

Animal symbols: lion, tiger, snake, bear, wolf, bull, goat, deer, fish, worm-chrysalis-butterfly (as symbols of transformation); birds (eagle, dove, etc.); animals (horse, elephant. dog, cat, etc.); and the egg.

Human symbols:

General human symbols: father, mother, grandfather, grandmother, son, daughter, sister, brother, child, wise old man, magician, king, queen, prince, princess, knight, teacher; the human heart, the human hand, the eye. Birth, growth, death and resurrection.

Modern human symbols: these include the mountain-climber, the explorer (including the space explorer), the pioneer, the scientific investigator (physicist, chemist, etc.), the automobile-driver, the aviator, the radio or TV technician, the electronics engineer, etc.

Man-made symbols: bridge, channel, reservoir, tunnel, flag, fountain, lighthouse, candle, road, path, wall, door, house, castle, stairway, ladder, mirror, bus, sword, etc.

Religious and mythological symbols:

Universal and Western religious symbols: God, the Christ, the Holy Mother, angels, the devil, saints or holy men, priest, monk, nun, resurrection, hell, purgatory, heaven, the Grail, temple, church, chapel, the cross.

Eastern symbols: Brahman, Vishnu, Shiva, the Buddha, etc.

Mythological symbols: pagan gods, goddesses and heroes; Apollo, the Muses (symbols of the arts and sciences), the three Graces (symbols of femininity in the refined sense), Venus, Diana (symbol of the woman who refuses her femininity), Orpheus, Dionysus, Hercules, Vulcan, Pluto, Saturn, Mars, Mercury, Jupiter, Wotan, Siegfried, Brunhilde, Valhalla, the Nibelungen, the Valkyries, etc.

Psychosynthesis

Abstract Symbols:

Numbers: in the Pythagorean sense of psychological significance – for instance, one symbolising unity, two – polarity, three – interplay, etc.

Geometrical symbols: two-dimensional; dot, circle, cross (various forms, such as the mathematical plus sign, the long-limbed Christian cross, the St. Andrew's Cross or multiplication sign), the equilateral triangle, the square, the diamond, the star (five-pointed, six-pointed, etc.) and three-dimensional; the sphere, cone, cube, the ascending spiral etc.

Individual or spontaneous symbols: these emerge during treatment or spontaneously in dreams, day-dreams, etc.

Roberto Assagioli (reprinted from the Psychosynthesis Research Foundation, 1969, first printed in the Journal of Transpersonal Psychology, Spring 1969)

Psychosynthesis

Psychosynthesis
Research
Foundation

The Repression of the Sublime

The title, *The Repression of the Sublime*, comes from the writings of Robert Desoille (*Le Rêve Éveillé en Psychothérapie*, Presses Universitaires de France, 1945). In the course of this paper, I am not going to offer you any really new ideas. Instead, I will try to bring together the ideas of a number of others in such a way as to make the concept of, the repression of the sublime so real and compelling to you that you will see it ever more clearly and inescapably in yourselves, in your patients, and in your associates.

I do not think it is necessary to define the concept of repression but I do want to go into the question of what is meant in this instance by the sublime. We can be ortho-dox-psychoanalytic about it and consider all higher artistic, social and spiritually ori-ented activities as sublimations of primitive erotic and aggressive drives. These would be sublime activities, but as sublimations of lower drives. But we could also consider that these same higher impulses, desires or motives exist in their own right and that they develop whether or not the sexual and aggressive drives are satisfied. In fact, one might go so far as to claim that the higher and more sublime needs of the person are more likely to be awakened and developed if the so-called lower, carnal drives are sat-isfied rather than if these are frustrated and 'sublimated'. For it is often out of a sense of boredom and dissatisfaction with the gratification of the senses that we begin to look for higher meanings to our life.

There are still other ways of looking at the term *sublime*. In its broadest sense it covers all of man's impulses, instincts, drives, urges to be something more, better, greater than he is. Personal growth and differentiation is part of the picture, to be sure, but beyond that, the concept of the sublime involves several other general areas. It refers to the true, the good, the beautiful. We orient ourselves towards the sublime when we disinterestedly seek to know things as they are, when we nurture others for the pleas-

Psychosynthesis

ure of seeing them grow, when we arrange physical events so that they are seen as beautiful or artistic.

Then, there is the tendency towards community, brotherliness, and caring. It is based on the feeling, the belief, the conviction that we all share the same fate, ultimately. In the thinking of Robert Desoille, in whose writings I first came across the conception of the repression of the sublime, the impulse towards the sublime demands that we be concerned with others, that we feel the need to communicate with others with the best of ourselves, and that we find our deepest satisfaction in service to others. I quote in translation the section of his 1945 book in which he says: "There are many forms of service and among them the disinterested efforts of the savant and of the artist are among the highest." The impulse to act in such ways is the expression of a profound urge to trust life, to give freely of oneself and to forget one's selfish concerns. These are among the traits of the sublime.

There is another aspect of the sublime which is confusingly called the religious. This is the inescapable need of every person to answer the existential questions for himself and to attach himself to a purpose, a goal, an ideal that he sees as greater and more important, more durable than his own transient existence and powers. When we sense the sublime as the feeling of communion with and devotion to something that is greater than ourselves, then we are experiencing this basic religious impulse. It may be theistic, agnostic or atheistic; it does not require a belief in God, but it is consonant with such a belief. According to Desoille it is the therapist's job to help his client to become fully aware of this basic and normal religious impulse and to help the client to clear his mind of any persisting infantile theological conceptions. Finally, the therapist helps the client to develop his primitive religious impulses to the level at which they are converted into reflective thought rather than being merely emotionally charged magic thinking.

Now to get back to the title of this paper, *The Repression of the Sublime*, I would like to demonstrate that it is an essential part of being fully human to feel the pull and the attraction of the sublime in the several ways that I have described. However, it is typically neurotic for us to avoid the responsibility of trying to answer this call of the sublime and, we often do repress it.

There are many ways in which we evade the call of the sublime. Why do we evade, for example, the challenge of personal growth? We fear growth because it means aban-

Psychosynthesis

doning the familiar for the unknown, and that always involves risks. I recently came across the same idea in the works of Andras Angyal (*Neurosis and Treatment*, Wiley, 1965) where he says: "Abandoning the familiar for the unknown always involves risks. When the changes are far-reaching or precipitous they are bound to arouse anxiety. The view that growth is inseparable from anxiety is shared by practically all thinkers who have substantially contributed to our understanding of anxiety...The anxiety felt at the prospect of dissolution of one's current mode of being has been related by some to the fear of final dissolution, of which human beings have the certain foreknowledge; since growth requires the breaking of old patterns, willingness 'to die' is a precondition of living...Excessive fear of death is often a correlate of the neurotic fear of growth and change."

Why do we evade the expression of care and concern for others? Often it is because we fear that we won't know where to draw the line and that we will find ourselves used and exploited by others. In the popular parlance, if you give a person an inch, he'll take a mile. Somehow we lack the stable sense of self which would limit us to have our 'yes' and our 'no' in such situations. I think that this fear is also related to the fact that as a part of the pattern of modern life, we know too many people too superficially – and we experience too little responsibility for each other.

I suspect that the loss of the security of a sense of community with others, the loss of the feeling of sharing a common fate, has led us to a state in which we are no longer able to commit ourselves to an ideal whose value, in our eyes, transcends that of our personal existence. This is the opposite of the situation that normally exists in primitive tribes. Today, the old tribal claims for loyalty in return for status and security are weak. We seldom experience a close relatedness to others for whose lives we are responsible and on whom we, in turn, can call for aid when we are distressed or threatened. Because of this loss, the motive for commitment of oneself to something greater than oneself must nowadays attach itself to something more abstract than one's tribe; something harder to define and to keep in mind and heart as a value.

Let's go back to the idea of repression. Desoille's idea that we repress the sublime can be found in the writings of current American psychologists. For example, Angyal (*ibid*) speaks of the defence mechanisms such as repression as exercising their effects not only on neurotic feelings and behaviour but on the healthy ones, too. To his way of thinking, two competing organisations or sets of attitudes or systems for attributing meaning to experiences are in competition with each other. One is healthy, the other

Psychosynthesis

is neurotic. Each system seeks to dominate the individual, and to do this, it must repress the other competing system. So when the neurotic system is dominant, the healthy system is *ipso facto* subdued and submerged, i.e. excluded from consciousness, or repressed. Angyal then says, "This conception is borne out by numerous observations that one can and does repress feelings and wishes that are in no way socially tabooed and are often considered laudable."

He calls this 'annexation' or 'appropriation' and he gives the example of an analytic patient who misinterprets his own natural and healthy friendliness as a viciously motivated exploitativeness.

There are a number of other current examples of the repression of the sublime. I would like to draw some from Abraham Maslow's writings. Recently he gave a lecture in which he included the notion of the Jonah Complex. To quote from Dr. Maslow ('Neurosis as a Failure of Personal Growth', *Humanitas*, 1966, Vol 3, pp 153-169):

"I'd like to turn to one of the many reasons for what Angyal has called 'the evasion of growth'. Certainly everybody in this room would like to be better than he is. We have, all of us, an impulse to improve ourselves, an impulse towards actualising more of our potentialities, towards self-actualisation, or full humanness, or human fulfilment, or whatever term you like. Granted this for everybody here, then what holds us up? What blocks us?

"One such defence against growth that I would like to speak about especially, because it has not been noticed much, I shall call the Jonah Complex.

"In my own notes I had at first labelled this defence 'the fear of one's own greatness' or 'the evasion of one's destiny' or 'the running away from one's own best talent'. I had wanted to stress as bluntly and sharply as I could the non-Freudian point that we fear our best as well as our worst, even though in different ways. It is certainly possible for most of us to be greater than we are in actuality. We all have unused potentialities or not fully developed ones. It is certainly true that many of us evade our constitutionally suggested vocations...So often we run away from the responsibilities dictated (or rather suggested) by nature, by fate, even sometimes by accident, just as Jonah tried in vain to run away from his fate.

Psychosynthesis

"We fear our highest possibilities (as well as our lowest ones). We are generally afraid to become that which we can glimpse in our most perfect moments, under the most perfect conditions, under conditions of greatest courage. We enjoy and even thrill to the god-like possibilities we see in ourselves in such peak moments. And yet we simultaneously shiver with weakness, awe and fear before these same possibilities.

"Not only are we ambivalent about our highest possibilities, we are also in a perpetual and I think universal, perhaps even necessary conflict and ambivalence over these same highest possibilities in other people and in human nature in general. Certainly we love and admire good men, saints, honest, virtuous, clean men. But could anybody who has looked into the depths of human nature fail to be aware of our mixed and often hostile feelings toward saintly men? Or toward very beautiful women or men? Or toward great creators? Or toward our intellectual geniuses? We surely love and admire all the persons who incarnated the true, the good, the beautiful, the just, the perfect, the ultimately successful. And yet they also make us uneasy, anxious, confused, perhaps a little jealous or envious; a little inferior, clumsy. They usually make us lose our aplomb, our self-possession, our self-regard.

"Here we have a first clue. My impression so far is that the greatest people, simply by their presence and being what they are, make us feel aware of our lesser worth, whether or not they intend to. If this is an unconscious effect, and we are not aware of why we feel stupid or ugly or inferior whenever such a person turns up, we are apt to respond with projection, i.e. we react as if he were trying to make us feel inferior, as if we were the target. Hostility is then an understandable consequence. It looks to me, so far, as if conscious awareness tends to fend off this hostility. That is, if you are willing to attempt self-awareness and self-analysis of your own counter-valuing, i.e. of your unconscious fear and hatred of the true, good and beautiful, etc. people, you will very likely be less nasty to them. And I am willing to extrapolate to the guess that if you can learn to love more purely the highest values in others, this might make you love these qualities in yourself in a less frightening way."

In another paper ('Self-Actualisation and Beyond' in *Challenges of Humanistic Psychology*, JFT Bugenta (ed), McGraw-Hill, 1967, pp 279-286) Dr. Maslow has brought up a different aspect of the repression of the sublime. He calls it desacralising:

"Let me talk about one defence mechanism that is not mentioned in the psychology textbooks, though it is a very important defence mechanism to the snotty and yet ide-

Psychosynthesis

alistic youngster of today. It is the defence mechanism of desacralising. These young-sters mistrust the possibility of values and virtues. They feel themselves swindled and thwarted in their lives. Most of them have, in fact, dopey parents whom they don't respect very much, parents who are quite confused themselves about values and who, frequently, are simply terrified of their children and never punish them or stop them from doing things that are wrong. So you have a situation where the youngsters simply despise their elders – often for good and sufficient reason. Such youngsters have learned to make a big generalisation: they won't listen to anybody who is grown up, especially if the grown-up uses the same words which they've heard from the hypo-critical mouth. They have heard their fathers talk about being honest or brave or bold, and they have seen their fathers being the opposite of all these things.

"The youngsters have learned to reduce the person to the concrete object and to refuse to see what he might be or to refuse to see him in his symbolic values or to refuse to see him or her eternally. Our kids have desacralised sex, for example. Sex is nothing; it is a natural thing, and they have made it so natural that it has lost its poetic qualities in many instances, which means that it has lost practically everything. Self-actualisation means giving up this defence mechanism and learning or being taught to resacralise.

"*Resacralising* means being willing, once again, to see a person 'under the aspect of eternity', as Spinoza says, or to see him in the medieval Christian unitive perception, that is, being able to see the sacred, the eternal, the symbolic. It is to see Woman with a capital 'W' and everything which that implies, even when one looks at a particular woman. Another example: one goes to medical school and dissects a brain. Certainly something is lost if the medical student isn't awed but, without the unitive perception, sees the brain only as one concrete thing. Open to resacralisation, one sees a brain as a sacred object also, sees its symbolic value, sees it as a figure of speech, sees it in its poetic aspects.

"Resacralisation often means an awful lot of corny talk – 'very square', the kids would say. Nevertheless, for the counsellor, especially for the counsellor of older people, where these philosophical questions about religion and the meaning of life come up, this is a most important way of helping the person to move toward self-actualisation. The youngsters may say that it is square, and the logical positivists may say that it is meaningless, but for the person who seeks our help in this process, it is obviously very meaningful and very important, and we had better answer him, or we're not doing what it is our job to do..."

Psychosynthesis

Here is one more quotation from Maslow (*Toward a Psychology of Being*, Van Nostrand, 1962) on another aspect of the sublime; one that is perhaps more prosaic. The title of the chapter from which it comes is 'The Avoidance of Knowledge, as Avoidance of Responsibility': "...lack of curiosity can be an active or a passive *expression* of anxiety and fear...That is, we can seek knowledge in order to reduce anxiety and we can also avoid knowing in order to reduce anxiety. To use Freudian language, incuriosity, learning difficulties, pseudo-stupidity can be a defence. Knowledge and action are very closely bound together, all agree. I go much further, and am convinced that knowledge and action are frequently synonymous, even identical in the Socratic fashion. Where we know fully and completely, suitable action follows automatically and reflexively. Choices are then made without conflict and with full spontaneity...this close relation between knowing and doing can help us to interpret one cause of the fear of knowing as deeply a fear of doing, a fear of the consequences that flow from knowing, a fear of its dangerous responsibilities. Often it is better not to know, because if you did know, then you would *have* to act and stick your neck out."

There is an interesting theoretical explanation of this idea of the repression of the sublime by Robert Desoille (*Le Rêve Éveillé en Psychothérapie*, Presses Universitaires de France, 1945), the French engineer who made it his avocation to develop the *rêve éveillé dirigé*, or directed daydream, as a psychotherapeutic tool. Desoille has woven theory and experience into a fairly elaborate explanation of how, why, and by what agency, the sublime is repressed. He has his own topographical description of the psyche, reproduced here:

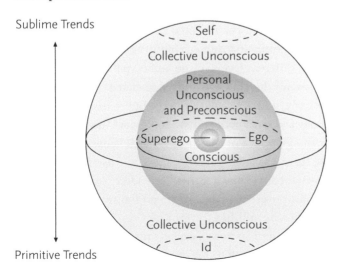

Sublime Trends

Self

Collective Unconscious

Personal Unconscious and Preconscious

Superego — Ego

Conscious

Collective Unconscious

Id

Primitive Trends

Psychosynthesis

It includes the usual Freudian trio – the id, the ego, and the superego; but they are now supplemented by a fourth agent, the Self. The area in the centre represents consciousness, the ego and the superego. Farther out, one finds the personal preconscious and unconscious. Beyond that is the collective unconscious. It should be noted that the superego does not partake of the collective unconscious.

Desoille borrowed Jung's concept of the self and modified it somewhat. For him, it means a state that represents the far limits of sublimation, a state that is the expression of the highest ideal that a person is able to entertain at any given moment. In this case, the id is the usual concept of our animal drive seeking expression. We experience it as it has been transformed in rising into consciousness, with all the associations that have been called forth by the stimulation of the primitive instincts. Desoille goes on to emphasise the unity of the psyche. The self and the id are considered to be two extreme limits, two opposite poles within the psyche; they never coincide. Each exercises its own attractive effect on the ego at the centre; and the ego oscillates back and forth between these two instinctual limits, the primitive and the sublime.

The superego is that arbitrary and infantile outgrowth of the ego that represents the strictures and demands of the parents and other authority figures as they were experienced primarily in childhood. Desoille sees it as a temporary structure that must eventually be dissolved and whose role must be taken over by the Self in the mature personality.

At this point, I would like to digress into a description of the types of imagery that Desoille has habitually found to occur in the directed daydream. As you may know, Desoille uses the imagery of ascending and descending in order to evoke images at different levels of the psyche, or different levels in the archetypal chain, as he puts it. The idea of ascending to heavenly heights he finds associated with sublimation, euphoria, serenity, and ultimately, with spiritual growth. But it frequently happens that the patient's ascent is blocked by a monster of some sort, perhaps a dragon. Desoille calls this character the 'guardian of the threshold' and considers it to be an agent of the superego, whose function had been in the past to frustrate a part of the child's self-expression, e.g. sexual behaviour. It is now the adult patient's task in his daydream to struggle with and to overcome this superego figure. If he succeeds in doing this in his daydream, he thereby nullifies the arbitrary restrictions set up by his parents and other authority figures, and so doing, accepts responsibility for directing his sexual and aggressive strivings according to his own judgments. At this point, the

Psychosynthesis

ego becomes animated by an intense aspiration to attain a sublime objective, which is still only glimpsed. The superego, which had been constructed from the introjects of the parents as a bulwark against oedipal desires and the like, becomes superfluous as the individual develops autonomy. The Self, with its higher, more sublime goals, supplants the superego.

Desoille (*Le Rêve Éveillé en Psychothérapie*, Presses Universitaires de France, 1945) draws an important point from Jung. He points out that Jung, among others, has emphasised the necessity of shedding one's own instinctive egotism. On this matter, Jung said that the ancient mystical precept, 'Get rid of all that you have and then you will receive' means, in effect, that one must abandon the bulk of one's most cherished illusions. Desoille says: "It is only then that something more beautiful, deeper, and more comprehensive will develop in one. For only the mystery of the sacrifice of oneself makes it possible for one to find oneself again with a renewed soul. These are precepts of very ancient wisdom which are brought back to light during psychotherapy...This aspiration, which must come to us from a region of the unconscious, arises from a deeper layer than the superego. That is why it needs a special name. We will go along with Jung and call it the Self. The conflict breaks out between the id and the Self. The Self tries to get the ego to satisfy its needs (for the sublime, its yearnings for growth) and the id, in opposing itself to the Self's desires, takes on the role of the repressive agent (and becomes) the expression of a new form of censorship, the *repression of the sublime*, in this case, of the urge to spiritual growth."

When the patient accedes to these intense aspirations of the Self which we mentioned earlier and attains certain levels of sublimation, the symbol of the guardian of the threshold changes. It is no longer that of a threatening dragon but takes on a different appearance in the daydreams. It generally appears now as a creature who is both kindly and firm, but still bars the route upward. In this situation the patient no longer feels threatened, but he does feel called upon to make a conscious choice between two equally possible attitudes. According to Desoille this is what is taking place. During the previous sessions the subject has become aware of the possibility of developing something more beautiful, deeper, more comprehensive within himself. There has been an intimation of the sublime, a call to become a finer person than he is. But for that to take place, the subject realises now that he must renounce old habits and stop following lines of least resistance. He must give up the gratification of impulses from the lower unconscious, *all of which have been tolerated and even encouraged by the superego* in the past, and accepted by the conscious ego. But the patient hesitates to take this path upward because he feels that it will restrain his freedom and diminish his range of activities. In some cases, the patient may even feel that these suggested renunciations have an inhuman character to them. This is when the guardian of the threshold appears – but no longer in a repulsive form. This time, it may take on the form of an angel, for example. The conflict between the Self and the id for possession of the ego, one might say between the sublime and the base, is no longer unconscious. It is now also taking place between the ego on the one hand, whose habit has been to accede consciously to those of the id's impulses that had been accepted by the super-ego, those impulses conforming to the lowest moral restraint of everyday life, and on the other hand, the Self, represented by the guardian of the threshold, the angel, whose call is felt to be ever more imperative.

In this case, we see that the id, acting through the ego and with the collusion of the superego, struggles against the demands of the Self. But at this stage, the struggle has become quite conscious; and the ego now seeks to suppress the sublime just as it represses what seemed to it to be base and vile.

Desoille says that there are three ways in which the patient may react to the image of the guardian of the threshold with its call towards the sublime:

1   During that very session, the subject may suddenly decide to give up his old habits because they now appear to him to represent non-values. These must be replaced by new values, which must be found and possessed. They are symbolised in the subsequent directed daydreams by such images as treasures that are hidden or guarded. Once this decision is made, the patient is again able to see himself ascending to greater heights in his directed daydream.

2   The subject may hesitate and the session may come to a halt at that point. Subsequently, while the subject is alone, during the interval between sessions, he may decide to take on the struggle. In subsequent sessions he is then able again to progress as a result of that decision.

3   Alternatively, the subject may flatly refuse, consciously or not, to give up his illusions. With this refusal he makes a negative transference on his therapist. Generally, it is rather discrete and of short duration, says Desoille, except in difficult cases.

Psychosynthesis (Assagioli, Roberto, Hobbs, Dorman, 1965) makes much of the fact that we suppress and deny our impulses toward the sublime. One possible reason why we do this is because the more that one is conscious of one's positive impulses, of one's

---

urges toward the sublime, the more shame one feels for one's failure to give expression to these impulses. There ensues a painful burning of the conscience, a sense of guilt at not being what one could be, of not doing what one could do. This is not superego guilt but rather the cry of the Self for its actualisation.

But we have available an 'easy-out', an escape from this sense of guilt, if we accept those popular intellectual arguments which reduce the call of the higher unconscious to nothing but sublimation of the impulses of the lower unconscious. Jung (*Modern Man in Search of a Soul*, Harcourt, Brace, 1933) decried this reductionism more than 30 years ago, but we still find it soothing and comforting to deny these instincts of the higher unconscious and to settle for a degraded self-image because, in some ways, it is an easier one to live with.

This is the self-image of the well-psychoanalysed man; he has undergone a sort of psychoanalytical lobotomy of the spirit, a deadening of his normal sensitivity to the higher unconscious and to the possibility of spiritual growth. The key to this denial is probably to be found in Freud's concept of sublimation with its emphasis on aim-in-hibited sexual and aggressive drives as the source of the kindly and generous acts of men. This emphasis denied the existence of autonomous impulses towards goodness, toward community. This dogma was especially useful for the reduction of anxiety because it automatically relieved the patient who accepted it of all sense of responsi-bility for spiritual growth, and of the normal anxiety attended on this quest.

Thus, the psychoanalytic theory of neurosis can be seen as a truncated theory of per-sonality which, in an ideological way, tends to relieve neurotic symptomatology by amputating or anaesthetising a portion of the psyche, the highest and most valuable functions, those which urge us on to be the most that is within our potentiality.

But perhaps it is better for the severe neurotic to temporarily put aside his impulses to the sublime. These impulses, if misused, can lead to ego inflation and solidification of one's pathological self-image. One classical picture of this is rigid self-righteousness. It may be that the severe neurotic should be prohibited from dwelling on thoughts of the sublime until he has uprooted the core of his neurosis, just as the aspirant is not initi-ated into the secrets of the society until he has developed the discipline with which to respect the facts and the skills with which to use them.

Psychosynthesis

The problem that psychosynthesis faces, and which I think that psychoanalysis in the classical sense avoids, is to provide a therapy for both the lower and the higher aspects of the personality. The needs of the lower unconscious are met more or less successfully by conventional forms of psychotherapy. Religious guidance seeks to enlarge the scope and effectiveness of the higher unconscious. Psychosynthesis provides a philosophy that aims to reach both the id and the Self. Psychosynthesis aims to help man to recognise all of his impulses, to accept the responsibility of deciding which to express and which to renounce, and to deal with the anxiety that is an inescapable aspect of the process of self-actualisation.

Frank Haronian (reprinted from the Psychosynthesis Research Foundation, 1972, presented at a seminar of the Psychosynthesis Research Foundation on December 15, 1967)

Psychosynthesis

SYNTHESIS

Dimensions of Growth

Modern Life has failed to meet the human need for meaning. The experience of meaninglessness, the lack of values and direction, has reached epidemic proportions. And yet our underlying needs persist, the urgent questions remain: 'What is really meaningful in life?' 'What is truly important for me to achieve?'

We need to find two different kinds of meaning: the meaning of *our own individual existence*, and the meaning of *the world we live in – ultimately of life itself.*

Personal dimension

Our first concern as developing individuals is the search for meaning in our personal existence. Whether as a child learning to walk, as a student struggling with a mathematical problem, or as a businessman closing an important deal, our experience of this personal meaning is similar. When we succeed in achieving a goal, we experience ourselves and our lives as having greater significance and value. Accordingly, we seek to accomplish larger and more important goals, and in doing so we develop our capacities and add to our skills and knowledge. This pursuit of personal meaning and goals leads us to grow as human beings, to form an increasingly well-integrated, creative personality which is more and more effective in the world. This process takes place along what we may call the *personal dimension* of growth.

Transpersonal
dimension

Psychosynthesis

But as the scope of our active involvement in the world increases, we find that our sense of world meaning also needs to grow. We leave the shelter of home and go to college, or we leave school and go to work, we get married and raise a family, we seek to make a worthwhile contribution. At each step, experience calls on us to clarify and deepen our values, to explore, to re-examine the beliefs we live by. If we respond to this call and pursue the quest far enough, we will eventually be concerned with such self-transcendent questions as: 'What is the true nature of the world?': Can there be a peaceful and loving humanity?' 'What are time, space, consciousness, good and evil?' 'Is the universe evolving in a positive direction?' We may approach questions of this sort intellectually, seeking insight into the truth, or we may reach for a direct experience, an expanded awareness that we hope will reveal the meaning and purpose of the larger reality. This search will lead us to the *transpersonal or spiritual dimension* of growth.

One Dimension or the Other

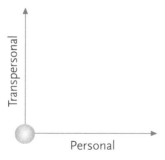

The personal and the transpersonal dimensions are *distinct but not separate*. Both are natural to human unfoldment. But generally a person will tend to be more in touch with one dimension, experiencing it as more real, more important. He may then tend to undervalue the other, and even to be critical of someone else who is oriented toward it.

Think of how a successful businessman and the follower of a spiritual movement might look at one another. The businessman, who has spent years creating a life for himself and his family by working hard to accomplish his practical goals, may look at the follower of the spiritual movement and say 'Why doesn't he come down from the clouds and do something with his life? All this talk of peace and love is just a way for him to avoid facing reality.' At the same time, the spiritual disciple may look at the businessman and say, 'He is too bound up in his ego, seeking power, prestige, and

material success. All this is an illusion he must let go of so that he can surrender to God.'

This tendency to favour either dimension is often reflected in approaches to growth currently offered in our own culture. Many of them have been categorised as following one of the two general orientations, which have been loosely described as 'eastern' and 'western'.

The 'western' view values most highly the person who is a strong individual, who can fully invest himself in his activities, function effectively, accomplish tasks and in general demonstrate skill and success in handling the practical realities of life. With his strong intentionality, he orients all the many aspects of himself toward a unified focus. He wastes little time and effort in internal conflicts, ambivalence or confusion. Accordingly, he has much energy available for the business of achieving a rewarding and productive life. To him the transpersonal dimension is likely to be a secondary concern, possibly considered a distraction from what is most important.

On the other hand, what is commonly described as the 'eastern' view values most highly the individual who cultivates the inner, spiritual life. Emphasis is placed on achieving clarity of vision, serenity, love and compassion, a sense of joy and harmony, and ultimately oneness with all life. To reach these goals the individual develops the ability to master his inner processes and to expand his awareness. It is considered necessary to simplify or even largely transcend daily life and the material world, attachment to which is seen as a distraction from what is more important. Thus the person who leads a contemplative life is most revered and valued – the wise sage, the guru, and the ascetic.

Despite the age-old tendency of people – and even whole cultures – to emphasise one dimension to the exclusion of the other, the possibility of unifying both has been splendidly realised by certain individuals throughout history. The foremost mystics, for example St. Francis of Assisi and St. Teresa of Avila, having achieved illumination, actively expressed their vision and their values in the world. One may also think of the great world teachers – for example Christ, Buddha, or Moses – all of whom became actively involved in the practical realities of their day. On the other hand, many of those most successfully concerned with the study of the material world – great scientists such as Newton or Einstein – were led by the very nature of their explorations into higher spiritual realms.

Psychosynthesis

Such illustrious figures of the past have pointed the way toward the needed synthesis. In our own times, increasing numbers of the many people involved in spiritual life are realising the need to develop well-integrated, capable personalities in order to make their spiritual values work. And more and more people who have been successfully expressing themselves in practical ways are reaching for the transpersonal to find deeper meaning, more certain direction, and greater effectiveness.

Unifying the Two Dimensions

In the last decades a growing number of psychologists have said that both dimensions are essential to full human growth, and have begun to explore the relation between them. Andras Angyal, for example, discusses not only the individual's need to achieve autonomy, but also his need for the experience of 'homonomy', of union with a greater whole. (A Angyal, 'A Holistic Theory', *Neurosis and Treatment*, Viking Press, 1965).

Similarly, Roberto Assagioli has recognised and developed two inter-related aspects of psychosynthesis: personal psychosynthesis which aims at fostering the development of a well-integrated, effective personality, and spiritual psychosynthesis which leads to realising one's higher nature.

Abraham Maslow, who introduced the term 'transpersonal', arrived through his observations at parallel conclusions (the similarity between Assagioli's and Maslow's conceptions is especially interesting, because while both men were deeply concerned with the spiritual nature of man and based their work on strong empirical foundations, they worked in very different environments and at different periods of time). In his later work Maslow recognised three groups of people whom he called respectively: self-actualisers, transcenders and transcending self-actualisers. Self-actualisers, Maslow found, are "essentially practical, realistic, mundane, capable and secular people", pragmatically concerned with "growth towards self-actualisation and freedom from basic deficiency needs. Such people live in the world, coming to fulfilment in it. They master it, lead it, use it for good purposes."

"Transcenders" are non-self-actualisers, "who have important transcendent experiences", and a strong contact with the spiritual dimension, but whose personalities are often underdeveloped. When compared to the transcenders, self-actualisers "tend to be 'doers' rather than meditators or contemplators, effective and pragmatic rather than aesthetic, reality testing and cognitive rather than emotional and experiencing." (A Maslow, *The Farther Reaches of Human Nature*, Viking Press, 1971, pp 280).

Psychosynthesis

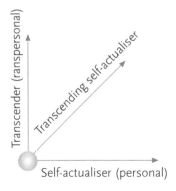

But Maslow found it necessary to differentiate between two kinds of self-actualising people: those who were clearly healthy but with little or no experience of transcendence, and those in whom transcendent experiencing was important and even central. These he called 'transcending self-actualisers'.

Transcending self-actualisers in *addition* to being well-integrated, healthy and effective, possess a number of other characteristics (Maslow lists 35 groups of them ('Various Meanings of Transcendence', *ibid*, pp 269-279)). For example, they are innovators and pioneers; they have a stronger sense of self, and yet at the same time are capable of transcending the limitations of personal identity; they have a sense for eternity, for 'the sacred'; they value and are more easily aware of truth, beauty, goodness, and unity.

Clearly, in order to realise more and more of our essential humanness, we need to include both the personal and the transpersonal dimensions. As personal meaning and world meaning develop and then fuse, as both the scope of our vision and our ability to express it expand, as our sense of individuality and of universality blend – we find that we move toward a lived unification with our higher human nature, toward realising our true Self. Therefore *self-realisation*, the realisation of our Transpersonal Self[2], involves the progressive unification, at higher and higher levels, of the two dimensions of growth (it is important to remember that self-realisation is not something we should 'do' or 'make happen'. Self-realisation is a natural process, and it

---

2   For discussions of the Transpersonal Self, see 'What is Psychosynthesis?' (*Synthesis*, 1977, pp 144-147, also reprinted in this book); Assagioli, Psychosynthesis, (Turnstone, 1965, pp 18-19); Assagioli, The Act of Will (Viking, 1973, pp 118-122); Betsie Carter-Haar, 'Identity and Personal Freedom (Synthesis, 1975, Vol 1, No 2, pp 89-90, also reprinted in this book); and Stuart Millar, 'Dialogue with the Higher Self' (Synthesis, 1975, Vol 1, No 2, p 131, also reprinted in this book).

occurs spontaneously. On the other hand, we can learn to better understand the process and thereby cooperate with it and facilitate it).

But before we can unify the two dimensions in ourselves, we need to develop them. Whether we develop both simultaneously or first develop one and then the other will depend on many different factors, such as our individual makeup, our awareness, our environment, and so on. In practice, people

often tend to proceed a long way primarily on either the personal or the transpersonal dimension before even becoming aware of the existence of the other.

If we feel more drawn toward one of the two dimensions and this seems right and fulfilling to us, clearly it is the path for us to follow. But at the same time, we will find it helpful to develop and maintain throughout, the awareness of the other dimension. Experience has repeatedly shown that if we proceed too far in one direction only, sooner or later we will need to become more inclusive and bring in the other. When that time comes, we can do so through a conscious, deliberate choice, provided we have the awareness and the understanding needed to recognise what is missing. Otherwise we may fall into a crisis of reorientation, one which will eventually lead us to the missing dimension, but often at the cost of much time, effort and pain.

So whatever path we may be following as individuals, it is best to keep in mind the whole picture – the entire 'territory' of human growth.

In this article, we will look more closely at both the personal and the transpersonal dimensions of growth: at how we experience them; at the crisis of reorientation that may occur if we proceed too far along one dimension exclusively; and at how we can increasingly unify the two dimensions in our lives.

Part One

The Personal Dimension

From the moment of birth we experience urges and needs, which motivate us into activity. What motivates us at any given moment is the sense that there is something worth achieving, something that has value and meaning. Our first and most basic meaning lies in simple physical survival. However, when this need is satisfied we do not merely sink into contented satiety. Rather something else arises, some new goal that has a different, or greater meaning.

To fulfil these goals we successively develop various aspects of our personality. As children we see that it is meaningful to master our body, to have physical competence, so that we can act effectively. The child's relentless urge to gain the ability to walk, his persistence through frustration after frustration, and finally the joyful elation that comes with success is a beautiful example of this process.

As we grow older it becomes increasingly meaningful to establish satisfying and warm relations with others. We learn to experience and share sensitive, deep emotions. During adolescence, relations with our peers, and particularly romantic relations, become the most significant focus of our life, and consequently the subtlety and richness of our feelings may flower.

During later adolescence, in response to the desire to understand ourselves and learn more about the world, our interest often shifts to developing the mind. At first, this motivation is likely to be motivated by simple curiosity. Gradually, however, we may become more and more involved in the pleasures of learning, and develop increasing mental discipline. When this happens, the mind takes a central place in our life.

With adulthood, we may find that in order to achieve most effectively the goals we set ourselves – whether pursuing a career, raising a family, or attaining success of any kind – we need to coordinate and integrate all our inner resources, so that they are working in a unified way and in line with our aims (this process of personality harmonisation, seen in terms of subpersonalities, is discussed in James Vargiu, 'Subpersonalities', *Synthesis*, 1974, Vol 1, No 1, pp 60-63 and 73-89 –reprinted in this book). The 'stages' he describes can be applied not only to subpersonalities but also to the integration of body, feelings and mind, and of any other personal element). Our feelings must be developed and harmonised so that we can avail ourselves of their energy and relate to other people in a satisfying way. Our mind must be further trained so that we can think creatively, flexibly, and with the power to do broad planning as well as work with specific details. Finally, body, feelings and mind must be harmonised and integrated with one another so that they can work synergistically.

Psychosynthesis

Growth along the Personal Dimension

In practice, development and integration of the personality does not always take place so easily or so completely. The body may be unhealthy, lethargic or hyperactive. The various feelings may be in conflict, they may be underdeveloped or overly intense, they may be ridden with inhibitions, anxieties, depression and fears – all of which interfere with full functioning. The mind may be too rigid or too unstructured, it may be untrained, overactive, out of balance toward the abstract or toward the concrete. Finally, all of these functions may not cooperate with one another. The mind may ignore both the feelings and the body. The feelings may cause stress and strain on the body, or might struggle with the mind about what is important, and so on. The full, harmonious integration of the personality functions is a long process, a goal toward which most of us are still working and moving. It is this process of integration which is represented by the horizontal arrow in our diagram.

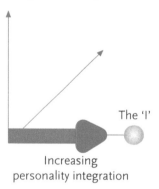

The 'I'

Increasing
personality integration

There are many approaches available to assist the various aspects of personality integration. The central concern of most forms of psychotherapy is to deal with deficiencies of specific personality functions, or with conflicts between them. The best approaches to self-actualisation that have appeared in recent years generally aim at the positive development of particular aspects of personality, and contribute to their gradual integration into a unified, dynamic whole. There is as well the growing recognition that self-actualisation consists not only in the harmonisation of all the aspects of the personality, but also in the gradual *emergence and empowering of the 'I'*, the centre of personal identity. It is through the action of the 'I' that the personality aspects are harmonised, so that the integrated personality gradually forms around it. (Two Workbooks provide many resources for this dual process of self-actualisation. The Workbook in *Synthesis*, Vol 1, No 1, 1974 focuses on the harmonisation of the personality through the integration of subpersonalities – the characters on our inner stage. The Workbook in *Synthesis*, Vol 1, No 2, 1974 deals with the means by which we can achieve the discovery of, and our identification as, the 'I' – the centre of personal identity, awareness and will.)

As we have seen, whether or not we deliberately seek self-actualisation by means of the various approaches available, it goes forward naturally through the pursuit of meaningful goals. In recent times, more and more people have achieved a high level of self-actualisation, and have become able to reach their goals with increasing success. This has led to an interesting phenomenon. Many people, when they have attained their personal or career goals, find that the satisfaction, the value, the meaning of these goals is *less than they expected*, and so eventually abandon them. And they often abandon them just when things seem to be going best for them, when they appear to be the most successful. Often, such people may take up a new, perhaps completely different pursuit – one that they believe will be more meaningful than the previous one. But as each new goal is successfully achieved, it also is likely to encompass only a limited or temporary satisfaction. Paradoxically, the greater the success, the more one is faced with the experience of finding that what was expected to be highly satisfying turns out to be uninteresting and empty.

After this happens a number of times, one may begin to simply imagine himself seeking new goals, pursuing new avenues to their conclusion, and realise before he even begins his pursuit that he will find no more meaning in it than in the previous ones. It is here that one enters a difficult period. If he has not yet made contact with the transpersonal dimension, the stage is set for what may be called the existential crisis: the crisis that challenges the meaning of one's very existence. (Viktor Frankl has written a great deal about the experiences of emptiness and meaninglessness. He describes this experience as the 'existential vacuum' which arises from the frustration of the 'will to meaning'. See his *The Will to Meaning*, New American Library, 1970, pp 83-98 and *The Unconscious God*, Simon and Schuster, 1970, pp 89-103. Roberto Assagioli also dealt extensively with this important topic, see for example, *The Act of Will*, Viking, 1973, pp 106-113 and his article 'Self-Realisation and Psychological Disturbances', *Synthesis*, 1977, pp 148-171 – reprinted in this book).

The person is now beginning to wonder if he is ever going to find fulfilment. An increasing sense of meaninglessness pervades all of his normal activities. Pastimes and interests which he formerly found rewarding do not bring the same pleasure they did before. His family, friends, and career simply do not interest him as they had. As this progresses, the person may experience at various times apathy, fear, and even despair. What is missing in his life? He has a strong identity, a well-integrated personality, and can function very well in the world. He is not neurotic; he has more than successfully attained the level of functioning termed 'normal' by modern mental health standards. Logically he should be happy.

But although he can seemingly accomplish almost anything he chooses, he now finds himself at a loss as to what or why to choose. 'I have been able to create a fine life for my family and for myself, but to what end? What does it mean?' As the educator and Gestalt therapist George Brown puts it, "After the individual can stand on his own two feet, what does he do then? Just stand there?" ('The Farther Reaches of Gestalt Therapy', *Synthesis*, 1974, Vol 1, No 1, p 33).

The Existential Crisis

The nature of this crisis and the pattern which leads to it is illuminated by Leo Tolstoy's striking account of his own struggle:

"Five years ago something very strange began to happen to me. At first I experienced moments of perplexity and arrest of life as though I did not know what to do or how to live, and I felt lost and became dejected. But this passed, and I went on living as before. Then these moments of perplexity began to recur more and more often…they were always expressed by the questions: What is it for? What does it lead to?

"At first it seemed to me that these were aimless and irrelevant questions. I thought that it was all well-known, and that if I should ever wish to deal with the solution it would not cost me much effort: just at present, I had no time for it, but when I wanted to I should be able to find the answer. The questions however began to repeat themselves frequently and to demand replies more and more insistently…I understood that it was something very important; and that if these questions constantly repeated themselves they would have to be answered. And I tried to answer them. The questions seemed such stupid, simple, childish ones; but as soon as I touched them and tried to solve them I at once became convinced, first, that they are not childish and stupid but the most important and profound of life's questions; and secondly that, try as I would, I could not solve them.

Psychosynthesis

"Before occupying myself with my Samara estate, the education of my son, or the writing of a book, I had to know *why* I was doing it. As long as I did not know why, I could do nothing and could not live. Amid the thoughts of estate management which greatly occupied me at that time, the question would suddenly occur: Well, you will have 6,000 desytinas of land in Samara Government and 300 horses, and what then?...And I was quite disconcerted and I did not know what to think.

"Or when considering plans for the education of my children, I would say to myself: what for?

"Or when thinking of the fame my works would bring me, I would say to myself, 'Very well, you will be more famous than Gogol or Pushkin or Shakespeare or Moliere, or than all the writers in the world – and what of it?'

"And I could find no reply at all. The questions would not wait, they had to be answered at once, and if I did not answer them it was impossible to live. But there was no answer."

All this happened to Tolstoy at a time of not only of enormous personal success, but also of great vitality and capability:

"All around me I had what is considered complete good fortune. I was not yet fifty; I had a good wife who loved me and whom I loved, good children, and a large estate which without much effort on my part improved and increased. I was respected by my relations and acquaintances more than at any previous time. I was praised by others and without much self-deception could consider that my name was famous. And far from being insane or mentally diseased, I enjoyed on the contrary a strength of mind and body such as I have seldom met among men of my kind; physically I could keep up with the peasants at mowing, and mentally I could work for eight and ten hours at a stretch without experiencing any ill results from such exertion."

Yet in spite of this fruitful life and his remarkable talents and abilities Tolstoy says, "I felt that what I had been standing on had collapsed, and that I had nothing left under my feet. What I had lived on no longer existed, and there was nothing left.

"My life came to a standstill. I could breathe, eat, drink and sleep, and I could not help doing these things; but there was no life, for there were no wishes the fulfilment of which I could consider reasonable. If I desired anything, I knew in advance that whether I satisfied my desire or not, nothing would come of it. Had a fairy come and offered to fulfil my desires I should not have known what to ask. If in moments of intoxication I felt something which, though not a wish, was a habit left by former wishes, in sober moments I knew this to be a delusion and that there was really nothing to wish for." (excerpt from *A Confession, The Gospel in Brief, What I Believe*, Oxford University Press, 1951, pp 15-19).

Tolstoy's account describes the existential crisis with penetrating clarity. It is a crisis in which the very basis of one's existence – an existence which had been unfolding primarily along the personal dimension – comes into question. The map of the two dimensions of growth suggests the basic strategy for the resolution of the crisis. This resolution is found when the individual is able to *expand the meaning of his existence beyond the boundaries of his own personality,* so as to purposefully participate in the life of the whole. This can begin as he reorients his attention toward the greater life revealed by exploration of the transpersonal dimension.

The period of the existential crisis is a particularly appropriate time to seek or renew contact with the transpersonal. Seen from the vantage point of the Higher Self, *the existential crisis is precipitated by an increasing flow of superconscious, or transpersonal, energy directed by the Self toward the personality* (for a discussion of the superconscious and its relation to the personality, see 'What is Psychosynthesis?', *Synthesis*, 1977, pp 16-21 – reprinted in this book; and Assagioli, *Psychosynthesis*, (Turnstone, 1965, pp 16-21). In particular, as the energy of the Self increases, it attracts the personal self or 'I' toward it. Before the existential crisis, the 'I' was attracted primarily by the pull of the personality life and of the environment (see 'Identity and Personal Freedom', *Synthesis*, 1975, Vol 1, No 2, p 75 – reprinted in this book). The existential crisis occurs when the increasing pull of the energy of the Self becomes equal in intensity to, and therefore neutralises, the pull of the personality/environment. Therefore this is a period of transition. It is like being suspended in space at a 'zero gravity' point, in which the earlier meaning of the personality life has vanished and a new meaning has not yet appeared.

So as the superconscious influence increases, the previously adequate sense of meaning begins to fade away, and a growing sense of 'something missing' develops. What is missing is the realisation of one's relationship with the greater life – a relationship that now needs to be recognised and acknowledged.

Psychosynthesis

This reorientation toward the transpersonal dimension can take many forms. For some people, superconscious energies break through to their consciousness suddenly and spontaneously – sometimes with great intensity – and then lift them out of the crisis into what can become a major, life-changing experience. Such a dramatic, spontaneous resolution is, however, relatively rare.

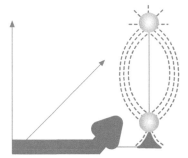

Reorientation after
the existential crisus

More often, the reorientation is gradual and involves our conscious and purposeful participation. Frequently, as the intimations of the approaching existential crisis are increasingly felt, past transpersonal experiences – which had been forgotten or even repressed, and had therefore gone unused – return to consciousness, and their meaning can now be actively explored and understood. This reowning of past peak experiences can provide a door into the transpersonal dimension and help one reduce the intensity of the crisis or even resolve it altogether. (As we shall see, most people have had transpersonal experiences of some kind. The exercise 'Integrating Transpersonal Experiences' in the workbook in *Synthesis*, 1977, p 129, is designed to help us recall such experiences and integrate them into our daily lives.)

As the crisis develops, people often experience a conscious urge for something beyond the worldview they have previously accepted. They may develop a growing curiosity about spiritual matters, philosophy, the metaphysical implications of modern physics, parapsychology, the occult – anything that, being mysterious, one hopes will contain answers to the basic unsolved questions of life.

It is important to realise that only some of the directions in which such a quest can be pursued are likely to be fruitful. Here, as spiritual teachers of all times have stressed, discrimination and motives are critical determining factors. In pursuing one's spiritual path, one needs to practise discriminations in a number of areas, for example interpreting transpersonal experiences and inner messages, determining the suitability of working with a teacher, the appropriateness of particular spiritual practices to one's needs, the usefulness of advice from friends and family and the value of other influences and potential resources (the matter of discrimination has been considered in 'Dialogue with the Higher Self', *Synthesis*, 1975, Vol 1, No 2, pp 131-132 – reprinted in this book). As for motives, to the extent to which one is seeking spectacular phenomena, whether for their own sake, for a kind of materialistically motivated need for reassurance, or for selfish or dubious purposes, to that extent the quest is not a genuinely spiritual one. When instead one is seeking for a fuller understanding, an enhanced apprehension of values, a heightened realisation of that intrinsic harmony which is ever emerging, then the quest is indeed along spiritual lines.

If such a quest is pursued far enough, it will result in a reorientation toward the transpersonal dimension, and the existential crisis can then be overcome. Its resolution is found in an expansion of our perception of who we are and of the world we live in. in other words, we begin the process of *disidentifying from our personality* and of achieving a broader, more inclusive state of awareness and identification, one that *includes* our personality *within a larger context*. It is from this larger context that, as individuals, we can begin to meaningfully participate in the greater whole. This expansion of identification is the turning point in the crisis. (The process of disidentification and identification is the topic of the Workbook in *Synthesis*, 1975, Vol 1, No 2. The Workbook includes a full description of this process, its right timing, and practical ways to accomplish it.)

More often the first experiences of disidentifying from the personality and expanding one's identification to more inclusive levels occur *after* some contact with the transpersonal dimension has been made, whether through a peak experience, or through a quickening of interest in spiritual matters. For when the transpersonal influence is consciously recognised, the expansion of identification is greatly facilitated. But sometimes, especially if the personality's attitude is *opposed* to spiritual matters, disidentification from the personality needs to occur *before* conscious contact with the transpersonal can be made. This can make the resolution of the existential crisis considerably more difficult. One has to let go of past satisfactions and pursuits, the fruits of many years of growth – all that one was attached to – because it has turned grey and barren, and there is simply nothing else to do. And the difficulty is that this must be done even though at the time there seems to be nothing of value to put in its place.

Psychosynthesis

At this point one may feel that his life has been wasted, that all he has achieved is empty. The fear one then faces is that one's very identity will be lost (on the fear of losing the sense of personal identity, see *Synthesis*, 1974, Vol 1, No 1, p 53).

But although disidentifying from the personality under such circumstances is a difficult step to take, we have in fact been prepared for it by a long sequence of lesser events that life provided for us. Whenever in the past we have given up an interest or a goal because it turned out to have insufficient meaning, we have in reality disidentified from it, and shifted our identification to a new one. With the advent of the existential crisis, we reach a further stage of this same process. Now the task becomes to disidentify from our personality as a whole. In this period of darkness, it is of great value to realise that we are already familiar in some ways with what is required of us, having successfully accomplished similar tasks in the past.

Disidentification from the personality needs to be clearly understood. It does not imply in any way, as some mistakenly believe, that we are to destroy our personalities, 'kill our ego', give up all our activities, resign from life, or take any similar action that would impede or even reverse the natural process of our growth.

Disidentifying from the personality means recognising experientially that our personality is not what we *are* but what we *have* – not the *source* of our identity, but our means to express that identity in the world. By disidentifying from it, we do not destroy or abandon it, rather we transcend its *limitations*, and the self-centred and separative tendencies they bring.

An attitude that can be of considerable help in disidentifying from the personality is to deliberately accept as a possibility – as a hypothesis to be entertained and verified – the existence of a realm of higher meaning we do not yet perceive. We can purposefully decide to turn from a relentless insistence on meaninglessness (like that of certain existentialists) and in an open-minded way, look to see if there is something greater than ourselves. This attitude is no less realistic than the physicists' search for the unseen principles of nature and the universe.

Countless people have borne witness to the fact that as we attempt to disidentify from the limitations of our personality and search for what is more than ourselves, we become increasingly able to see the world as an interconnected and unified whole – one in which our personality can find its rightful place, just like everyone else's. Then

Psychosynthesis

all which *as an end in itself* had lost meaning, acquires a new and much greater meaning, because it is now recognised to be an intrinsic part of the larger whole.

For Tolstoy, light broke in on his despair as he walked one day alone in a forest. He tells us that he began thinking about his life and that which was greater than his life, as yet undiscovered, the lack of which was the source of his despair. There, in the naturalness of the woods, he sought to trace in himself this sense of something greater. Suddenly he experienced the first awakenings of a renewed sense of meaning and purpose in life. This something greater was life itself, and it was all around him. He was filled with an appreciation of the richness and depth of life, and of his own place in it. After this experience, Tolstoy wrote, "Things cleared up within me and about me better than ever, and the light has never wholly died away. Just how the change took place I cannot tell. As insensibly and gradually as the force of life had been annulled within me, and I had reached my moral deathbed, just as gradually and imperceptibly did the energy of life come back." (*A Confession*, Scribner's, 1923).

So the existential crisis is, fundamentally, an opportunity to expand our sense of reality. Once resolved, it allows purpose, meaning and values to become part of our lives in a new way – as our personal life takes its meaning from a more universal, inclusive and lasting source.

(When one reaches the existential crisis it is possible, although rather uncommon, for the personality to be impervious to the influence of the superconscious. This is especially so when a strong, well-integrated personality is fed by an overwhelming drive for personal power, and as such power is seen as either as the source of meaning or as the way to gain that which one considers to be meaningful. In such a situation, the existential crisis probably will not be felt very strongly, and the personality is likely to be well equipped to resist it. The resistance of the personality is greatly increased if one is working with a guide who does not recognise the crisis for what it is, and thus fails to encourage, or even allow, the emergence of the superconscious energies (see also Roberto Assagioli, 'Self-Realisation and Psychological Disturbances', *Synthesis*, 1977, pp 167-168 – reprinted in this book). One's development may then tend to continue solely along the horizontal dimension. If followed for too long before making a stable connection with the superconscious, this path leads one in an antisocial direction, to seek more and more personal power, and can be harmful both for oneself and others. In extreme cases it can even lead one, eventually, to draw on superconscious

energies and use them to achieve personal, separative goals, thus perverting their essential nature.

There can also develop, as Assagioli says (see *Synthesis*, 1977, pp 155-156), a confusion of levels and an illusion, by which one attributes to his personal self, or 'I', the qualities of the Transpersonal Self. One then unwittingly arrogates to himself – and *himself only* – those powers which justly belong to the Transpersonal Self: the transcendent focus in which *all* humanity participates. In other words, such a person sees his personal identity as the ultimate reality and, to use a current phrase, 'goes on a power trip'. He increasingly perceives other people and his environment as mere objects to be used in support of his personal identity, and may even go so far as to see them as extensions of himself. A most extreme example is that of a political dictator who has exaggerated his sense of identity to the extent that he sees it as absorbing even his country – such as Hitler who stated, 'I am Germany.')

After the Existential Crisis: Problems and Strategies

But what happens next? What happens after the self-actualising individual has begun his reorientation? Through a transpersonal awakening, whether gradual, or more dramatic like Tolstoy's, he has seen the need to achieve the synthesis of the transpersonal dimension with his practical life in the world. This is a most rewarding enterprise – perhaps the most fascinating of all human adventures. As we take our first steps toward such a synthesis, even what may appear to be relatively small accomplishments are significant, because we are becoming the conscious agents of that creative energy which underlies the development of nature and man. The great cosmic play of creation, one pole infusing and transforming the other, is being visibly enacted in our ordinary lives.

Much more could be said about the joys of such accomplishments, increasing as they do with the magnitude of the reconciliations we are able to bring into being. But there is also another side to things, one which can accompany or alternate with the new sense of progress. At first, one's contact with the transpersonal is necessarily imperfect, and therefore can generate difficulties of various kinds. Sometimes a transpersonal vision may be powerful and seem complete when it occurs, but later turn out to be lacking some all-important aspect, or be very difficult to interpret in practical terms. At other times, the vision may simply begin to fade and become more and more remote without one's knowing how to recapture it. In other cases, rather than a sud-

Psychosynthesis

den and full picture, one may have received only a sequence of faint hunches, flashes of insight, glimpses that appear sporadically over a considerable period of time, so that one can barely recognise them or grasp them. Or again still, a sense of joy, harmony or love may pervade one and lift him so he can see life as more than the problems, the struggles, the doubts of his everyday existence. But then gradually this exalted state may fade, and things *apparently* revert to just what they were before – with an added sense of loss.

It is generally realised that these periods of darkness, of aridity, doubt and uncertainty are common phases of spiritual unfoldment. But what often is not understood is that they are valuable and necessary to our development. In fact they are brought about, in many cases, by the Transpersonal Self in order to facilitate the eventual fusion between our personal and transpersonal natures.

This is an important insight, because all too often our tendency is to feel that such withdrawal of energy is unnatural and therefore must be a punishment for, or at least the consequence of, our having failed in some way. This can cause us to search – sometimes frantically – for the mistake we need to correct. These difficult phases may in fact be the result of wrong action – or of failing to act on what we know is right – and identifying the cause and correcting the situation will then usually re-establish our superconscious connection. But at least as often, periods of darkness are normal phases of growth – analogous to the natural cycles of day and night. If we can recognise them as such, we will see that they are useful opportunities, and will be able to use them most effectively and also, in many cases, shorten their duration. While the specific purpose of such periods is unique in each situation, three common patterns are worth mentioning.

In the early stages of transpersonal contact, the withdrawal of energy often serves as motivation for the individual *to reorient his personality* more firmly and decisively toward the transpersonal realm. When, after his first awakening, the individual is thrown back on his own resources, he may understandably find himself unsure of his future direction. He may distrust his earlier more self-centred or socially determined habits and impulses, without yet knowing which behaviour would be more in line with his new perspective. He may be afraid to use his personality, his old powers, in case what he uses them for be inadequate or even contrary to his vision. He may even experience guilt at not knowing what to do (Assagioli discusses in depth the reactions to spiritual awakening and methods for dealing with them in his article 'Self-Realisation

and Psychological Disturbances', *Synthesis*, 1977, pp 148-171 – reprinted in this book). It will become apparent to him before too long that he needs, with enduring determination, to seek and apply the best available means of contact with the transpersonal. His personality can then be increasingly guided and transformed, as the light of what the transpersonal reveals becomes a steadier source of direction for him.

Later, once this transformation is well underway, the purpose of periods of aridity is often to *increase the sensitivity* of the personality to transpersonal intimations. This the Self does, not by remaining completely silent, but rather by 'whispering', by sending us insights or hunches that appear when we least expect them, and that are barely above our 'hearing threshold'. This leads us to pay closer attention, and develop an increasingly keen sense for such messages as we 'hold still' trying to hear them.

Finally, especially in the more advanced stages of development, an already well-established contact with the transpersonal may disappear altogether – sometimes gradually over a long period of time, sometimes suddenly at a crucial moment. When we need to act in such a situation, we have to depend only on our personality, without being able to tap the higher sources we had become accustomed to rely on. We need then to draw on our past experience, and on our best understanding of what we have already learned about the transpersonal realm. Fundamentally, it is a matter of asking, 'If I were to face this situation with the benefit of the wisdom and love of the Higher Self, what would I do?' and of acting as much as we are able, in such a way. The purpose here is the reorientation and eventually the unification of the personal will with the Transpersonal Will (see Assagioli, *Act of Will*, Viking, 1973, pp 106-131). This unification is a culmination of the process of self-realisation – a process which began with the reorientation of the personality toward the superconscious.

Part Two

The Transpersonal Dimension

The reorientation that saved Tolstoy from his 'moral deathbed' is a dramatic example of one person's encounter with the transpersonal. It should not be thought, however, that transpersonal experiences are only the results of life crisis, of pain and struggle, or that they are reserved to the exceptional few – great artists, scientists or religious

Psychosynthesis

figures. In actual fact, experience of the transpersonal dimension is nothing exotic or unusual. It is a characteristic part of being human.

Recently, social scientists McCready and Greely conducted a research study on mystical experiences in which they interviewed 1400 persons chosen as a representative sample of the population in the United States (A Greely, *The Sociology of the Paranormal: a Reconnaissance*, Sage Publication, 1975, pp 58 and 65). To a key question, "Have you ever felt as though you were close to a powerful spiritual force that seemed to lift you out of yourself?" As many as thirty-five percent replied 'yes'. Of these, half also indicated that such experiences had occurred 'several times' or 'often'. Almost as many said they had experienced 'feelings of peace, a certainty that all things would work out for the good, a sense of need to contribute to others, a conviction that love is at the centre of everything, and a sense of joy and laughter.' Twenty nine percent also stated that during their experience they had a 'sense of unity of everything and my own part in it'.

Description of transpersonal experience	Percent of those reporting experience
'A sense of deep and profound peace'	55
'A certainty that all things would work out for the good'	48
'Sense of my own need to contribute to others'	43
'A conviction that love is at the centre of everything'	43
'Sense of joy and laughter'	43
'A great increase in my understanding and knowledge'	32
'A sense of the unity of everything and my own part in it'	29
'A sense of a new life or living in a new world'	27
'A confidence in my own personal survival'	27
'The sense that all the universe is alive'	25
'A sense of tremendous personal expansion, either psychological or physical'	22
'A sensation of warmth or fire'	22
'A sense that I was being bathed in light'	14

Their findings, which are consistent with those of a recent Gallup Poll (G Gallup, 'Year 1976 Could Mark Beginning of New Religious Revival in America', *American Institute of Public Opinion*, Princeton, New Jersey. 1976), are of considerable interest because of the quantitative, statistical approach taken in researching these experiences, and because the study is based on a large cross-sectional sample of the American

population as a whole.[3] It is also significant that the people surveyed describe their experiences in ways that were similar to the autobiographical accounts of many great spiritual figures.

The following report of one woman's peak experience shares many or these characteristics: 'I was sitting quietly in the kitchen after getting the kids off to school. I was alone in the house and in the quiet I began thinking about my life, where I was now, and where I was going. Gradually, I began seeing my life as one flow, a flow which was only one stream in the larger flow of life in the universe. Suddenly I was unexpectedly overwhelmed by an intense feeling of joy; I felt intensely alive and saw my life filled with meaning and direction. Mixed with the joy was a deep love – a love for my life, my family, and a love for humanity as a whole with its struggles to grow and change. I felt that all of us were moving toward this joy and love.'

Clearly, during her experience she moved into a state of consciousness beyond her everyday awareness, in which she saw deep meaning not only in her own life, but in the life of humanity as well. The experience was indeed transpersonal; in it she transcended her normal identifications, saw her connection to a larger system of life, and a deep sense of love and joy arose from feeling this connection.

The orientation toward the transpersonal may begin in different ways and at different times. The various periods of life – childhood, adolescence, and adulthood – all have typical patterns of transpersonal activity that are well-known, although not often recognised for what they are.

That the child is often a 'philosopher' has been observed by such widely disparate figures as Piaget and Wordsworth. Wordsworth's description in his 'Ode: Imitations of Immortality from Recollections of Early Childhood' is classic: "Thou best philosopher...Seer blest! On whom those truths do rest; Which we are toiling our lives to find..."

---

3 There have been many other studies of transpersonal experiences from the point of view of the psychology of the normal individual. This tradition in psychology, which goes back as far as Richard Bucke (*Cosmic Consciousness*, EP Dutton, 1901) was carried forward by William James (*Varieties of Religious Experience*, Modern Library, 1936), Roberto Assagioli, Carl Jung, Abraham Maslow, and others. A good description of the characteristics of transpersonal experiences by Maslow is to be found in his previously cited article 'Various Meanings of Transcendence' (*The Farther Reaches of Human Nature*, Viking Press, 1971).

Psychosynthesis

A child's intense curiosity and wonder about life as he sees his first snowfall or takes apart a flower are often examples of natural early interest in the transpersonal dimension. Even a very young child may sometimes seem the true philosopher, delving into the meanings of things, the nature of birth, death, space and time, An example was shared by a mother whose five-year-old son came home from school one afternoon, dropped his jacket and lunch box on the kitchen table and asked, 'Is there anything to eat?' She gave him some cookies and as he finished eating, he very matter-of-factly asked, 'How did *all this* begin…I wonder if it will ever end?' And then in the next breath said, 'See you later, Mom, I'm going out to play.' And he was up and gone almost as quickly as he had mused about the nature of the universe.

Spiritual orientations also frequently arise during adolescence, as a teenager becomes increasingly interested in the meaning and possibilities of life. His interest may be kindled while experiencing an expansive and joyous wave of feelings, or when faced with a life situation or a philosophical question that he thought he knew the answer to but found he really didn't. He may become aware, sometimes acutely, of the confusion, pain and disorder in the larger world. He realises more and more that the answers he had been given are no longer always right, or not always right for him. So now he must find new answers. He may seek out parents, teachers, friends and others he trusts, to guide him and help him understand these mysteries. If his experiences and questions are treated seriously and with respect, his interest will be nurtured and grow. Then the emergence of his higher values and ideals can occur smoothly, and as his transpersonal nature develops, he can more easily integrate it with his personality. Too often, though, his questioning is responded to with embarrassment, condescension or even ridicule. When this is the case, he will feel that it is better not to bring up such concerns, and may keep to himself or even repress this whole area of his life.

Transpersonal awareness in adults emerges in different ways and at different times. It is important to realise that the spiritual quest is not always along traditional religious lines. A physicist may search for meaning by attempting to unlock the mysteries of matter, space and time; a biologist the inner workings of life and evolution; an artist the experience of transcendent beauty; a historian the underlying patterns and forces that have determined the development of mankind; a dancer the more profound rhythms of life; a psychologist the true nature of consciousness. In many cases, after a long process that builds up in the unconscious, spiritual realisations arise spontaneously as peak experiences.

Psychosynthesis

It is also not unusual for interpersonal interests to be kindled by a serious disruption in a person's life, one that compels him to disidentify from much that he was attached to. A divorce, an accident, a natural disaster may shake apart so much that seemed stable and certain, that one is forced to ask, 'If all this can change, then what is it all resting on? What, if anything, can I be sure of?' Similarly, experiences through which a person comes close to his own death will cause him to question the significance of his life and to look for answers beyond himself.

In general transpersonal experiences have a reality about them which seems deeper than our normal day-to-day existence. They carry an intrinsic validity – a noetic quality – and convey a broadened sense of meaning and values.

(Simultaneously with this sense of greater reality may come a seemingly paradoxical sense that one cannot possibly speak about the experience, that words fall short and can only point to the understanding. William James described this as the ineffable quality of the spiritual dimension. A word of clarification on this point is needed. Many of the greatest mystics agree that experiences that reach a certain level – that of the Transpersonal Self – are suprarational, above the level of the mind (see *Synthesis*, 1975, Vol 1, No 2, p 43), and therefore impossible to communicate in words or even to conceptualise correctly).

But this fact has been confused with another phenomenon – the difficulty of the inability to describe, *at first*, transpersonal experiences which are well within the reach of our cognitive ability, but which by their very nature expand our awareness, perhaps for the first time, into new regions of our mind. In such situations we feel unable to describe or even conceptualise an experience not because it is ineffable in substance, but simply because we do not yet have at our command the symbols, concepts and words needed to first interpret and then express it. Many people report, for example, that they have had an experience which seemed to them completely indescribable, only to later find it beautifully described in someone else's writing – whether poet, psychologist, mystic or physicist. This question of relative versus absolute ineffability is a complex one. It has been considered in detail by Charles Muses (Charles Muses and Arthur Young (eds), 'The Exploration of Consciousness', *Consciousness and Reality*, Avon, 1974, p 111) who goes as far as affirming that no experience is ineffable in the absolute sense. From a practical point of view, the art of conceptualising and expressing our transpersonal experiences is of great value, as a most effective means of facilitating further experiences, of increasing our working understanding of the

Psychosynthesis

spiritual dimension, and of developing the higher, more inclusive regions of our mind (see 'Keeping a Psychological Workbook', *Synthesis*, 1975, Vol 1, No 2, p 110 – reprinted in this book).

On the other hand, it is well known that the transpersonal dimension is a subtle one. Our connection to it can be tenuous at first, and may have to be nurtured and deliberately strengthened. We can do this by first learning to *recognise* such experiences when they occur, then exploring the experience, whether through meditation, introspection, or other means, and finally, as we have said, by *integrating* the experience, by *expressing* in our life and activities what it brought us.

The Path of Transcendence

When people turn to pursue their search for meaning along the transpersonal dimension, the results will vary greatly. For some the attempt is slow and laborious. For others the process moves quickly and spontaneously. Whatever the rate of progress, many people sooner or later go through a phase where they are able, for a time, to have increasingly frequent transpersonal experiences with decreasing effort.

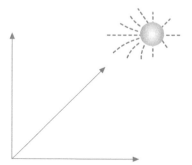

The path to transcendance

But because these experiences of transcendence are so fascinating, gratifying, even ecstatic, some people are gradually drawn more and more toward them, and may in the process turn away from their personality development and participation in the world. By comparison, the world and one's personal existence in it may begin to look ugly, drab, even unreal. If at this point the individual's personality is not sufficiently integrated, he may tend to increasingly neglect everyday life and activity. Eventually he may come to ignore his personality and its further integration altogether.

Psychosynthesis

This of course tends to further increase the imbalance between personal and transpersonal development. His whole life may become devoted to penetrating into more and more exalted superconscious levels. In his attempts, such a person will often find that he can best further his climb along the vertical dimension by utilising one specific aspect of his personality – usually the one he is most identified with. If, for example, that aspect is his feeling nature – as is often the case – he will work single-mindedly on purifying, transmuting and harmonising his feelings, and focusing them upwards towards the transpersonal. This is an approach which has been successfully used by the mystics of all cultures – and it can, indeed, result in ecstatic experiences of great power and meaning.

In general, working for a time primarily on purifying, transmuting and harmonising the feeling nature can be a valuable phase in the growth of almost anyone. But to more easily accomplish this, an individual may also push the other aspects of his personality – such as his physical needs, sexual drive or intellectual curiosity – out of the way, ignoring them, quieting them or even forcibly repressing and 'starving' them. The integration of the personality may then come to a stop – or may even regress. The mistaken assumption behind such a course of action is that if one can experience the transpersonal intensely enough, he will be able to maintain that state indefinitely, and live all his life in the higher consciousness thus achieved.

One young man reported his difficulties in pursuing this exclusively vertical direction. He had a peak experience in which, he said, he perceived a transcendent goal, an ultimate reality, a point of consummation toward which he was moving. As he felt he was on the verge of becoming one with it, it eluded his grasp. Afterward, he was filled with reverence and longing for that vision. He felt enriched by it – was a more complete human being for the experience. He also had a strong sense that if he could only have 'another experience like that', he would actually achieve union with that transcendent focus, he would *become* it and be completely and permanently transformed. In fact, after strenuously following various spiritual disciplines, he eventually did have another experience where, in his words, he 'went much higher' than in the first one. But he was still unable to fully bridge the gap between himself and that transcendent focus. He pondered his disappointment and took stock of what he had gained. The sense that one more such experience would lead to a permanent unification was even stronger in him. However, when his third experience at last occurred, despite the fact that 'its beauty and power were far beyond' the previous one, the final consummation that had appeared 'almost within reach' was not any closer than at the beginning.

Psychosynthesis

He realised then that no matter how much further he might go, and no matter how vividly he might see the grandeur of the universe, he would never 'get there' in this way, never achieve the state of being he sought. As he recognised he was making no real progress toward the goal he had set himself, he entered a deep crisis, finding it unbearable that what he saw as the ultimate reality seemed to be forever beyond his grasp.

This kind of experience – the futility of trying to achieve transcendent unity by leaving behind the everyday – is not uncommon. It is as if one sees an image, a reflection of the Self and moves directly toward that, not realising that it is a reflection, that the real state of unity inherent in the Transpersonal Self, and the joy, the serenity it brings about, must necessarily include the integration of what one is trying to leave behind.

Some people who pursue the path of pure transcendence can be, temporarily, more successful than the young man we have just described. They may be fortunate enough to actually bridge the gap and have experience of unity with the Transpersonal Self. But when the unity is achieved in this way, the experience is only a transient one, and is inevitably followed by the same profound and painful sense of loss. Assagioli points out that "one cannot go to the Goal directly, except momentarily. In a moment of ecstasy, it can be done. But one must distinguish between mountain climbing and airplane flights. You can fly to the top, but you cannot remain always on the airplane, you have to go down. The flight is very useful in order to show you the reality of the mountaintop, inasmuch as there are clouds and mists which prevent one from seeing it from the plain. One also sees the road better, the different steps and so on. But eventually one has to come down, and go through the laborious process of gradual organic development, of real conquest." (*RM Bucke Memorial Newsletter*, Vol 1 No 2, September 1966, pp 11-12).

If one persists exclusively along the path of pure transcendence, the increasing awareness of what appears to be an unbridgeable gulf between oneself and the transcendent goal will lead to the crisis of duality.

The Crisis of Duality

Like every other crisis, once correctly understood, the crisis of duality is fundamentally an opportunity for growth. The one-sided, single-minded focus along the path of transcendence that leads to it can be a necessary, appropriate, and even important

---

phase of development. But sooner or later, the inevitable pull of nature to re-establish balance will require the shift of one's orientation to include the personal dimension as well.

The first sign that one is entering the crisis of duality is an ever-increasing difficulty in proceeding further along the vertical dimension. The difficulty, and the ensuing realisation of the need to include the personal dimension, can be experienced in a number of different ways. One we have seen – the young man who could never quite achieve the experience of unity with the transcendent. Others report that eventually their higher experiences stop happening, and after a period of depression they realise both the necessity and the wisdom of accepting their personality and the world in which they find themselves. After this acceptance, contact with the superconscious gradually returns.

Other people experience that, beyond a certain point, the way is barred as long as they tread it alone. Yet others see the way to be wide open before them, but out of a powerful, deepening love and compassion for humanity and its suffering, freely make the choice to turn back toward the world and help others in their own journeys. Still other people, by proceeding in this direction, recognise that the transcendent unity toward which they are yearning is the culmination of a process of unification in which all mankind participates. So they see that without 'getting there' all together, getting there has no meaning. Attempting to reach and maintain this unity by oneself is seen to be not only a practical impossibility, but a contradiction in terms. (There is a fascinating paradox involved here. Because the Higher Self is in fact our true being, and transcends normal time and space, there is a sense in which 'we are there' already and eternally. From this very high point of view there is nothing to seek, nowhere to go. There is however, the gradual process of *becoming aware* of who we really are – and of learning to act accordingly. The apparent paradox is resolved by distinguishing between what in philosophical terms can be called 'life' and 'consciousness': what is, and our *awareness* of it. The process of reaching toward the self is thus a very real one: one that involves the expanding of our consciousness to become increasingly aware of that which eternally is.)

Another experience of reorientation – one that is perhaps most characteristic, that gives the best insight into the nature of the reorientation itself – has been reported by a mystic who had reached great purity in his love and devotion. The more he gave his love to God, the more that love brought him near to Him. One day, as he was project-

ing his love upwards, he heard God explain, with great gentleness, that in fact he was the Source of Love, and the mystic was actually receiving it from Him and reflecting it back. So he did not need the mystic's love, but humanity did. And now that he had learned to receive it so well, God said, it was time for him to learn also to transmit it to other human beings – to give it to those who were further away from it, or not yet able to reach for it directly themselves.

After the Crisis of Duality

Once having made the decision to reorient his life to include the personal dimension, the individual typically encounters a number of problems and opportunities.

After making significant progress in exploring the transpersonal realm, he has now turned to the task of expressing his vision in the world. Full of that vision of the way things could be, he may approach the task of transforming the world with great confidence and enthusiasm, assuming 1) that he can do it alone and 2) that he can do it this week. At first he may believe that all he needs to do is tell others what he has seen of the right way to do things, and they will speedily and gratefully follow. When they do not respond, he may begin to become more zealous, assailing and haranguing them. With the best of motives, he may even get angry, take a militant approach, and proselytise to the point of fanaticism. Clearly, if he is to make progress and be effective, he must accept that the world is slower and more resistant to his vision and ideals than he expected.

This naïve expectation is most often due to the lack of a working *sense of proportion*. A good sense of proportion is always important, but at a certain point in our lives it becomes essential. It derives from such factors as a clear sense of values, an understanding of the relationship between causes and effects, a recognition of the various patterns and levels of organisation, and a sense for the meaning of the various trends and processes that are emerging in ourselves and in the world. Developing a working sense of proportion is as essential to expressing our vision effectively as knowing the scale factor of a map is to the successful completion of a traveller's journey.

The parallel is important because from one important point of view, transpersonal experiences often are *visions of a map, plan, or 'ideal model'* and not of the actual territory that needs to be traversed. This fact often goes unrecognised, however, because transpersonal visions can be so vivid, immediate and all-engrossing that they are

Psychosynthesis

likely to be experienced as much more real than 'ordinary reality'. Here again is the underlying paradox: what we experience may in fact exist now in the transpersonal dimension, although it may be only an ideal, a potential, in the dimension of daily life. So at first we may not perceive correctly the proportion between the experience of the vision (the map) and the scope of its expression and implementation in the world (the territory). For example, one may suddenly have the direct and powerful experience of love as the sustaining and unifying principle in the universe, together with the clear, intense, and quite accurate perception that in order to cure the ills of the world what we need to do is 'be more loving'. But then as a result one may expect to make this happen simply by telling everybody to do it.

Unfortunately, as has been repeatedly shown, this won't work. Expressing a transpersonal vision requires considerable skill and experience, as well as a well-integrated personality. So it is understandable that people who have focused their attention mainly toward the transpersonal are especially prone to such difficulties. This is the case with many idealistic people, and tends also to be a common pattern among the young. Often young people have not yet had a chance to develop through life experiences the needed sense of proportion, the inner resources and the necessary worldly skills. At the same time, they have an intense idealism, which often has its roots in a great sensitivity to the transpersonal: a sensitivity that gives them a strong feeling for the potential richness and beauty of human life, but at the same time the acute and often painful realisation that this potential is not yet being actualised. One young man expressed his dilemma by saying: 'How can I know beyond any doubt that I am one with the Universe and still get uptight talking to my mother on the phone!'

So it is important to recognise the need to cultivate a sense of proportion and patience, and then set about the task of actualising one's vision in a realistic and effective way.

As our sense of proportion develops, we become better able to see that many needed changes are already taking place, that the world is evolving, and that there are many forces at work for positive transformation. One woman, deeply impatient with the world, had an imaginary dialogue with it. The world told her, 'You don't need to feel responsible for solving *all* my problems – I'm already working on my problems – but I could use your help.' In examining the world from this perspective, one can get a clearer sense both for the positive trends that are already occurring and for the further steps that are needed. Then one may see how he can contribute to this process and what changes he needs to make in himself in order to make that contribution possible.

Psychosynthesis

Thus the individual who becomes filled with a love for mankind, or who has clearly seen that all people need to become more loving, may discover that it takes considerable examination of the nature of love, and many changes in his own life for him to actually become more loving himself. For example, he may discover that he needs to overcome his fear of loving and being loved, and choose to do work on personality patterns developed in childhood. Clearly, *experiencing* love in a peak experience is very different from making one's personality and life an *expression* of love.

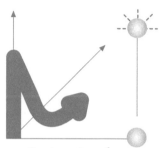

Reorientation after
the crisis of duality

To take another example, the person who has a vivid insight into what society would be like if it recognised our deeper humanness, may see the need to improve our social structures. In looking carefully, he may see that one of the things needed is a more positive approach to the development of the human being. He might then decide that if children were raised with their higher potential in mind, many of the ills in society would fall away, as we produce healthier human beings. Understanding now the scope and the complexity of the task of actualising his insight, he might start by searching out the best of what is already known in psychology and education, and begin to develop his own understanding and knowledge with which to create a better educational approach.

By developing a realistic plan in this way, the person who had been oriented toward the transpersonal dimension moves closer to making his vision happen. While taking time to balance transpersonal growth with personal development may seem, at first, to be a sacrifice of the glories of transcendent experience, as the needed personality functions and skills are gradually developed and the vision begins to become a reality, one will gain access to vaster reaches of the transpersonal than ever before, as well as an increased communion in the evolution of the larger whole.

Psychosynthesis

The Dynamics of Your Higher Energies

As we have seen, no matter which path we have been following, sooner or later we experience a compelling pull to include both the personal and the transpersonal dimensions of meaning – the horizontal and the vertical, self-actualisation *and* transcendence. Adopting such a fully integrated approach to living, encompassing both dimensions and uniting them in one's life, is nothing less than reaching toward self-realisation. To best proceed along this new, most inclusive path we will need to comprehend the underlying relationships between the personal and the transpersonal aspects of our nature.

Major psychological thinkers from Kurt Lewin to Sigmund Freud have repeatedly pointed out that all psychological relationships are fundamentally energetic in character. Thus the fundamental interaction between the personal and the transpersonal can itself be best understood dynamically, in terms of energy. Let us consider in some detail the phases of superconscious energy flow through our personality, and the means by which that energy can be enhanced, enabling us to move forward to self-realisation.

Self-actualisation: growth along the horizontal dimension – consists essentially in coordinating and integrating the energies of the personality, and in the emergence of a strong self-identity, or 'I', capable of effectively expressing those energies.

Transcendence: progress along the vertical dimension – consists primarily in reaching for the energies of the superconscious, which then flow into, and pervade, the personality.

Growth toward *self-realisation*, then, occurs as the personality becomes both well-integrated in itself, and in harmony with the transpersonal, therefore *capable at the same time of receiving the superconscious energies, and expressing them in action.* (Parallel to this transformation of the personality is a growing intensification of the 'I', and its gradual disidentification from the personality itself. This, in turn, leads to the experience and recognition of one's personal will as distinct – and free – from the often separative desires and urges inherent in the personality. This process of increasing inner freedom culminates as one achieves the capability of aligning one's personal will with the *transpersonal* will – the will of the Higher Self.)

Psychosynthesis

Development along the path of self-realisation is a process full of adventure and joy, one which results in a continuous, unimpeded flow of higher energies *through* the personality and into the world. This has been recognised from the earliest times as the developmental goal of the human personality. It is implicit in the etymological meaning of the word 'personality' itself, which goes back at least as far as the masks of the ancient Greek drama. It derives from *per-sona* – 'to sound through' – thus implying the flowing through the personality of a more essential, or higher energy.

To follow the path of self-realisation, then, it can be seen that we have three fundamental tasks:

1 *To eliminate the obstacles within our personality* so that the transpersonal energy can flow through more freely and without distortions.

2 *To reorient our personality patterns and habits* in harmony with the superconscious, so as to reach upward and increase the flow of energy that can be received.

3 *To develop the needed channels and skills* by means of which the energy can be harmoniously expressed.

Eliminating the Obstacles

The energies of our higher nature, such as love, joy, compassion or serenity, are always present, and are continually being generated in our superconscious. However when they first begin to flow toward our personality, they are often stopped from reaching it by psychological 'blocks' of various kinds. So they remain in our superconscious, where they steadily build up and form actual *reservoirs of accumulated energy*. As time goes by these energies will slowly but, happily for us, inevitably, increase their potential, and thus their pressure against the obstacles that are in the way.

As the accumulated energy increases, it may gradually surmount an obstacle, just as a mountain lake fed by a spring will *gradually* rise, overflow its boundaries, and flow onward into the valley below. On the other hand, an obstacle to the flow of superconscious energy may be removed suddenly by the mounting pressure of the superconscious energy sweeping it away. Such a *breakthrough* can also be produced by a life experience, the action of a therapist, or some initiative of our own. In such a case, a sudden and greatly intensified flow into the personality occurs, until the accumulated energy is spent. These abrupt eruptions of energy constitute the 'peak experiences' described by Maslow and others. It has been repeatedly observed that peak experi-

ences often occur spontaneously after a catharsis or other psychological breakthrough by which a personality 'block' is removed. And after the accumulated energy is released, the *decreasing* flow that inevitably follows is often experienced as the depression, or 'let down' known to frequently occur after a peak experience. It is interesting to observe that many times peak experiences following this pattern occur even though the person involved has no expectation of them, and even no belief in, or knowledge of the transpersonal dimension. (A belief *against* the existence of the transpersonal dimension, however, does in itself form a serious obstacle to the inflow of superconscious energy, and thus can inhibit peak experiences. Consequently, the importance of an open-minded attitude when exploring the transpersonal dimension cannot be overstressed.)

But what are the obstacles to the flow of superconscious energy? They can be the problems and difficulties dealt with in psychotherapy (fear, doubt, shame, guilt, a sense of inferiority, and other complexes, phobias, undesirable patterns, or such larger formations as subpersonalities at certain stages of their development). Or they may be the barriers to spiritual experience which are commonly defined in many religious or ethical traditions (for example pride, anger, sloth and the like in Christianity. Or the 'fetters and hindrances' in Buddhism, and so on).

These patterns and traits can be conceived of as organised structures in our personality which resist the flow of higher energy. Rather than transmitting the energy in its original form, they *absorb* it and break it down into 'lower' forms. For example, an inferiority complex can absorb and transform the superconscious energy of love into feelings of possessiveness.

This *de-graduation* of energy has many well-known counterparts in the physical world (it can be seen to be the psychological counterpart of the principle of entropy expressed by the second law of thermodynamics, according to which physical energies are transformed into heat under the effect of friction). If, for instance, the plug of a heavy electric appliance is poorly connected to its wires, it will warm up, sometimes considerably, as some of the electricity flowing through it is absorbed and transformed into heat. To use another such example, the food inside a microwave oven absorbs electromagnetic energy and so becomes hot, while the oven walls, being metallic and good conductors, present little resistance to the energy flowing through them, and remain relatively cool. In our personality, the process analogous to this 'heating up' is usually experienced as pain, in one of its many forms. Often, through this pain we gain an enhanced awareness of the undesirable habit pattern or other trait which absorbed the energy, and which therefore needs to be changed or eliminated. (Psychologically, energy degradation has its converse in the process of the sublimation of energies (see Assagioli, *The Act of Will*, Viking, 1973, pp 62-65.) Thus, while degradation is entropic, sublimation is anti entropic, or syntropic (see *Synthesis*, 1974, Vol 1, No 1, pp 12 and 18).

A growing awareness of undesirable traits to be corrected is often a first sign that superconscious energy is beginning to flow into the personality. If we do not take adequate steps to correct such limitations, more and more of these higher energies will be absorbed and transmuted in painful 'lower' feelings, for example shame or guilt. Such feelings of inadequacy, sometimes developing to an acute stage, are frequently reported by many people as having preceded some of their most important spiritual experiences. Often, as the intensity of these negative feelings grows, it forces us to mobilise our resources and eliminate the undesirable patterns from which the feelings originate. But even if we are unable or unwilling to do what is needed, the process of eliminating obstacles can continue, and be achieved in another way. As the 'heat' continues to increase, it eventually can reach the point of a real burning away of the obstacle – the actual breaking down of the pattern. Interestingly enough, the symbols of 'purifying fire', the 'burning ground'; and other beneficial aspects of fire in general, are very common in certain kinds of transpersonal experiences and in much mystical literature. And in alchemy, fire itself is a fundamental principle of transmutation and sublimation. Spiritual 'fire' can thus be considered not only as a metaphor but also as a psychological reality, a true correspondence to the physical process of combustion.

It should be pointed out that we experience this process as painful only as long as we are either unaware of the undesirable pattern needing to be changed, or psychologically identified with that pattern. Thus psychological pain is often simply an alarm bell, a means of capturing our attention, a warning that all is not well and that reactive action of some kind is needed. Once we recognise the cause of the pain, succeed in disidentifying from its source, and cooperate with the forces within us which aim at remedying the situation, then the same process is experienced as liberating, uplifting and joyful.

Reorienting Our Personality

We have seen how energy accumulates in the superconscious when its flow is impeded by obstacles. The amount of energy that is stored, and the ways it can be released by

removing the obstacles, differ for different individuals. Two factors are important: the extent to which the Transpersonal Self turns its attention 'downward' toward the personality thus directing more superconscious energy toward it, and the extent to which obstacles in the personality resist the flow of that energy.

Some thinking will make it clear that when in an individual there is both a strong superconscious influence *and* a highly resistant personality, large amounts of energy will be present – but blocked – within the superconscious. This is in fact the situation for many people in our Western society, at the point when they consciously orient themselves toward spiritual pursuits. Because of obstacles caused by the materialistic influences of our culture, many people will turn to the transpersonal only after considerable pressure has built up within them. This is why techniques to remove obstacles and release blocked energy, and emphasis on catharsis, breakthroughs and peak experiences, have become increasingly widespread and successful in recent years. For many, such approaches have been appropriate first steps in purposeful spiritual development.

But eventually most of the superconscious reservoirs are discovered, and the energies stored in them released. Today, increasing numbers of people have reached this stage. They have had a sequence of breakthroughs and peak experiences which helped them, sometimes considerably, in their growth, but after a few months or years the intensity of such experiences has tapered off. None of the familiar techniques now yields the old results, and gradually the process comes to a halt. What is needed now is to reach beyond the spent reservoirs, to the *actual sources of energy* in the superconscious and increase their flow – while continuing to eliminate new obstacles to that flow as they become apparent.

One now enters upon a new mode of development, one that will tend to be less dramatic and may *appear* to be more laborious, but which will produce over the long run steadier and more serene progress, and ever more significant and rewarding results.

The difference is due to the special dynamics by which the release of transpersonal energy occurs. Fundamentally, this release is beyond our *direct* control. This is a sharp contrast to the more familiar process of personality growth and self-actualisation. Especially in its more advanced stages, personality growth – including the elimination of undesirable patterns – is more and more the direct result of conscious decisions and deliberate action, of which we become increasingly capable as we realise our identity as the 'I', the personal self. [The functions of the 'I' in regulating and promoting the growth of the personality are more fully discussed in Betsie Carter-Haar, 'Identity and Personal Freedom', *Synthesis*, 1975, Vol 1, No 2, pp 74-81 – reprinted in this book.] From the vantage point of the 'I', we see a personality pattern that needs to be changed, and can then take direct action to make that change.

Transpersonal unfoldment is different. While we can do much to deliberately facilitate the superconscious energy flow and to maximise its beneficial effects *once it has been released*, the release itself is initiated by an act of the Transpersonal Self. This has been recognised in many spiritual traditions, and expressed with such concepts as that of *Grace*. But these concepts have frequently been misinterpreted – despite much experiential evidence and spiritual teaching to the contrary – as representing the action of an unknowable, unpredictable, mysterious and even capricious Source, which *may* bestow upon us its guidance and help, but which we can only wait for hopefully, without being able to influence its action in any significant way. Yet the similarities that cut across the many different types of spiritual experiences and methods of transpersonal unfoldment are a strong indication that the life and processes of the superconscious realm proceed according to universal principles and laws that are reliable and can be increasingly be understood and trusted, just as is the case with the laws governing the physical world.

One of these principles can be stated in this way: *the Transpersonal Self is, in its own high sphere, an Ontological Reality, a centre of Being, awareness and will.* It is therefore more than a source of energy: it has intentionality – including the enduring intention to send us the energy we need to grow and evolve. In the deepest sense, *we are that Self*; it is our true nature, although we may not yet experience and live that fact. It is to bring us to this realisation, to assist us toward eventual unification with it in consciousness and action that the Self wills us the energy we need.

Accordingly, the problem of how to 'convince' the higher Self to send us its energy is an artificial one. The Self already has the fixed intention to send us superconscious energy, and it will do so just as soon as we are *willing* to receive it and *capable* of using it constructively. So what is needed is to establish the right conditions, the right orientation in our personality – and over this we indeed have much real control. These facts have been repeatedly stated in the major scriptures and by the greatest mystics. In Christianity, for example, it is the fundamental meaning of the affirmation, "seek and you will find; knock, and it will be opened to you." (Matthew 7:7). *In other words,*

Psychosynthesis

as the personality orients itself toward the Self with sufficient intensity and focus, the response of the Self inevitably follows.

Of course, like everything else in nature, the evocation of superconscious energy into the personality is a gradual process, one that proceeds according to the ebb and flow of inner rhythms of maturation. As a consequence, when we consciously and earnestly turn toward the Self, its response may not follow immediately, and may not be in the form we asked for. But when the response does come, it comes with the benefit of the Self's deep wisdom, and therefore – as many have the occasion to acknowledge after the fact – at the time and in the particular form we most need and would in fact have chosen if we had known enough.

After we have made the decision to reorient ourselves toward the Self, there are many techniques we can use to achieve that goal. Let us consider the principle underlying many of the most common and effective methods: it is to *form in our consciousness patterns that can reverberate to corresponding patterns in the superconscious* and thus 'evoke' their energy, and draw it into the personality. Establishing such a reverberation is a primary effect of all useful forms of meditation, prayer and certain types of imaginative techniques (for an extensive description of how such inner creative acts are based on the formation of mental patterns that can reverberate to superconscious energy fields, see James Vargiu, 'Creativity', *Synthesis*, 1977, pp 17-53 – reprinted in this series). A practical example is the technique of 'Dialogue with the Higher Self' (see *Synthesis*, 1975, Vol 1, No 2, pp 122-139 – reprinted in this book. This reverberation is also the basis for 'the Blossoming of the Rose' and the 'Inner Silence' exercises in this issue. Other practical examples of this process of reverberation are discussed later in this article). Here the image of the Wise Old Man is a *mental pattern* which, experience has shown, can reverberate to the corresponding energy of loving wisdom in the superconscious. Our desire for the Wise Old Man then becomes capable of being 'heard' or 'seen' by the Higher Self, which responds appropriately, making the image 'alive' with its own energy.

The same reverberation can be set up along primarily cognitive lines, for example by reflecting upon the meaning of certain geometric symbols (three such symbols of profound integrating value are a square, a triangle, and a circle with a point in the centre), or ideas ('Infinite space is the only space there is', 'Time must have a stop', 'The most incomprehensible fact of Nature is that Nature is incomprehensible').

Psychosynthesis

This reverberation becomes a channel or path through which superconscious energy can flow. This energy then has an integrating, synthesising effect. It strives to bring the personality – or that aspect of the personality into which it flows – to the higher level of organisation, one that will contain patterns even more responsive to the superconscious energy itself.

The formation of reverberating patterns can also be initiated by our Higher Self. For example, it is well known that transpersonal symbols can emerge spontaneously in our consciousness – at times with dramatic effect. And as we have seen, at the core of the existential crisis is our experience of a spontaneous, impelling urge to find answers to the most basic, most universal questions.

But whether the process appears to be initiated from below, by action of the personality reaching toward the Self, or from above by an impulse of the Self sending its energy toward the personality, the result will be the same: action by one side will evoke the response of the other side, in a two-way interaction which builds upon itself. This leads to a 'virtuous circle' through which personality and Higher Self interact more and more with one another, creating a growing reverberation, a path through which the superconscious energy increasingly pervades the personality, as the personality proceeds to reorient itself in harmony with the superconscious.

This deeply fulfilling interplay usually begins long before one recognises it for what it is, although it may be apparent in its early phases to an experienced observer or guide. Much evidence, such as the Greely study discussed earlier, indicates that this profound interaction is in fact present and growing, although still largely unrecognised, in a considerable proportion of the human beings alive today.

There is also a complementary aspect to this fundamental reorientation. As we turn more and more toward the Self, we find that we also need to turn away, and disidentify from certain negative personality traits – for example selfishness, or pride – that form patterns incompatible with the flow of superconscious energy. Here a *choice* is required – a choice between two aspects of our nature that may be in conflict with one another. But choosing to align ourselves with the more spiritual aspect does not have to imply the rejection of the other. On the contrary, that choice often gives us the opportunity of transforming it, as we have seen, in such a way that it too can then become a channel for transpersonal energy.

Psychosynthesis

As we proceed in the work of reorienting our personality in harmony with our spiritual nature, we face many such conflicts, requiring us to make corresponding choices. Eventually, as we move closer and closer toward self-realisation, all the patterns and tendencies in our personality that remain opposed to the influence of the Self may be experienced as one purposeful, well-organised formation. At this very advanced point, we see that we have the choice to either acquiesce in its urgings, or to deliberately and irrevocably align ourselves with our higher nature. To bring about this culminating alignment we find that we need the help of our Higher Self – a help that we must ask for by drawing on the totality of our resources. In doing so we disidentify fully from those tendencies of our personality that would separate us both from our fellow men and our higher nature. Achieving this consummating act of disidentification – an act of will which is made possible by many earlier efforts and numerous smaller achievements – is the necessary condition which finally enables the Self to reach us with the fullest impact of its energy. As a result we achieve complete identification as the Self, and the realisation of Being. The energy of the Self then pervades the remaining parts of our personality that still oppose it, transforming them, and integrating them with the rest into a harmonious, unified whole which becomes our willing instrument of expression in the world.

Expressing Superconscious Energies

Fortunately for us, we do not have to await this culminating transformation in order to express the energy of the superconscious: we can and need to express it as we go. We have seen that enabling such energy to flow *through* the personality is a basic aspect of the entire process of self-realisation. The expression of this energy may often be unconscious at first, in the same way as its reception can be. One of the first visible manifestations is a broadening of our sense of responsibility. Typically, this develops into a rising concern for, and dissatisfaction with, the existing state of things – whether in our environment or our personality – and a growing urge to improve them. This urge for improvement according to the best we know becomes increasingly conscious, taking on greater meaning, and becoming a central purpose of our life. Eventually, it is also recognised to be a central purpose of human and world evolution, of Life itself (this universal urge for improvement is beautifully described by Albert Szent-Gyoergyi in 'Drive In Living Matter to Perfect Itself', *Synthesis*, 1974, Vol 1, No 1, pp 14-26 – reprinted in this book).

Psychosynthesis

In essence, the way we express the energy of the superconscious is by making our *patterns of action* more and more consonant with the new vision and the transpersonal qualities which are becoming a normal part of our conscious existence. As we do so, we gradually transform the patterns of our environment, so that they too become more in tune with the superconscious energy and better able to receive it. Whether it be the patterns of our relations with those near to us, of the groups to which we belong, or of the social institutions in which we participate, the influence we have on our environment becomes increasingly harmonising and integrating. This is because *it is intrinsically the same as the influence that the superconscious has on our personality.*

We are dealing here with two successive phases of the same process: *the flow of energy between two reverberating patterns.* Our perception of this process is primarily from the receiving end of the flow in the first phase (from the superconscious to our personality) and from the *sending* end in the second (from our personality to the world). These two complementary vantage points give us a broader perception and a deeper understanding which has practical usefulness, because many of the principles, dynamics and laws that apply to one phase apply to the other as well.

Let us look at one such correspondence which is especially important. We have seen that if inner obstacles prevent the superconscious energy from reaching the personality, it will accumulate in 'reservoirs' within the superconscious. But what happens if the energy is able to reach the personality yet lacks the channels to proceed further? As long as it is not expressed in action – keeping the flow through the personality going – the energy will, once again, accumulate – but this time *within the personality itself.* Eventually, it will create a congestion that will actually prevent further inflow from the superconscious.

Interestingly, this congestion is often experienced as a state of emptiness and aridity quite similar to the experience of being cut off from the energy source. This is because when we experience energy, what we experience is not so much its intensity as its *rate of flow.* (This is the case for the awareness of superconscious energies – which represent the majority of people's transpersonal experiences. The experience of the Transpersonal Self (and of the 'I') on the other hand, is complementary: it relates not to the rate of energy flow, but to its *intensity* or potential. (See also *Synthesis*, 1975, Vol 1, No 2, p 131)). And when the personality is congested no energy is flowing through it, *just as when it is cut off.* Understandably, we are then likely to mistakenly interpret

the experience of a diminished rate of flow as a *lack* of energy. As a consequence we may seek to draw more energy from our superconscious, while instead what we need to do is express the energy we have already received.

This important but little recognised fact can help us to understand and work through many common difficulties along the path toward self-realisation. It is a matter of determining whether the main obstacles to the flow of energy are *between the super-conscious and the personality or between the personality and our environment*. The latter is usually the case when our orientation and the focus of our interest have been, for a considerable time, primarily toward the transpersonal dimension. In fact, the crisis of duality often turns out to be an extreme case of this situation: an acute energy congestion in the personality. As we have seen, it leads to a fundamental reorientation, through which the limitations to the *expression* of energy are recognised and overcome.

Part Three

Toward Self-Realisation

Throughout history, mankind has used a very wide range of methods to reach for superconscious energies and facilitate their flow and expression. Among these methods we find the myriad forms of prayer and of meditation; chanting, dancing and rituals; the many types of yoga; purification and sublimation of the emotions; mental training; group experiences and activities; different kinds of psychotherapy and a variety of approaches to action and service to one's fellow men. In older times, such methods were known only to an initiated few, who were also limited by the cultural traditions of their particular society. Today, because of the rapidly growing knowledge in such fields as psychology, sociology, anthropology, history and comparative religion, combined with the modern communications explosion, these techniques are becoming increasingly accessible to every person, and in greater quantity than at any other time in history.

This unprecedented circumstance furnishes us with great richness of opportunity, but also presents its own unique problems. There are many methods, especially those of recent development, that tend to be relatively – or in some cases excessively – specialised, to address only one part of the overall process of self-realisation. Thus they may be very well suited to one's needs during a particular phase of growth, but not during another. Clearly, such techniques can be effective, but only temporarily (however, if the focus of a method is on shortcuts or quick results for their own sake, it may have dangerous, or even harmful side effects. For example, striving to increase an already adequate inflow of superconscious energy if we have not yet learned to utilise what is available, can be irresponsible and dangerous – even though, because of the inherent synthesising nature of the higher energies, the results may still turn out to be positive. There are also popular methods, notably some which focus on the physical body (special diets, taking particular postures, and so on) that can have a useful part to play in preparing one's personality to handle superconscious energy, but cannot in themselves get that energy to flow. So these can be useful at the right time, if used in conjunction with other techniques. But by themselves they are eventually sterile, and often lead one either to discouragement, or to the illusion that just because one is making a considerable effort, he must be making progress). There is in fact today a growing number of people who have become involved in one method of growth after another, often deriving benefits from each, but in each case eventually gaining all the particular method had to offer them, and finding the need to abandon it and look for something else.

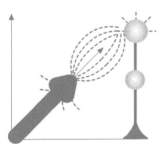

Toward self-realisation

To use the many available methods most effectively and according to one's individual need, it is most helpful, as we have seen, to have a basic understanding of one's development in terms of the energetic processes of human growth. A study of the great spiritual traditions and the lives of the people who have followed them reveals that the integrative path of self-realisation has always taken into account all phases of the process of energy flow. This is true for example of the Raja Yoga of India, the Eight-Fold Noble path of Buddhism, and a number of parallel approaches in the Judeo-Christian tradition. All these traditions show that as we proceed along the path of self-realisation we need to avail ourselves, *simultaneously but in various proportions*, according to our point of development, of the three complementary aspects of that path, corresponding to the three fundamental tasks outlined before. These are:

Psychosynthesis

Reaching upward toward the superconscious, through various methods of meditation, visualisation and prayer.

Understanding the nature of the superconscious, our personality and the world, so as to be able to increasingly harmonise them with each other.

Service, or the expression of the best we know so as to achieve the greatest good.

Let us examine each of them, and some of their main methods.

Reaching Upward

Prayer is a universal method of reaching upward. Seen psychologically – that is, independently of the validity or non-validity of specific religious beliefs associated with its particular forms – prayer can be described as that inner action in which our feeling function is directed toward our higher nature or, through it, to even higher realities or powers. It is a bringing together of the many divided aspects of our emotional nature, first through desire, then aspiration, affirmation, dedication and gratitude.

Consequently, prayer has a *harmonising and transmuting effect* on our feelings. Whether or not in our prayers there is the conscious desire that we will obtain something or that it may 'descend' on ourselves or others, the upward projection of our feelings has the effect of 'lifting' our centre of consciousness in some measure on to the subtler levels of our inner world. It is a process of *elevating* our feelings and desires, thus transmuting them into aspiration toward higher goals.

This elevating process can lead to an appreciation of the beauty and wonder of the world around us. We might call it 'joyous admiration' of the unknown Life or Reality which has created and continues to sustain the universe and all its component parts – including ourselves. It is not surprising that many people who do not think of themselves as 'religious', or who would not literally subscribe to the beliefs inherent in many forms of prayer, do in fact pray.

Imaginative techniques are another means of reaching upwards to contact realms of superconscious inspiration and insight (see the series of articles on The Purposeful Imagination, *Synthesis*, 1975, Vol 1, No 2, pp 119-151 and *Synthesis*, 1977, pp 17-53). These techniques are based on *visualisation*, the conscious and deliberate use of

images. It is by visualising the appropriate image or symbol that we establish with the corresponding superconscious pattern a reverberation through which the needed energy can flow. The visualised image then takes a life of its own, and the energy reaches our personality with beneficent results.

This purposeful use of the imagination is particularly valuable owing to the breadth of its effects. Because it utilises our mind as well as our feeling nature, it can tap a very wide range of superconscious energies, and can be used with great flexibility and precision. For example, while the symbols that are formed by our imagination are often polyvalent – carrying many meanings, reverberating to many energies – and therefore full of surprises in their effects, they can also have selective properties and specialised uses, giving access to *specific qualities* of transpersonal energy. The ascending flame, the sturdy rock, the tranquil mountain lake and the energetic whirlwind are four such symbols taken from nature which can be used to evoke and explore corresponding aspects of our transpersonal nature (for a more complete list of the main categories of transpersonal symbols see Assagioli, 'Symbols of Transpersonal Experience', *Journal of Transpersonal Psychology*, Spring 1969, also reprinted in this book). Imaginatively evoking and then focusing on the flame can help give us insight into the aspiration in all things for what is better. Contemplating the symbol of the rock can put us in touch with the firm basis and order underlying the apparent flux of existence. The mountain lake may speak of the serenity behind all movement. And the whirlwind may call up that great power and motion of which we are all a part. What we visualise conditions and affects our feelings, thoughts, and actions. Therefore as we contemplate such symbols and experience their meaning, our own nature itself can be gradually transformed.

Meditation, in one of its most basic forms is well described in the following account about Robert Frost, written some time ago when the poet was still alive:

"When Frost was a freshman in college, his fraternity brothers worried about him because he took long walks alone in the woods. Finally a delegation of seniors waited on him and after some fumbling preliminaries, one asked, 'Frost, what do you do walking by yourself in the woods?'

Freshman Frost looked at them and replied, 'Gnaw Bark.' Thereafter, they left him alone.

Psychosynthesis

Actually, what Frost was doing in the woods was meditating. He still takes long walks and he still meditates. In part, it is his ability to do so which makes him America's greatest living poet.

There is one kind of meditation which is passive, a quiet sinking into the self, a sort of contemplation. But with most of us, what passes for thought is a purposeless stream of consciousness, like an uncut motion picture with our own confused inner dialogue attached.

Robert Frost's kind of meditation is neither passive nor meaningless. It is directed, tenacious and purposeful. He is able to take a word, or an idea, and hold his mind to it while he looks it over from all angles, turns it inside out, dissects it. By doing so, he sees new aspects, new meanings, new beauties even in tired and timeworn phrases." (CW Cole, *This Week Magazine*, March 1960).

This focused and purposeful type of mental activity is one of the most effective forms of meditation. It has enabled men like Einstein or Teilhard de Chardin to gain direct awareness of what they called the 'Universal Mind'. Its patient and regular application has proven invaluable in establishing a rich and reliable channel between the personality and the superconscious.

This channel can enhance our perception of reality in many ways. When the energy induced by contact with the superconscious flows into our minds, we experience flashes of intuition, illuminations and a wider and more inclusive understanding. Our consciousness is lifted toward this broad perspective, and the events and problems of our own existence and of the world then make increasing sense as we begin to recognise the deeper patterns underlying them. We begin to see the evolving whole, its meaning, and the meaning of our role in it as individuals.

But meditation can lead to more than purely mental activity. For example, it frequently calls down energies which are also received in our feelings – energies which can uplift our emotional nature. Through meditation we can come in touch with such transpersonal qualities as joy, beauty, compassion or serenity, and we can contact the underlying vitality and sweetness of life. Meditation, increasingly sustained by the power of our will, can be deliberately combined with the focused energy of our feelings in a powerful and synergistic method that enables the fullest kind of access to our higher nature (a brief exposition of techniques for such a unified approach to medita-

Psychosynthesis

tion can be found in Assagioli, 'Thinking and Meditation', *The Act of Will*, Viking Press, 1973, pp 218-231).

Understanding

The development of a reliable and inclusive understanding, which grows as we grow, is the second essential aspect of the integrative path of self-realisation. It is the understanding of the nature of the transpersonal realm, of ourselves as personalities, and of the world in which we live, in light of our best awareness of the purpose of the larger whole. It can be achieved by seeking the deeper meaning, the hidden causes of outer events. If, for example, we understand the world as moving toward transcendent unity, then we will examine particular events to see how they relate to that unity. Do they, as is true in the case of many historical occurrences, reveal obstacles to evolution with which individuals and society must deal? Or do they indicate positive and growing trends which we will choose to encourage and support? Events having great impact on society – like the Renaissance, the American Revolution, the Great Depression, and such contemporary ones as the Civil Rights Movement, the Vietnam War, or Watergate – can be examined in this way, as can events and turning points of a more personal nature.

It will be seen then that study of the outer world and the inner world are parallel and complementary. We can then use our understanding more and more to bring our personalities and the world into meaningful correspondence, or reverberation, with transpersonal reality. In this way, the generalised visions we have attained in our transpersonal experiences become particularised, and can be practically applied to ourselves, society in general, and our part in it.

But in order to build this progressive and dynamic understanding, our thinking must be, in the most profound sense, our own. For much of our lives our primary source of learning has been what we absorb, as if by osmosis, from the ideas, feelings and actions of others. Through this contact we gain access to the combined experience and understanding of humanity over many thousands of years. This is both inevitable and good, provided that this great richness is neither lightly accepted nor automatically dismissed. Rather, at each important step, we must strive to be aware of what we are exposed to, what idea or new knowledge is becoming available to us, and decide whether or not we want to accept it. We need to develop the awareness of what flows into us and the capacity to regulate that flow. (Just as regulating this inward flow is our responsibility to ourselves, so regulating the *outward* flow is our responsibility to others. This is the significance of such traditional spiritual watchwords as 'right speech' or 'harmlessness'.) The issue is not only whether a certain idea, principle or value is good or bad, true or false, but even more, that *we cannot truly make it our own, if we absorb it without understanding it.*

It is interesting to observe that many spiritual guides of the past, whose followers were oriented primarily along the vertical dimension – that path of transcendence – emphasised devotion, unquestioned belief, acceptance of the teacher's authority and obedience to his wishes and precepts. Today, as more and more people reach this path of self-realisation, spiritual guides are increasingly abandoning such approaches, and adopting techniques more appropriate to this path. Rather than asking for unquestioned belief and obedience, they stress the importance of clear thinking, of ascertaining for oneself what is true or false, important or trivial, and of acting on what one sees. They emphasise the individual's inner resources and responsibility, and guide him to rely more and more on himself, and eventually on his Self. While this orientation is rapidly spreading today, it is far from new. It has always been at the core of the greatest spiritual teachings, and was, for example, a central teaching of the Buddha at least twenty-five centuries ago: "We are earnestly enjoined to accept nothing whatever on faith; whether it be written in books, handed down from our ancestors, or taught by sages. The Buddha has said that we must not believe in a thing said merely because it is said; nor in traditions because they have been handed down from antiquity; nor rumours, as such; nor writings by sages, merely because sages wrote them; nor fancies that we may suspect to have been inspired in us by a Deva (that is, in presumed spiritual inspiration); nor from inferences drawn from some haphazard assumption we may have made; nor because of what seems an analogical necessity; nor on the mere authority of our own teachers or masters. We are to believe when the writing, doctrine, or saying is corroborated by our own reason and consciousness. 'For this,' says he in concluding, 'I taught you not to believe merely because you have heard, but when you believed of your consciousness, then to act accordingly and abundantly.'" (see the Kālāma-sutta of the Anguttara Nikāya as quoted by HS Olcott in *A Buddhist Catechism*, Quest Books, 1971, pp 62-63).

Service

This action, abundant and according to one's best vision, is the essence of service. It completes the path through which the superconscious energies can flow, in the same way as completing the circuit at an electrical power station energises and illumines a city.

Just as breathing is a natural activity of our body, service is a natural activity of our Higher Self – and at a certain point of development, it becomes natural to the personality as well. Its precursor in the personality is the urge to make things better. This is perhaps our most human tendency, that which most clearly distinguishes man from animal. And as we make contact with the superconscious and begin to understand the larger whole as it is and as it is evolving, we are spontaneously drawn to use our energies to assist that evolution, to help the gradual work of perfecting man and his world. We recognise that service in line with our transpersonal vision is the most effective way to make things better – therefore the best, the most meaningful thing to do.

We can also be drawn to service before having made a clear contract with the transpersonal, perhaps out of a sense of obligation or guilt, or following the example of others, or feeling for the pain of those in need. Many people are motivated in these ways at first, and much that is good and of real value has been accomplished out of such motivations. But in the long run, if the transpersonal energy is missing, difficulties will occur. If one gives more and more of one's energy, the need to refill oneself will inevitably emerge. If one acts only out of an emotional urge, without a clear vision and plan, one may find that the results, although worthwhile, may not be commensurate with one's effort. Increasingly, there will develop the sense that our work is more difficult, more unconnected than we instinctively know it should be. We feel that something is missing, which needs to be found. What is missing, of course, is our connection with the transpersonal vision and source. And as we search for what is lacking, we will reorient our personality and make that connection possible. As our vision and knowledge of the whole then becomes clearer, and we become able to express the energies of our superconscious as well as those of our personality, we can serve more freely and energetically. We see the forward moving currents in the larger world and we are nourished, sustained and strengthened by them – and by the knowledge of their inevitable triumph. Our feelings and our mind become aligned with each other and with our higher nature, and the work of perfecting the whole then becomes at the same time the most reasonable and also the most desirable thing we can do with our lives.

This leads to a new and more realistic perspective on our own growth. We discover that there is no contradiction between serving the whole and developing our individuality, because as we serve the whole we also develop our unique gifts and overcome our particular limitations. Gradually, our individual growth becomes integrated with our commitment to do useful work in the world. But no longer will we strive to improve our personality *for its own sake*. We see clearly that our personality could be improved, but we also see that there is an almost endless possibility for improvement. Although there are many ways our personality could grow, and many limitations we could get rid of, we find it most practical to work on some and postpone dealing with others on the basis of what specific service seems particularly right for us to do. The man who is shy but who sees that having direct contact with people is an intrinsic part of his next contribution, will choose to work on his shyness. But another shy man, one who sees that writing is his next best vehicle, may ignore his shyness for the moment, and work on other limitations like a lack of persistent will.

Interestingly enough, people invariably report that after having made their individual growth dependent on the needs of their service, not only did that growth not slow down, but rather it gained increasing breadth, momentum and ease. The apparent paradox is resolved if we keep in mind that the commitment to serve our larger vision and express our transpersonal values in action calls for the sustained flow of superconscious energy out into the world. Thus service becomes the most effective and most direct way to organise the patterns of our personality in harmony with the superconscious, so as to best transmit its energy. And that energy will now work with us – and also spontaneously, by itself – to remove blocks and clear the way.

The integrative path of self-realisation has in it, then, an inherent *joyousness*. It is the joy of becoming who we really are by living our higher lives – the joy of *self-expression*. It arises from the increasingly immediate sense of our true identity, as we learn to manifest it in daily life. We realise that as the Self, we are one with the larger whole, that our essential nature is what we would have to describe by such words as 'transcendent', 'immortal', 'divine'. Yet we deal with such joyous realisations realistically, because we also understand our need to progressively cooperate with and find our place in the larger context, as it is continuously revealed to us.

With this double perspective, this 'bifocal vision', we see our own spiritual dignity and essential divinity on the one hand, and on the other our need to grow in order to express those qualities. We see the essential divinity underlying the whole of the world's process of growth, and the fundamental rightness of helping that immense work forward as best we can in the time we have. As we bring that knowledge into our

Psychosynthesis

lives, what results is a spontaneous resolution of contraries. Work and play were earlier experienced as antagonists, then we 'time-shared' between them, and now they tend to merge so that one's work in service comes to seem more 'right', more authentic, and at the same time more satisfying and enjoyable than anything else. The dichotomy between self and others, between responding to others' needs and taking care of one's own disappears, as one acquires the practical wisdom to see the intrinsic legitimacy of both and the relative priority of each, from an objective perception of the circumstances at any given moment.

With all this comes maturity – not the drab and mere 'getting older' that is often falsely taken to be 'maturity', but something rich and ripe – an enlightened maturity, full of joy and will, acceptance and discrimination, wisdom and love.

We may well end with Goethe's thought: "Everything that changes is a symbol." In other words any action, habit pattern, feeling, thought or word, all processes, indeed our life as a whole, can be seen as symbolic patterns. As we learn to live the patterns of our life according to our best values and vision, these patterns become more attuned to the higher patterns of our superconscious energies. The Hermetic aphorism, 'As above, so below' becomes then not only an inclusive description of reality, but also a fundamental method of unfoldment, and at the same time an affirmation, an imperative, a way of life. As we increasingly identify with the whole and help to create it, any sense of separateness, of alienation, gradually fades away and is replaced by a certain knowledge of being at home, indeed, of being at one, both with ourselves and with the world.

John Firman and James Vargiu (reprinted from Synthesis, 1977)

Chapter 6 The Will

"Will is neither origin nor end in itself but only a means, expressing the origins and the goals of human life, which is essentially a deep breath of love and freedom." (Alberti, Alberto, Psicosintesi, April 1999)

At the core of our Being is a dynamic energy – a life force recognised by many different disciplines which seek to know the nature of the human being. Freud spoke of this force as libido, spiritual disciplines in the East speak of Chi. Over time, this force takes on form and differentiates into consciousness which covers the spectrum from the most universal and general to the most individual and particular.

This Being, in incarnating, subjects itself to a series of steps via the Universal Self, to the Transpersonal Self to the Personal Self. It is as if that Consciousness becomes stepped down via each of these centres and in that process becomes more and more limited and loses perspective. As it loses perspective and becomes bound to the principles of each of those centres it takes on the form of consciousness of each. In doing so, it identifies with each dimension and 'forgets' more and more its Universality or sense of wholeness.

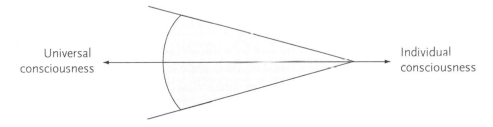

Universal consciousness ⟷ Individual consciousness

Psychosynthesis recognises the ontological reality of Self - that Self is – with the Will as the closest expression of Self. Will therefore is always expressing the Self, at whatever level we are identifying with or experiencing. The essence of Will, within psychosynthesis, is not the strong forcing, 'Victorian' will, so often associated with writings on the Will. It is, rather, the means whereby spirit or life expresses itself. Will is therefore not a physical drive or action, nor an emotional desire nor a mental focus and direction. It is prior to all of these levels and like the Self acts on and through each of these levels.

Psychosynthesis

As with the Self it is easier to talk about what the Will is not because mental constructs cannot effectively grasp the nature of the Will. We can only approximate its reality through the use of metaphor and images. To use the wind as an analogy, we only 'see' the wind when the trees, branches and leaves move; the wind itself acts but cannot be seen or understood at the level of its phenomena.

So why is the Will so important in psychosynthesis and psychology? Because in the process of Self awakening and becoming an authentic being, there is increasing awareness of history and how identifications have both served and now may limit. As we learn to disidentify from these identifications the awareness that accompanies this process does little to transform how we act and behave in the future; only the Will can ensure that this transformation happens.

Two functions serve the 'I' – Awareness and Will. Paradoxically, if we only allow awareness without Will, it often means that we become paralysed, immobilised by awareness. Nothing actually changes and we fail to realise more of ourselves. Similarly with an overdeveloped Will we need to develop increased awareness to ensure the appropriate consciousness is present.

Let us look at how this seems to work. As we disidentify from strong identifications, the observer function of the 'I' comes into play. We observe, see how limiting this identity is and how it can be different. At the same time as the 'I' experiences more freedom we realise there is within our power the energy to act differently and we direct ourselves to do so. It is as if we choose to will and yet the choice in effect follows the energy or will to express ourselves differently. Here we begin to see that not only is Will the closest expression of Self, it is fundamental to the process of self-realisation, in that this is only possible if, following each step of realisation, there is self-expression.

If the Will is so obscure and intangible how is it developed? Assagioli reminds us that even though we may not know the Will we can experience the energy of it. In effect we get to know the experience of Will by understanding its qualities such as persistence, courage, tenacity etc., and forms of expression such as strong will, goodwill and skilful will.

So, for some of us who struggle to allow the Will this may mean training ourselves to ask, after a significant insight, 'What does this mean for my life right now?' and start-

Psychosynthesis

ing to act accordingly. For others it means acting in order to know, rather than awaiting awareness before acting.

As we learn to use and direct the Will, so we realise that Will acts through different levels of Self. At the personal level of 'I' we have the Personal Will serving to express the 'I' and at the level of Self we have the Transpersonal Will, serving the Self and bringing spiritual Will into all we do. At the level of the Universal Self, the Universal Will brings a universal connectedness and context to the life of Self.

The Self *(Roberto Assagioli)*

The Transpersonal Self is an ontological reality, a being, and is on its own level a stable Centre of Life, from which it radiates energies. The personal self, the self-conscious 'I', is a projection or reflection of the Self into the normal human level.

An analogy may help understanding, although, as are all analogies, it is only approximate and partial. The relationship between the Transpersonal Self and the personal self, or 'I', can be compared to that between the Sun and a planet, let us say the Earth. From the Sun emanate many powerful radiations, which affect the planet and all the living beings on it, producing the conditions for evolution, development, growth. In the same way the Self projects a small portion, a spark, a tiny centre of self-consciousness. This self grows in self-awareness, intelligence, power to act, etc., under the combined influence of 'nourishment' from the environment, the soil where it exists, and from the vivifying impact of the descending energies radiated by the Self. One might say that the Self becomes aware through the self of what exists and occurs at the personal levels (physical, emotional, mental). The personal self, in its turn, becomes aware of the Self in two ways:

1 By opening itself consciously to and recognising the radiation from the Self

2 By rising towards and eventually contacting and merging partially with the Self

This conscious experience of the Self is feasible, and many witnesses have testified that the Self can be experienced as a living reality, even more as a living being. It has functions, but is not a function. It is essence – substance – transcendence.

A clear and full experience of the Self gives at first such a strong sense of self-identity that it is felt as something sure, permanent, unchangeable and indestructible. It is

Psychosynthesis

realised as such an essential reality that all other experiences and realities appear, when compared to it, as changing, impermanent and of lesser value and significance.

Some of the qualities manifested by the Self are: pure initiative and free will, creative impulse, wisdom, altruistic love, and a sense of concentrated power at rest, yet ready to express itself dynamically at will.

Some of the effects of the realisation of the Self are: a sense of inner guidance, of strength, of purpose, of responsibility and of joy.

Further Reading

Assagioli, Roberto, *The Act of Will*, David Platt, 1999 (Chapters 11-16)

Ferrucci, Piero, *What We May Be*, Thorsons, 1995 (Chapter 6)

Psychosynthesis

SYNTHESIS

Dialogue with the Higher Self

The long night of reductionism is over. Its product, *homo reductus* – the reduced man captive to his instincts, a mechanical toy with a computer for a brain, is losing his sway over the contemporary imagination. Increasingly, knowledgeable and sober men and women are re-admitting the higher human attributes into their visions of themselves and others. The evidence for this shift is to be found on every hand, particularly its spiritual aspect – the study of religious experience, and the increasing disenchantment with world leaders who can envision no more than merely cynical power relations between the fellow men and women who constitute the nations of the world.

Hopeful as this emerging trend is, it causes for the individual new problems that the pessimism fashionable some decades ago did not present. One is annoyed, troubled, perhaps even tormented by a sensed inner division – and inner division along a 'vertical' dimension.

'I know I can be a better person, but I don't know how to get there.'

'I know what is right to do, but I fail to do it.'

'I have a sense for the way things should go in order to be better, but I cannot translate it into a practical direction for my own life.'

'I know that the pulls of instinct and my social conditioning are often wrong, but I cannot quite see what to do instead.'

It is as if we know that our present personalities, the sums of our lives as we have led them, are not what they could be, and yet we don't know where to turn for guidance. In earlier times we might have relied on older relatives, ecclesiastical authorities, or political leaders to answer such questions. But if there is one lesson that we have learned, it is the inadequacy and sometimes the outright harmfulness of external authorities, when we rely on them without the benefit of our own independent think-

Psychosynthesis

ing. The task is one of discovering and developing a clearer contact with one's own inner source of wisdom. But frequently it is not easy to know where to start.

An extremely simple method within easy reach of most people can be used as a way of beginning. It is the technique of 'Dialogue with the Higher Self'. This technique, which is being increasingly adopted by a number of people, emerges out of the psychological study of various philosophical and spiritual traditions. It is a practical application of the ancient and nearly universal twin belief – that man has a higher aspect, or soul, and that this higher aspect can be contacted by the personality and asked for guidance. It has been said that the fundamental goal of psychology, one only now beginning to be realised, is the understanding of the relationship between these higher aspects of human nature and the personality as we understand it. Those who hold this view call our attention to the root meaning of the word psychology. In Greek 'psyche' means 'soul', and so 'psychology' means the *science of the soul*.

The technique of Dialogue with the Higher Self is, in its essence, simple and straightforward. It consists of the assumption that within each of us is an endowment of wisdom, intuition, and a sense of purpose, which can become a source of guidance in everyday life. The next step is simply to begin to dialogue with it, trusting that it is there and it will answer.

In the Hindu tradition, this higher aspect is sometimes called the Atman. As is well known, Mahatma Gandhi, a practical and most successful political leader, used to talk to the 'inner light of universal truth', which he would consult on important matters. When confronted with such important issues, about which his colleagues were pressing him for decisions, he would retire into meditation to consult this 'inner light', and would emerge after he was rationally satisfied that with the help of this higher inner guidance, he had arrived at the best answer he could. The great Indian saint of the nineteenth century, Ramakrishna, used to practise a similar technique, having talks with Kali, the Divine Mother. In the midst of a crisis, he would go into the temple and talk to her.

In the Eastern tradition, there has been for thousands of years an ambiguity about such dialogues. On the one hand, the various deities involved are symbolised as being outside the person; but, on the other hand, they are considered to be within the person's own psychological and spiritual nature. The *Bhagavad Gita*, the most revered of Indian scriptures, is presented as a dialogue between a young man in crisis, Arjuna,

Psychosynthesis

and the great Lord Krishna, a major Indian deity. But interpretations of the Gita going back over 2,500 years have described it as an internal dialogue – a dramatic presentation of the dialogue between the aspiring personality and the divine light, or Higher Self, symbolised by Krishna. Arjuna is in real-life crisis – required to take a crucial role in battle, he demurs and questions his role and destiny. In the midst of his crisis and despair, he turns to his inner light, personified by Krishna, to find a solution.

In the West, the tradition of dialogue with the Divine is at the very foundation of the Old Testament. The notion of dialoguing with a part of oneself that is attuned to the Divine is also found in the Jesuit practice of 'Discernment of Spirits' – where the student attempting to decide upon his religious vocation seeks to discern, to distinguish the action of the 'good spirit' within him from the selfishness that is a reflection of the 'devil'. One reads, similarly, of the 'indwelling of the Holy Spirit' as a psychological condition to be sought. The New Testament also speaks of receptiveness to 'Divine Providence' as a technique where, having exhausted the ordinary and rational ways of wrestling with a problem, one turns to a higher source for an answer.

As we have said, such practices as these can be seen as attempts to contact an *otherness* full of power and wisdom. Or, they can be thought of as attempts to reach those parts of our own psyche that are not available in our ordinary social lives. There are also more inclusive interpretations, according to which both the inner and the outer models are, in fact, complementary forms for the expression of the same formless reality. Using the psychosynthesis model, we can say that one makes contact with universal archetypes – which are in the higher collective unconscious – by means of their reflections or projections in one's own *individual* superconscious. And it is the organising and integrating energy of these archetypes that provides the mind with the needed solution.

Whatever the precise explanation, the answers that come may be seen as the result of letting go of our identification with the analytic mind, thus liberating creative aspects that are usually blocked. This does not mean rejecting the mind, only disidentifying from it. Certainly, the common practice among creative people of wrestling with a problem, reaching a point of frustration, letting go, and then simply waiting for a solution, is structurally similar. And in this creative process, many report that when the answer does come, they experience it as coming from 'outside' themselves, with, as one writer put it, 'source-less connotations of authority'.

Psychosynthesis

So the notion that there is a source of such wisdom and guidance – a Self, or Essence, Soul, Spirit, Atman, or Ruach – is certainly not to be cavalierly thrust aside. But, as the experience of a great number of people has shown, it is not necessary to believe in a Divine organising entity in man for the technique of Dialogue with the Higher Self to work. It is enough to accept the entirely reasonable proposition that there are aspects in each of us which are higher than many of which we are normally aware. In short, it is enough that we believe there are in us positive human potentials for more wisdom, love, strength, compassion and growth, than we have yet discovered. If we believe these are accessible and that they can be explored, that is enough.

The Technique Itself

Assume, with many ancient traditions, that you have within you a source of understanding and wisdom that knows who you are, what you have been, and what you can most meaningfully become in the future. This source is in tune with your unfolding purpose. It can help you direct your energies toward achieving increasing integration, toward harmonising and unifying your life.

Having made this assumption, close your eyes, take a few deep breaths, and imagine that you are seeing the face of a wise old man or woman (the results of employing the symbols of the Wise Old Man and Wise Old Woman are different and complementary. The reader may want to try both and find out which is more useful for different purposes and circumstances in his or her life) whose eyes express great love for you. (If you have difficulty visualising this, first imagine a candle flame, burning steadily and quietly, and then let the face appear at its centre (See *Synthesis*, 1974, No 1, Workbook 48 on how to visualise)).

Engage this wise old person in dialogue, in whatever way seems best: use the presence and guidance of the sage to help you better understand whatever questions, directions or choices you are dealing with at the moment. Spend as much time as you need in this dialogue, and when you are finished, write down what happened (see 'Keeping a Psychological Journal', *Synthesis*, 1975, Vol 1, No 2), amplifying and evaluating further whatever insights were gained.

◆ ◆ ◆

The technique has the advantage of wide variation. While this particular form is useful to many people, there are many others that can be used. The Wise Old Man and

Psychosynthesis

Wise Old Woman are symbols of archetypes in the Jungian sense. As we have said, they can allow us to contact parts of our psyche that ordinarily may not be so accessible – that belong to our higher unconscious or superconscious. Symbols are the language of the unconscious, and there are a number of these higher symbols that can sometimes work as well as the Wise Old Man. Some people have used a lotus, a rose, the sun, a diamond, a flame, a silver cloud, a star, a fountain, an angel, an eagle, a dove, a phoenix, the Christ, or Buddha, among others. These symbols can also be used dynamically, and in combination. For example, many have found it very effective to imagine the bud of a lotus, or rose, that gradually opens, and then a Wise Old Man appearing inside it. Different images often emerge spontaneously to meet different needs, though the one most commonly associated with the inner source of guidance is the wise and loving old man.

A number of people who have used the technique over a period of years report that they have spontaneously developed several different symbols of inner guidance. This is experienced as the Higher Self reaching us by assuming different forms at different times. One psychologist reported these diverting variations:

■ Usually he is a Wise Old Man who looks something like Lama Govinda, whose pictures I have seen. He is old, slender, bearded and dressed in ritual robes. He is Tibetan and ascetic, and has a very loving and blissful expression

■ Another one is of fuller face and looks more like a Hindu swami. He is less ascetic, and though he is also old, he is not as old as the Tibetan

■ Another person has a Moses-like appearance; he is more of the Charlton Heston type

■ A fourth one is a sun symbol; round like the sun, an overlay of a face on the sun. He has eyes, a nose and mouth, but that's all

■ Another person describes at least three varieties of her Wise Old Man: The first is my 'best self' – he is rather comic, and appears only with eyes, shoulders, and hands. He delivers a lot of 'one-liners', and they are usually about things going on in the immediate situation; things like, 'Forget it!' or 'Keep going!' or 'Hang in there!' This one usually accompanies his terse remarks with a hand gesture of a very emphatic sort. He is an old man with a great sense of amusement; Then, there is a young man. He is dressed like a monk and talks about larger issues than the first one. He doesn't communicate in many words, either: he indicates an experience to be had. For example, if I ask him, 'Where do I have to go next in my development?', he would say just a couple of sentences: 'You need to integrate your personality', or, 'Think deeply on the meaning of the word Love'; There is also a third kind. This is a group. They appear as a cluster of white-robed old men who talk among themselves and give me advice. They are very joyous and very supportive. They are less 'high' than the second one and more interested in me – less impersonal. They give me advice about groups of individuals or groups in general. I do a lot of work with groups of people, and they are sort of specialists in groups. They are more loving than the second symbol. He is more wise, and kind of abstract

After some practice, one may prefer not to use any visual symbols; and indeed they are not necessary.

An interesting variation of the technique is to write a letter to one's Higher Self and then to expect that the Higher Self will write back through you. For this, simply switch role and 'answer' the original letter as if you were the Wise Old Man. (This procedure clearly has nothing to do with reported cases of 'automatic writing', trance mediumship or any phenomena of that type. These are of a completely different nature. In such cases the person is unconscious or deliberately passive, while in the kind of dialogue suggested here, there is a normal, and often greater than normal, awareness and attention, and the mind can be *receptive* but is in no way *passive*.) This version is especially appealing to people who are used to a high degree of precise verbal exchange. As can be seen from the preceding examples, however, with other people the verbal interaction with the Higher Self can frequently be very brief, and others report that the communication from the Self is often primarily visual, e.g. hand gestures indicating 'Stop' or 'No' or 'Yes' and so forth. Still others, especially after a certain amount of practice, report a kind of direct knowing of what the Higher Self is saying and that the interchange is then beyond both the visual and the verbal mode.

Whether symbols are used or not, whether they are animate or not, whether the exchange is verbal or not, let me stress that for the technique to work, it must be tried. Of those who have used it fruitfully, many say that the technique, although extremely simple, seemed strange to them at first, but when they gave themselves to it, the procedure worked quite well. Others already believed that they had such positive potentialities within them, but were pessimistic about being capable of contacting them. Sometimes they expressed feelings of being unworthy of such contact. In all of these cases, however, all that was called for was, in Coleridge's phrase, 'a willing suspension of disbelief.'

Psychosynthesis

To put it another way, in attempting this or any other technique for self-realisation, one needs to trust that it can work. As the Jaina philosophers of India have emphasised, trust is a precondition for any real progress in a given philosophy, approach, or path. Not blind trust, of course. Not trust that it will work, but trust that it can. Later on, one checks the preliminary results of the technique to see if the trust has been rewarded or not. All spiritual and psychological schools – from the sages of India to the Catholic mystics; from the exponents of the psychoanalyst's couch to those of the Gestalt therapist's empty chair – stress the limitations of efforts made without such commitment.

Accordingly, if the idea of a dialogue with the Higher Self is new, or strange to you, it may be worthwhile to begin by simply thinking through the reasonableness of the idea that there are latent parts of yourself wiser than your daily self. This kind of thinking helps to quiet scepticism and the tendency we all have, in one degree or another, to repress the sublime within us. For most people, taking this attitude of 'provisional belief' is simply a matter of deciding to do so, and if they do so, they often discover that over a period of time the Higher Self provides better and better answers, surer guidance and more loving impulses. There are some people, perhaps because of temporary crises or simply earlier conditioning who have trouble giving even this provisional belief to a Higher Self within them. These may be people who are tormented by guilt and depression, a sense of worthlessness, and the like. Naturally, these are the people who most desperately need to cultivate an awareness of their higher inner aspects. Those in the helping professions – psychologists, counsellors, teachers and others – have found it very helpful to use this technique with people in such crises, doing it first together, and recommending that they continue practising it at home. (Note to professionals: a number of therapists report that consulting their own Higher Self to activate their intuition and gain insight about their clients has been quite successful. Naturally, such insights – like all therapeutic intuitions – must be scrutinised and evaluated before being put into practice.)

The technique very often yields useful results at the first try, although occasionally it may take longer.

One client got an answer for the first week after daily attempts to contact his Higher Self. He didn't dare hope such an inner Worthy would talk to him. But with the encouragement of his therapist, he persisted in the attempts. His written letters to the Higher Self during the first few days were simply emotional, despairing pleas; 'Help

Psychosynthesis

me, Higher Self; give me your advice! Appear to me, talk to me! I need you!' Gradually, attempting to write these 'letters' led from this very needed emotional release to a more reasoned approach; a detailing of the young man's real-life dilemmas, and finally his coherent examination, for the benefit of the Higher Self, of his troubles and their particular causes. At the end of the week, the young man discovered he could assume the position of his Higher Self and answer his letters.

An important first result of this work was that he began to achieve an inner position that was detached from the turmoil of his problems. (In general, the use of the technique of Dialogue with the Higher Self is of help in achieving disidentification from problems and in cultivating the attitude of observer. Disidentification and the attitude of observer are discussed extensively in Betsie Carter-Haar's article, 'Identity and Personal Freedom' in *Synthesis*, 1975, Vol 1, No 2 – reprinted in this book (see also the exercises, pp 94-114)). One of his future discoveries was the difference between the Higher Self and his 'superego'. It turned out that part of his resistance to making contact with his own inner source of wisdom was owing to the fear that all he would discover in his quest was not a Higher Self, but, rather, a Higher Superego – a 'super Top Dog', to use the language of Gestalt Therapy (see the conversation with George I Brown, 'The Farther Reaches of Gestalt Therapy', in *Synthesis*, 1974, Vol 1, No 1, pp 25-41). In the process of attempting his dialogues with his Higher Self, however, he soon realised that the Higher Self was of an altogether different nature.

The Higher Self, insofar as I know him, is not like the superego. The Higher Self does not issue orders, he is not compelling, he is not harsh. He makes suggestions, he indicates ways – he is more mental, in a pure sense of the word. The superego, on the other hand, has a lot of emotional voltage – often negative. He pushes and urges...

The Self appears serene, clothed in white...strong (though dimly seen) and radiant – like the Christ in Fra. Angelico's 'The Transfiguration'. He speaks to me...He has the quality of a teacher. Interested and concerned, but detached. If he demands anything, he demands to be embraced. He opens himself to that. Take him or leave him, is what he says. He shows me directions and possibilities, leaving me to follow them or not. He is there. He is to be chosen.

My superego, instead, is dark, more fleshy, and even stone-like. There is a scowl on his face, a hammer in his hand. He bangs and chips away. He threatens and coerces. He exhausts me and he compels me. One is the principle of freedom and Love, the other

the dark principle of Bondage...(The example illustrates a common tendency in many people to fear that their higher nature will be of a critical, authoritarian, puritanical and frequently life-denying character. This misconception is often a cause of the 'repression of the sublime'. Another example of a person discovering this error is reported in Betsie Carter-Haar's paper on 'Identity and Personal Freedom' in *Synthesis*, 1975, Vol 1, No 2 – reprinted in this book).

One may look upon the superego as a shadow, a degenerated image of the Higher Self. We absorb our superegos from outside ourselves, from society, our parents, and so on. Such a 'construct' may well have a role to play in our early development and may be temporarily necessary. But when it becomes rigid and restrictive it must eventually and gradually be replaced by a much more genuine and 'adoptive' inner source of wisdom, ethics, and good judgment. In cultivating the dialogue with the Higher Self, therefore, one should be careful to identify voices answering our questions that are not really coming from our authentic higher selves. Sometimes this may be the voice of a subpersonality that pretends to be the Wise Old Man, or the voice, introjected from childhood, of an angry or ambitious parent, and so forth. Discrimination, then – what the Hindus call Viveka in their spiritual tradition – must be used to identify critical and authoritarian figures who impersonate the wise and loving Higher Self.

Discrimination

When engaging in a dialogue with the Higher Self, we must test *any* message we receive in the 'fires' of the mind's critical discrimination. We must ask: is this advice really wise? Does it really make sense? This is a vital step, for it is clear that any such message can come from a variety of sources, not only from the Higher Self or from the lower unconscious, but also from many intermediate ones, where wisdom is combined with varying amounts of distortion, unmet needs and desires, unrelated thoughts and emotions.

(This discussion of discrimination provides a useful place to make a precise theoretical discrimination concerning the way we have been using the phrase 'Higher Self' in much of this paper. The Dialogue with the Higher Self is not *directly* with the Higher Self. Rather *it is with one or another element in our superconscious, which itself is activated by the Higher Self.*

Psychosynthesis

An analogy will help explain these distinctions and the reasons we choose to ignore them in the rest of our discussions. When we dialogue with another person, we are not usually conversing with his essence, his person-ness, so-to-speak. He doesn't present himself in his essence nor do we perceive him that way. Rather, he presents us with an intermediary – a subpersonality or a feeling, for example. And, in turn, that subpersonality or feeling expresses itself through still other intermediaries such as his voice, facial expressions, and so forth. So, in actuality, a large part of our ordinary dialogues or conversations in everyday life are carried on by us at two removes at least from the personal essence of the conversants.

Similarly, the image of the Wise Old Man is not the same as the energy which animates that image, and that energy in turn is not the same as its source – the actual Higher Self. But just as in ordinary conversations, it would be awkward, if not paralysing, to keep in steady awareness of our two-fold removal from the other person in his essence, so it is generally unhelpful, in entering into dialogue with the Higher Self, to keep in steady awareness that we are not in direct communication with the real article. On the other hand it is important to know, and to keep in the background of our minds, that the Wise Old Man and the 'Higher Self' with which we may dialogue are not the actual Higher Self. This recognition helps us to have an accurate sense of proportion. For example, at times people have the experience of 'becoming' the Wise Old Man. This can occur spontaneously on occasion, or it can be achieved intentionally, after practice with the technique of Dialogue. Such an experience can be an exalted one, charged with deep and beautiful feeling, and it can result in significant assistance to our growth. But as a result, many people tend to the erroneous belief that they have actually become identified with their Higher Self. It should be said, however, that the actual experience of direct contact, and eventual identification with Higher Self is one of profoundly greater moment than these other experiences, no matter how authentic, valuable and important. The experience of contact and identification with the Higher Self in its true essence has an altogether different quality and opens the door to new dimensions of awareness that are – in experience and by definition – ineffable.)

Of course, the very fact that we consciously and deliberately address ourselves to the Higher Self has the result of weeding out many of the lower 'voices'. And with continuing practice we become increasingly able to recognise the 'voice' of our true source of wisdom and to build a reliable channel of communication with it.

Psychosynthesis

But we can never be *completely* sure that we are in touch with the genuine article. This is especially so in our first experiments with the technique, or during periods of intense conflict and crisis when many of our inner voices are clamouring at the same time. So we need to treat the answers we receive just as we would the advice of a good friend. We consider it, make sure we understand it, and try to decide whether it is useful or not. If the answer is really from the Higher Self, our tasks is likely to be easy, because it will often have some 'peculiarly good' quality. This quality may be the very essence of common sense, it may be 'just the solution I would have chosen if only I had thought of it'; it may be a simplicity that is profoundly beautiful; it may be the answer accompanied by a vision of the good that will come out of it, which becomes a source of joy. In these cases, the course of action is likely to be clear.

At other times, it will be obvious that the source is not the Higher Self. This will undoubtedly be the case if the message clashes against our best and highest values; if following it would lead to needlessly hurting ourselves or others; if its main effect is to inflate (or deflate) our ego; if it is mostly self-serving; if it has an autocratic, dictatorial character. One student lamented that in the early days of her using this technique, what she believed to be her Wise Old Man had the quality of 'a New Age Top Dog', urging her relentlessly and heedlessly toward more and more transpersonal attainments before she had built a sufficiently steady base in the personality life of every day. She recalled that she had not been discriminating enough to reject such pushy and harsh messages, messages without the mark of a loving acceptance coupled with a desire to be of help.

Many times the message comes either from the Higher Self, or from a source at the opposite extreme, and then it is easy to discriminate. But some situations are less clear, and may need to be examined carefully, especially if they deal with important issues. Some messages are 'mixed', and we need to separate what is useful from what is irrelevant, or even harmful. In such cases, the earliest and most abstract part of the message is often the valid one. The elaborations and details that may follow are more likely to contain distortions, or to be voices of subpersonalities masquerading as the Higher Self. But sometimes, it is not possible to tell whether an answer is or is not valid by thinking it through. This can be because its content is 'supra-rational', beyond what the mind can reach. Or it can be because the results of the suggested action are unforeseeable, and will be apparent only after the action is accomplished. In these cases, we must decide whether we are willing to take the chance of trying it out, taking into account any intuition or hunch we may have, our past experience in similar circumstances, the possible consequences of a mistaken action, and whatever other factor may be relevant, including – and especially – our common sense.

If we do decide to go ahead in such a situation, it is important that we do so with an open-minded, scientific attitude. We are, in fact, running an experiment: we are trying something to find out whether it will work or not. Maintaining such a scientific attitude has a value over and above the results or outcomes of our actions. This attitude allows us to learn from our choices, to better know the sources of our inner messages, to discriminate the voice of the Higher Self from other voices. In time, through repeated trials of this process, we come to have a clearer and clearer channel for the messages of our Higher Self. Such a channel can be of precious value in our future choices of action.

Interpretation

Once we have satisfied ourselves that the message does come from the Higher Self – and sometimes in the course of determining whether it does or not – we often need to 'interpret' the message. For the Higher Self does not always give simple, concrete answers to simple, concrete questions. Frequently an abstract, symbolic message needs to be examined to find out how it applies specifically and concretely to the issues of the moment. Or the opposite may be true: an apparently plain and simple message can hide an important insight that has broad relevance to our life as a whole. An example may make this clear. A woman was lying on the back porch and attempting to talk to her Higher Self about her life purpose. She had been thinking for a long time about changing her career, perhaps going back to school in one or another subject; but she was uncertain about how to begin, which path to follow, or even whether to make such a change. Her Higher Self answered her question about purpose with a single word, 'Harmony'. The woman realised this message needed to be interpreted and began thinking about harmony. She entertained various images of harmony, including herself as a Pied Piper, sprinkling musical harmonies into the world. Another image was the turning fork, which she interpreted as tuning the personality to the soul so it could be receptive to its energy. Eventually, she came up with the abstract thought that 'the personality is an instrument through which the soul plays its music'. By interpreting this, in turn, she saw that the choice of one or another career pattern was not as relevant as the cultivation of an inner attitude of harmony within herself that would let her be as fully human a persona as she could be. As she began to cultivate this inner attitude, problems with work, family, and friends gradually began to disappear. But for all these positive results to happen, it was first necessary for her to have sufficient determination to use her mind to think things through, and then to gradually find ways to implement the wisdom of her Higher Self.

We see from this example that a fundamental goal of interpretation is to recognise at which level of generality the answer pertains, and at which level it is to be applied. Clearly, interpreting a message as belonging to the wrong level can have harmful, even dangerous effects. Many cases of fanaticism, ego inflation, or delusions of grandeur have such a mistaken interpretation at their roots. Such a mistake is possible even for very advanced people.

A famous example of wrong level interpretation is that of St. Francis hearing God say to him, 'Go and rebuild my church.' At first, St. Francis thought this meant he should rebuild the little ruined church of San Damiano, outside the walls of Assisi. It was only later that he realised its true import – to rebuild the venal and corrupt Catholic Church of his day, by means of examples of love, frugality and charity. It is interesting to consider here what would have happened to Saint Francis if the message had indeed meant to rebuild the church in San Damiano, and he had tackled the entire Catholic Church!

One can also experience different levels of the Higher Self's wisdom in a single dialogue. A very busy man described the following interchange:

'I was feeling very speedy, off centre and unstable. So I talked with the Wise Old Man about it and at first he said things like: "You need to rest, to trust the process; everything will take care of itself. If you overwork yourself now you won't be able to do the things you're worrying about". But I simply kept waiting for more; opening myself in a kind of silent expectation.

After a few minutes, I experienced a quantum jump in understanding. I saw that my worries had a purpose. The Wise Old Man enabled me to see that the worries of today were a necessary part of the 'process' he had talked about. "This is where you fit now – you're irritable and strained, and that's because you're going through a *process of learning to work with people* and you don't know how to do it yet. But that process is very important in the development of yourself as a person who can give something good to the world. It is, as you well know, the necessary step beyond your sweet but ineffective idealism. It is the step to make your idealism practical and useful in the

Psychosynthesis

world. That's why you can be patient with yourself and even take the day off. You're doing fine.'"

The Role of the Mind

As we have seen, the use of the technique of Dialogue with the Higher Self does not in any way call for an occlusion of the mind, far from it. The intellect can be and ought to be involved not only in the phases of discrimination and interpretation, but from the very beginning, and at every stage of the process. It is important to use the Dialogue with the Higher Self in conjunction with hard critical thinking, and not as a substitute for it.

But overthinking is not necessary. It is not necessary to feel that before we deserve the privilege of addressing the Higher Self, we must carry out extensive brain-racking. As usual common sense is needed to keep the golden mean between excessive and insufficient mental work. (If in doubt, this is a good issue about which to ask the Higher Self for feedback.) For important situations it is generally advisable to think through the ins and outs of a problem as much as we can before presenting it to the Higher Self. Writing a carefully thought-out description of the circumstances, or silently speaking the essence of the problem to the Higher Self is the best preparation in these cases. Not only does this exercise the mind, it also mobilises the superconscious, or higher unconscious, to produce a more creative solution, and at the same time puts the mind in an expectant attitude, making it most receptive to the answer when it arrives. In the language of creativity, having dealt with the problem extensively on the 'horizontal' level (at which it presently exists), one can then more effectively turn 'upward' for illumination.

To take a concrete example, one man is worrying about whether to take Job A or Job B. 'A' is more financially remunerative and secure but 'B' is more creative. He begins to think about the consequences of each choice; more opportunity to grow and express himself in the creative job, but more money to save toward the education of his children in the other. Having listed all the arguments on both sides, he refers the answer to the Wise Old Man, who says, 'Your main service to the education of your children will be through the quality of your being.' The problem has been implicitly solved by an answer at a higher level. Duty to children and his personal growth are not contraries. Thus, his initial thinking assembles the basic information with which the Higher

Psychosynthesis

Self can work. Frequently this kind of deliberate thinking things through is enough for the Higher Self to offer the solution to the problem without actually being invoked.

In general, then, we may say that the most effective use of this technique occurs when the mind is well developed, or when there is the will to use it and develop it. Making contact with one's own inner wisdom through the various symbols of the Higher Self is itself a strong motivator for developing the mind. With the assurance that we have an inner core which is wise, good and loving, we have a basis upon which to build a coherent program of self development. We experience our intrinsic worthwhile-ness, and we hear its gradual and gentle call. We can then increasingly align our will, our intellect, and our emotional nature to fulfil the best that is in us.

As this process continues, people report that they can turn to their Higher Self to answer more and more profound questions. They come to see that the ultimate usefulness of this technique (though not necessarily its best usefulness at first) is to pierce beyond the outer form of specific life problems (Job A or Job B), to the meaning, the principles, and the qualities behind them. This transition upwards in the use of the technique is generally a gradual thing. It is a natural transition, which can be encouraged but need not be forced. The process may start by asking the Higher Self about tiny dilemmas – 'How can I make myself feel better now?' – but it will lead to seeking the underlying causes of the dilemmas. One use of the Higher Self technique that need not be reserved for later, however, is to ask it for understanding and awareness about various abstract qualities – as in the Harmony example. Other qualities to explore are Love, Joy, Wisdom, Compassion, Courage, and Serenity; in fact, any of those qualities that the wisdom of mankind has identified as being close to the centre of our highest humanness. Because it is in these qualities that the real solutions to our life problems will ultimately be found.

This technique has helped many people to recognise that the dimensions beyond their ordinary selves are real and living aspects of existence. And as they come gradually to know their Higher Self more and more, they find that their lovingness and wisdom, compassion and serenity are increasingly available. Some people who have used the technique for a long time report eventually being able to dispense with symbols for the Higher Self, such as the Wise Old Man, and with instruments of communication like writing, or formal dialogue. They speak of knowing the 'note', 'quality' or 'flavour' of messages from the Higher Self very well, and of simply wanting to be in touch with their Higher Self, and then 'being there'. For example, a number of therapists who have used this technique for some years report that when they do therapy, the voice that used to belong to the Wise Old Man talks to them spontaneously, and simply operates in them – at times, they are even able to let it become their voice, to have it merge with their personality and inform it.

Such levels of realisation may not be quick in coming, but they are possible. One important aid in that direction is writing – the practice of writing down our dialogues with the Higher Self. This can include, as I have already noted, writing the preparatory mental considerations – the thinking through of the problem – and then recording the actual answers, the work of discrimination and interpretation, and any other mental elaboration of what the Higher Self has said. In this process of writing things down, one is attempting to establish a palpable connection between the wisdom of the higher unconscious and the conscious mind. Another useful way to facilitate the process is to imagine that one is in fact building a 'channel' or 'path' through which superconscious energies can flow – and to actually visualise such a path with one's imagination.

At times, when we pose a question, or express a need to the Higher Self, the answer comes in the form of energy of a particular quality. Thus people report a sense of joy, of illumination, flashes of light, an infusion of courage, and many other subtle and very positive experiences. But these tend to be short-lived and ephemeral, unless we 'ground' them, expressing them in our actions and making them part of our everyday life. Writing and recording the insights and their later mental elaboration helps to do this, and seems to open the way for progressively higher illuminations. It is as if the work of introducing superconscious material into the activity of our lives makes room for more to emerge.

Such high experiences as feeling the Higher Self speaking through us, or seeking to build a bridge between the superconscious and the daily personality, or expressing progressively higher and higher intuitions, are ones that we have been used to imagine as being reserved for a specially gifted few. And yet it would appear, in practice, that the simple technique of affirmative inner dialogue with our best self helps open the doors of the transpersonal to many who previously had thought them locked. Many who begin using the technique of Dialogue with the Higher Self become more and more aware of the value of connecting their personalities with their higher natures. For pragmatically educated contemporary persons, it provides a fully pragmatic approach to domains that used to be reserved primarily for formalised religion. This

can lead to more systematic explorations, through meditation and other techniques, for opening broader channels to the higher aspects of individuality. Eventually, this in turn may lead to an experience beyond dialogue, an experience which has been referred to as the ground of all wisdom, purpose, and love. People then will talk about the Self, the soul, the divine spark, the Atman, as an inner entity – a reality and not a metaphor, an experience of real livingness, beyond duality, the 'place' where the individual and the universal are reconciled. And they will speak of such experiences as giving them a kind of ultimate fearlessness, a direct knowledge of their true nature, of the ontological reality of their very souls, and of their immortality.

The double beauty of this simple technique is that while there are many who look back on it as having started them toward such exalted heights, it is just as useful in helping to solve the simple problems of everyday living.

Stuart Miller (reprinted from Synthesis, 1975, Vol 1, No 2)

Psychosynthesis

Chapter 7 Synthesis and Evolution

The process of synthesis is in essence the evolutionary process which involves discrete individualities organising themselves into greater and greater wholes. Teilhard de Chardin describes this process in far greater detail including chemistry and mineral composition – he calls it the process of complexification; the organisation of higher levels without the negation of previous levels. Buckminster Fuller describes it as 'negative entropy' or 'syntropy'.

When we look at our bodies, they are well synthesised, working as coordinated wholes.; our arms and legs don't go in different directions. Looking at the psyche it is not so well organised at this point of its evolution. We find discrete parts which rather than choosing to act as part of a unity, do not recognise that there could be a larger whole. We have a level of organisation of the parts within us – some of which are fighting it out between each other. So there is conflict *horizontally*. Those parts fear losing their individuality if they come together. What is unrecognised is the higher potential, the higher synthesis.

Psychosynthesis

The process of psychosynthesis is focused on working on conflicts in such a way that more inclusive patterns come into manifestation. We do not work on conflicts for the sake of it.

If you are only aware of the parts the potential still exists in the same way as the answer to a maths problem exists whilst you are working on the problem. So the larger whole, the future exists, now even though it is not in manifestation. Freud proved the past exists and influences us now. In psychosynthesis, we say that both the past and the future are affecting us simultaneously.

So, in the 'here-and-now', we ask the question 'to what purpose am I working on this conflict?' The psychoanalytic 'why' goes backwards – 'Why? Because...Why? Because...' In that way the past, one's history, becomes causal to one's life now. The psychosynthesis 'why' brings the potential into expression. Why for what reason. This gives a sense of direction and at the same time, allows one to see the obstacles to the future manifesting.

Psychosynthesis

Top Down or Bottom Up

We can look at this process as parts uniting and becoming something greater, or as the wholes descending and becoming manifest. In the latter, the whole already exists and manifests in the parts.

The Self represents the highest pattern of unity in the psyche. Its potential is a reality which exists now and can be connected with. As we have seen, it manifests via an energy field which we call the 'superconscious'. Thus the Self expresses itself through qualities – transpersonal qualities – which become the higher organising principles. These principles draw the various disparate elements of the personality in their direction thus effecting a drawing together of these elements towards synthesis.

We have elaborated the process of self-realisation and self-expression in previous chapters, whereby the parts function more and more together and in an integrated fashion to become a whole, that is more than just the sum of the parts. At a macro psychosocial level there is the process of realising the Universal Self and its expression through the individual selves acting interdependently to become a whole – the Universal Self – which is more than the sum of these selves. The selves of humanity, acting together in this way, express more of the universal.

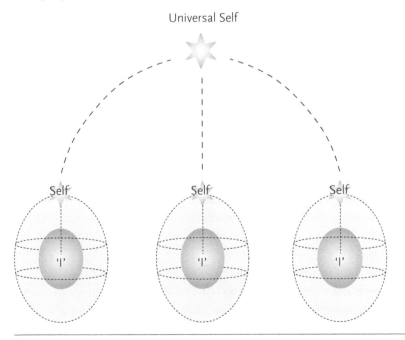

Psychosynthesis

This many-levelled synthesis also predicates a context for evolution, whereby the individual self acting the best it can as the 'I', asks, 'How on earth can I make a difference, what can I do?' As we see from the simple model below – the more that I am realising and expressing myself to the best I can, the more I am participating as an integral part of the whole and expressing the whole in what I do by being myself. So within a synthetic and a holographic context the whole – universal and self – is being expressed now by how I am and what I do in the now.

Interdependence

As we turn from inner reflection towards the outer world, we must inevitably begin to address questions of purpose and meaning beyond the context of individual development. We come to see, through the models of Body, Feelings, Mind and Subpersonalities, how the parts carry and are in service of the whole individual. In the same way we come to reflect upon the relationship of individuals to one another, and beyond that we consider how groups and nations may relate, and ultimately how humanity relates to the universe.

By reflecting upon the question, 'For what?' we begin to look beyond personal wishes and desires and may in this way begin to transcend the sense of personal limitations and personal differences; to focus not on our struggles and on how we compete with one another, but on our capacities and on what we might be able to do together.

As we connect with transpersonal qualities which may have been dormant within the personality, and as we awaken to the potential of the Self, it is important, ultimately, that we find some way of expressing these transpersonal qualities and this energy towards some purpose beyond self-awareness and beyond self-actualisation. The consequences of ignoring or repressing this dimension are increasingly evident in the world around us: in individuals who are in despair at the lack of meaning in their lives; in societies where information and technological skill grows ever more rapidly while any sense of confidence about purpose and direction diminishes; in peoples and whole cultures who are in conflict with one another and out of relationship with their larger environment.

Important as it is to avoid the dualistic and ultimately destructive and self-destructive position of narcissism and hubris, of acting as if 'I' and 'other' are not interdependent, of acting as if 'I' can be in control of others or my environment, determining outcomes without reference to any sense of higher values and purpose; nevertheless it is equally important not to make the converse mistake of acting as if what I do makes no difference to the other, or that my limitations are such that it is not 'worth' my doing what I can. Not being powerful enough to accomplish everything can easily become an excuse for doing nothing, for withdrawing one's energy from the world altogether. This position is, in the end, no less self-centred than believing that I can control everything.

In fact, everything I do makes a difference at some level and scientific research indicates that humans as individuals use only a fraction of the resources available to them. If we are willing to make full use of our inner resources, and then to consider how these resources might be used in co-operation with others, unexpected things may be achieved.

In *What We May Be* (Thorsons, 1995) Piero Ferrucci invites the reader into a meditation on 'Humankind's Potential'. He asks the reader first to consider the suffering of humanity, the pain and darkness, then to direct their attention to the immense latent resources of humanity: the yearning for peace, the drive towards the unknown, the sense of wonder, and the artistic creativity, and to imagine how these potentialities, if released, could generate countless beneficial effects. This method of looking, both 'downwards' at the suffering which is experienced at the level of the personality, and 'upwards' at the potential which may be released, is crucial in the psychosynthesis approach to understanding and working with human development.

Further Reading

Assagioli, Roberto, *The Act of Will*, David Platt, 1999 (Chapter 10)

Eastcott, Michal, *The Silent Path*, Rider, 1979 (pp 127-141)

Ferrucci, Piero, *What We May Be*, Thorsons, 1995 (Chapter 18)

Russell, Peter, *The Awakening Earth*, Arkana, 1988

Psychosynthesis

SYNTHESIS

The Synthesis of Nations

The planetisation of our consciousness – expressing our oneness with humanity and accepting the whole planet as our home – involves a process of change to be undergone both by ourselves as individuals and by our largest functioning groups, the nation-states. *The stages of this process are essentially the same for individuals and for nations.* In both cases, this change is manifested by the gradual emergence of the same qualities: community-mindedness, inclusiveness, and shared responsibility.

As individuals, we must struggle to end the 'divided house' of conflicting goals, wishes and desires within our personal lives. We must struggle to harmonise and integrate our many subpersonalities – the local dominions within our selves – whose conflicts dissipate our energy, by preventing its effective focusing and expression.

The same is true with nations. For example, divided energies in the national life may be represented by the many internal groups which have different and conflicting values, concepts or goals. Thus, the energy of an ethnic or minority group which has urgent unmet needs will be largely lost to the nation until that group is accommodated and its reasonable needs satisfied.

Or, powerful special interest groups can be laws unto themselves in the corporate personality of national life. Thus, for instance, economic interests with narrow and self-oriented goals often wield sufficient power to convince the leadership of a nation that their wishes and well-being represent the interests of the nation as a whole. They 'impose' their value system on the society and interfere with the direction and utilisation of energy, distorting the note sounded by that nation. In this instance – and, too often, in general – the leadership of a nation is narrowly *identified* with a particular group or tendency. It is the same as with an individual whose personal centre, or sense of self, is habitually identified with only one, or at the most a few, of the many elements or tendencies within the personality.

Psychosynthesis

In both cases – individual and national – *disidentification* is needed, and leads to the emergence of the true identity: one that is capable of accepting and integrating all separate elements (see 'Identity and Personal Freedom', *Synthesis*, 1975, Vol 1, No 2, p56 – reprinted in this book). Only when such an integral self-identity is established and a self-actualisation process entered into – whether consciously or not – can the individual or the nation begin to climb the Jacob's ladder of more appropriate energies – those with higher intensity and value content – and to express them in the individual life or in the world community.

The qualities or energies which nations present to the world and to each other give clues to the 'place they are' collectively speaking – to when the dominant emphasis is on the personality wishes and desires of the nation, and when it is beginning to show evidences of response to some deeper pull within the national being; when the nation is fundamentally materialistic and self-centred, and when it is identified with the good of the whole.

It may be very difficult, looking from within a particular nation, to distinguish among the tendencies in other nations, for precisely the same reasons that a self-centred personality cannot secure an accurate impression of those around him, but rather projects his own attitudes on others. From a trans-national vantage point such as that afforded by the United Nations, where the behaviour of each member state is easily seen, it is not as difficult.

Many of the large and industrialised states are primarily interested in the maintenance of privilege. Many of the smaller and newer nations are naturally interested in a world system which would supply them more equity and justice than the present one does. Some newer countries tend to exhibit a spontaneous idealism and concern about the world community as a whole. And a few are unique in their commitment to general world well-being, often at considerable sacrifice to themselves. Their enlightened international policies are based on the will of populations which support world-order values and goals. These countries particularly, and others, show evidence in specific and important respects of the birth of a planetary sense of responsibility – which a very wise person has said is 'the first indication of divinity'. A comparison of the voting behaviour of the member nations at the UN will easily demonstrate the values by which nations live and through which they express themselves in the world community – which often, unfortunately, is at variance with their public pronouncements.

Psychosynthesis

To what extent are nations prepared to relate to the world through values of caring and sharing? To what extent are they prepared to express communion rather than charity? Planetary identification rather than separative selfhood? By these measures one can determine when nations are still using old energies marking the nation-state as tribal God, and when the newer energies are related to the human community as a whole.

The condition of nations presently is often not very encouraging; and if we were to measure progress toward planetary consciousness only on the basis of national behaviour, we might often be down-hearted. Not so long ago I had a good visit with one of the top people in the Secretary General's office, an extraordinarily ebullient person, especially for someone who's been with the UN for about twenty-five years. He said, 'You know, Don, I've never been so optimistic.' 'Optimistic?' I said. The Middle East was about to flare up again, the Vietnam war was in full swing at the time, things had been going from bad to worse at a number of different places. He said, 'Ah, but you don't understand – these are the frictions brought about by the shrinkage of the globe which we're experiencing. They are inevitable surface confrontations. These are not the long-term, deep-lying trends. The deeper, persistent trends have to do with all this business of knitting the world together, of growing trans-national activity which is beyond the control of any special group.'

Fortunately there are many elements to the picture and many processes in motion, which individual nations do not and cannot control. Some of these factors are historical and technological; others are psychological and even transcendent. Together, they are fostering the emergence of a new consciousness. We are, as a result, facing a situation absolutely unprecedented in human history:

"It is an amazing thing that in less than a million years the human species has succeeded in covering the earth, and not only spatially. On this surface that is now completely encircled, mankind has completed the construction of a close network of planetary links, so successfully that a special envelope now stretches over the old biosphere. Every day this new integument grows in strength. It may be clearly recognised and distinguished in every quarter. It is provided with its own system of internal connections and communications, and for this I have for a long time proposed the name 'noosphere'. (P Teilhard de Chardin, *Activation of Energy*, Harcourt, Brace, Joranovich, 1970, p 285).

Psychosynthesis

The noosphere in fact physically requires for its maintenance and functioning, the existence in the universe of a true pole of psychic convergence: a centre different from all the other centres, which is a super-centre by assimilation: a personality distinct from all the other personalities it perfects by uniting with them. The world would not function if there did not exist somewhere ahead in time, in space, a cosmic 'Point Omega' of total synthesis (P Teilhard de Chardin, *Human Energy*, Harcourt, Brace, Joranovich, 1969, p 145).

No one has more adequately or more eloquently sketched the existing situation than did Pierre Teilhard de Chardin, in the above words, written prophetically many years ago. Mankind is clearly moving, willy-nilly, towards that one united body, through the construction of a seamless web of planetary interconnections which is beyond the domination of individual nations. Man, the species, is in the amazing process of becoming self-knowing and self-aware. He is waking up as a global entity – a Rip Van Winkle who has been asleep for millions of years. For the first time in all human history we as individuals can consciously participate in human-Humanity relationships. We have the possibility to describe, delineate and experience the participation of the individual within the global entity. This is, without doubt, the most staggering event of human existence. Man, the magical weaver, is spinning out of himself the planetary nervous system – the neural network. He is travelling anywhere at a planetary constant – the speed of sound. He is communicating anywhere at a universal constant – the speed of light. He is no farther from any member of his race than the electrical distance of his finger from his brain. The same time span for communication is all that is required. What is immanent as a result is the organisation and birth of a new entity – World Man.

The sudden discovery and understanding of planetary ecology is intrinsic to this development. Ecology is nothing less than the science of the wholeness and relatedness of all planetary life. We find ourselves the custodians of a living spaceship, and understand for the first time the real meaning of the world being round. Man the individual set off across the globe, and now he has met mankind coming back. His new meaning, his deeper meaning, lies in the whole of which he is inescapably a part. The activation of the noosphere – the neural envelope of the Earth – and the discovery of ecology mean that mankind as a whole is on the 'path of return': he is consciously engaged in simplification and in reintegration into that of which he was at one time an unconscious part, and then later an estranged and prodigal son – reintegration into planetary life.

Psychosynthesis

The evidence of this inter-relationship and the obsolescence of separateness are everywhere to be found. Most dramatic have been the object lessons resident in environmental degradation and depredation: the bathtub ring around the Mediterranean, the acid snows of Sweden caused by sulphuric clouds from the Ruhr; radioactive fallout raining across the globe; exhaustion of fishery stocks; extinction of animal species; the energy crisis; the depletion of mineral resources. The newly discovered limits to food and natural resources and a host of other factors all indicate the sensitivity with which mankind will have to regulate his planetary interference and stewardship in the future. While World Man slept, spaceship Earth was on auto-pilot. In a half-waking state, he pressed some technologically augmented controls which have thrown the ship seriously off balance. Now in a full waking state, Mankind must accept the responsibility for his actions and consciously control and guide the planetary craft.

A positive response to the new inter-relatedness and its consequences has begun. A UN World Population Conference took place this year to sensitise the world to the limits of population expansion. Later in the year a World Food Conference was held in Rome to begin the long process of facing up to the question of dwindling stocks, diminishing arable lands and spreading famine. A Law of Sea Conference has been convened to establish laws and a mechanism for the governance of seventy percent of the earth's surface and to provide for equitable use of its resources beyond the limits of national jurisdiction as the 'common heritage of mankind'. A major world conference on human settlements to treat the increasingly inhuman problems of urbanisation – as serious for the developing countries as for the developed – is planned. A special session of the United Nations General Assembly – only the sixth such session to be held, was devoted to initial conceptualisation of a new and more adequate world economic system. The rapid growth of multi-national or trans-national business corporations which are beyond the control of nations has caused the United Nations to develop a programme for monitoring their activities and for elaborating a body of law governing such activities. This is not to say that the best deliberations of any of these efforts will be immediately and enthusiastically implemented by governments. Those which feel they have more to gain from the status quo in the short run (among which are many of the present heavily industrialised nations) will obstruct and delay such implementation. But in the end they will have no other choice.

The integration of World Man as a functioning being presupposes and implies a super centre (Teilhard de Chardin) and a new energy which embodies centripetal, relational and purposive characteristics as well as inclusive love. Where do we look for these?

Psychosynthesis

As regards a world super centre integrating the localised centres of human action and organisation, the United Nations is its representation in human affairs. The United Nations is an imperfect and partial manifestation of that transcendent super centre, largely because the member nations are not yet ready, prepared or willing to see the UN become its fuller manifestation.

Nevertheless, the UN itself has become a vast drafting board for sketches and plans of a future world order. These plans are under preparation less because of any far-sighted initiatives of member nations than because there are a large number of conscientious, world-minded people working in and contributing to the secretariat who share a common vision of a more effective and just world order. The United Nations is in fact elaborating a series of 'departments of planetary management'. They are embryonic, they are half-starved, but they exist; and at any time that nations can summon the global will to implement them, they can be brought into full function and full size. With some of them we have long been familiar, such as the World Health Organisation, the Food and Agriculture Organisation, and the UN Children's Fund. Others, such as the UN Environmental Programme and the UN Fund for Population Activities, are very new. The Regime for the Sea Bed is the most important new department currently projected. The sheer inability of nations to deal effectively any longer with any of their major problems on a unilateral basis, whether it be energy and resources, the world monetary system and inflation, peace and disarmament, or population and food, is forcing a turn toward development of international organisation and to processes related to and centred in the United Nations. The imperatives of the human condition and world conditions are forcing mankind along the path his idealism and vision have shown him long ago.

Is there also a special impingement of higher energy upon the United Nations as a vortex of human unification, representing goal and purpose for human and planetary life? Can it be recognised, can it be tapped, can it be utilised? The answer is yes, beyond all doubt.

It is appropriate and useful here to take a concept from General Systems Theory and to note that when discrete individual organisms are approaching a time of organisation into a super organism, a new system of which they will henceforth be constituent members (as nations are now preparing for participation in a planetary structure), they create a unitary field upon which newer and more cohesive, inclusive, goal-oriented energies can impinge. Such energies must, by their very nature, be attuned to a higher goal, one that is new and as yet incomprehensible and unknown to any of the separate elements. The UN is the precise location where enough 'inter-nation' substance is lodged for it to provide a focus for the down flow and expression of such energies.

The preparation of such a 'field' or focus is deceptively simple. Quite apart from the surface phenomena of the United Nations, the crises, conflicts and confrontations that get headline treatment, there is something else occurring which might hardly occasion comment, but which has a magnificent subjective component. It is the simple fact that the elements of humanity physically meet at the UN. For the first time in human history elements of all humanity can be found continuously in the same spot. The representatives bring the multihued waters of their national, ethnic and cultural lives and pour them into a common crystal bowl. Thus, the UN is a place where we can experience the first intimations of what humanity itself as an entity and a species really is. Humanity as differentiated from this person, that person, group, tribe or nation is a quantum jump different from anything heretofore experienced. It is not uncommon for visitors or short-term delegates to experience a sudden, overwhelming realisation of *Mankind* – very similar to that which has struck moon-travelling astronauts.

In the United Nations secretariat staff we find mainly unconscious representatives of the energies of human unification. They are animated by it, act on it, but are not given to lives of contemplation or speculation. Their work, to which a large number are utterly dedicated, can be equated to continuous meditation on human unification, not in the abstract, but in action. Among them are the grand Karma Yogis [Karma Yoga is the path to enlightenment and self-realisation through selfless and dedicated action.] of the age, who hear nothing, see nothing, feel nothing, apart from what they are doing to manifest the vision of planetary justice, freedom, order and peace.

Occasionally, there are conscious representatives of that process and of those energies. One most notable, who anchored the six-ton lodestone of pure crystalline iron ore in the U.N. meditation room, was Dag Hammarskjold. Do you think he was not conscious of his inner reality and its relation to his world-serving role? Hammarskjold wrote:

"You are not the oil; you are not the air; merely the point of combustion, the flashpoint where the light is born. You are merely the lens in the beam. You can only receive, give

Psychosynthesis

and possess the light as a lens does. Sanctity either to be in the light or to be self-effaced in the light, so that it may be born. Self-effaced, so that it may be focused, or spread wider.

The uncarved block. Remain at the centre, which is yours and that of all humanity. For those goals which it gives to your life, do the utmost which at each moment is possible for you, without thinking of the consequences." (D Hammarskjold, *Markings*, Knopf, 1964, pp 155, 159).

This Dag Hammarskjold, second Secretary-General of the United Nations, wrote in his spiritual diary, shortly before he was killed on a mission trying to bring peace to the Congo.

Another conscious server of the greatest stature, and nearly unknown in the western world for the magnificence of his inner dimensions was the late U Thant, the third UN Secretary-General U Thant, who skilfully and quietly guided the UN through the most difficult decade of its existence, was a devout, practising Buddhist, who deeply searched himself in meditative practices native to him every morning before he went to the Secretary General's office on the 38th floor of the UN.

The energy of synthesis focusing in the United Nations, seeking to make its harmonising, relating, integrating, goal-oriented impact, now has another champion. He is Sri Chinmoy, a dear friend, a colleague and teacher, who in addition to his offerings to young people seeking the golden door of freedom, has accepted a responsibility in relation to the United Nations. As director of the UN Meditation Group, he is undertaking to construct a consciously cooperating meditative network throughout the UN of persons training themselves to be better representatives of the soul of the UN and better receivers to manifest and dispense the energies of human unification. Sri Chinmoy conducts meditations in the United Nations, attended by delegates, staff, and representatives of non-governmental organisations, and once a month gives a lecture in the Dag Hammarskjold auditorium on some aspect of the significance and subjective life of the UN. [Although the meetings of the UN Meditation Group are open only to those closely associated with the UN, Sri Chinmoy conducts other meditation meetings which are open to the public. For information, write: Sri Chinmoy, 85-45, 49th Street, Jamaica Hills, New York 11435.]

Psychosynthesis

A quote or two from lectures by Sri Chinmoy on the United Nations will provide something of the flavour of his presence there: "A spiritual goal for the United Nations is practical. Without the least possible hesitation I venture to say that it's highly practical. It is not only practical, but also practicable: something more, it is inevitable. We have to know what the spiritual goal for the United Nations is. Its goal is to become ultimately the saviour of the world's imperfection, the liberator of the world's destruction and the fulfiller of the world's aspirations. My heart tells me that the United Nation has a divine idea. My soul tells me that this ideal is going to be transformed into reality. Soulful concern is the essence of the United Nations ideal. Truthful patience is the substance of the United Nations ideal. Supernal fulfilment will be the essence of the United Nations reality. Today's United Nations offers hopeful and soulful advice to mankind. Today's United Nations feels fruitful and [offers] fulfilling peace to mankind. Today's United Nations feels truth and light in its loving heart. Tomorrow's United Nations will manifest truth and light in its all-embracing soul." (*The Garland of Nation-Souls*, Lighthouse Press, 1972, p 27).

"This meditation is not only for the United Nations but for the world at large. This meditation is for the God-lover and the man-lover. If we really love God, and if we really love mankind and consciously believe that we are responsible for mankind, then we feel that our aspiration and dedication to the soul of the United Nations and our Inner Pilot is of paramount importance. Please feel that it is your own aspiration that will expedite the vision for the United Nations. And when the vision is transformed into reality, the Inner Pilot will know our contribution whether or not the world ever recognises it..." ('Invitation to Meditation', *Meditation at the United Nations Bulletin*, May 27, 1974).

The little people and the big people are important in implementing the United Nations' vision. Every year the UN receives hundreds of thousands of applications from highly qualified people that it cannot possibly employ who are responding to the magnetic pull of the new vision of global mankind. Two incidents related to UN peacekeeping also show the instinctive (or if you like, institutional) response to the meaning of the United Nations. The first occurred at the transfer of British troops on Cyprus to UN command. There was some concern among the officers as to how this would be received by the Tommies. After review the new commander asked, 'Any questions?' He became apprehensive when one soldier said, 'Yes, sir.' But the question was, 'When do we get the blue UN berets?' The same unit petitioned for, and received

Psychosynthesis

permission to wear them back to the United Kingdom for one final review before they were retransferred.

Recently, when a terrible earthquake struck Peru and disaster units were needed, Sweden asked UN permission to send a contingent it had trained for UN peacekeeping missions, which wished to serve in disaster relief as a UN unit. Permission was granted.

Another aspect of UN life is almost totally unknown. The UN Charter, which begins with the words, 'We the Peoples...' not governments, has made room for direct citizen participation in its affairs. Qualified NGO's (non-governmental organisations) may become consultants to UN agencies and to the Economic and Social Council, and may make statements or circulate their views to some UN bodies. Several hundred citizen groups have accepted this opportunity, and have a direct and important impact on what the UN is doing. Cooperating also, is an informal 'mankind under-ground' of delegates and secretarial personnel who are wholly dedicated to the construction of the City of Man.

We are watching in the United Nations the vivification of a new centre and the manifestation of a new energy. We are participating in the organisation of a new entity: *Mankind*. This is not only a hopeful prospect. It is in the process of occurring.

The integration of the human individual in his physical, emotional, mental and transpersonal aspects, and world unification are not separate processes. They interact and reinforce each other. The soul of man and the soul of mankind are not separate. Marked in the substance of each one of us are the gashes and scars which afflict mankind, resulting from discrimination, tyranny, injustice, inequity. We will always be incomplete until the song celestial of World Man is finally heard. The individual human bells will not ring perfection by themselves. If you seek deeper or higher self-linkages; if you undertake meditative or spiritual practices as part of your personal life, you will soon find that the partitions in the 'farther reaches of human nature' are thin, and discover your essential identity with all persons and with Mankind.

If, on the other hand, you decide to act on behalf of human need and in support of planetary unification – the next step for mankind – you will also discover our relationship to the whole: if you give your life to selfless service to mankind, you will find that you yourself are also on a path of self-transcendence and spiritual growth,

Psychosynthesis

because you will find the necessity for drawing on ever deeper aspects of yourself. The two approaches, vertical and horizontal, to our Soul and to Mankind, are not at all separate paths. No matter which one you take initially, they will soon converge and eventually coincide. That they were ever separate was an illusion. They were one path from the beginning.

Furthermore, every individual, no matter how obscure he may feel, and regardless of along which arm of the cross he enters into the process, will, as he grows and works, contribute far more than he may realise to the process.

There is something every person can do, beginning from where he or she presently is, by following the wonderful old aphorism of 'Advance without, retreat within'.

You will begin to act out your responsibility not from duty, not from zealousness or even the search for martyrdom, but out of the spontaneous integral-ness of your own nature, which is Humanity. So, tune up and tune in, and assist in the interception, reception, circulation and re-radiation of the newly arriving energies of human unification. Your resonant achievement will be Mankind's blessing.

Donald Keys (reprinted from Synthesis, 1975, Vol 1, No 2, adapted from an address to the VI Menninger Conference for the Voluntary Control of Internal States, Council Grove, Kansas, 1974)

Goodwill. The Only Hope for the World

We all realise that the world is a terrible state, and in our hearts most of us admit that we have all contributed towards it directly or indirectly by our selfishness, mistrust and often hatred. In so doing we have created wrong human relationships and in consequence mankind has become a house divided against itself. This state of affairs has led civilisation dangerously near the abyss. Unless we can stop the rot soon the results could be catastrophic for us all.

It is obvious that we cannot afford to be complacent about it any longer. Immediate action by all men and women is needed.

But what action?

We need to realise that no individual is an island unto himself; that we are all part of the one human family. Whether we like it or not we are all interdependent and inextricably bound together for better or for worse. Therefore our primary object must be to establish *right human relationships* in all fields of endeavour and thus make the world a better place to live in.

How can we do this?

The answer is almost too simple. It is by the spreading of Goodwill, for we can only achieve peace through Love and Goodwill and these must begin with each one of us.

What will Goodwill achieve in practice? Here are some of the qualities:

▮ Goodwill is the prerequisite to *right human relationships* based on caring and sharing

▮ Goodwill is essentially a creative force and it oils the wheels of life

▮ Goodwill acts as a leaven bringing about co-operation and harmonious relations between individuals and nations

▮ Where Goodwill is present, the walls of separation and of misunderstanding fall and confidence is restored

Psychosynthesis

▌ Goodwill promotes and nourishes understanding between individuals which is the greatest need today

▌ Goodwill is contagious, for Goodwill in action can be inspiration to others

The above qualities indicate what a powerful tool Goodwill is. Therefore we must make the fullest use of it in thought, word and deed.

Goodwill, which is the prerequisite to *right* human relationships, must become a built-in quality in our lives. This calls for a change of heart, of attitude and approach towards all whom we meet in our daily round; I our families, our places of work and our social contracts.

Thus, by spreading of Goodwill between individuals and nations, we shall be creating a happier world for our children and our children's children. Then peace more real than any known before, will come to pass.

Gregor Norman

Chapter 8 Creative Expression – The Act of Will

After a period of reflection, retreat or crisis leading to change in one's life, steps may be taken to give expression to what may have been learned, discovered and experienced. How will spirit come into matter and how will matter find form? If a seed has been planted, how can we help the seed to grow? If there has been inspiration, how can we find ways of realising this in our actual lives, in our work and play and relationships?

The Act of Will as described by Assagioli offers a framework for bringing inspiration into form. As a practical tool, it invites the user consciously and deliberately to identify their Purpose and to explore, through consideration of each of the further stages of the Act of Will – deliberation, choice, affirmation, planning and implementation – how intention can be manifested in the world.

The step decided upon may be large or small. The point is to find a way of beginning to create, in reality, what has been envisioned. This means clarifying and concretising ideas about intended courses of action which may at first be comfortably vague. It means taking time to think carefully about options and recognising that choosing one path means renouncing another. It means working out not only how I may do something, but also how I may actually avoid doing it or neglect to do it.

In one way it is an extremely simple model which is easy to use. Yet it is very challenging because it invites the user out of the world of ideas and into the world of action – of risk and commitment; it invites the user to confront the gap which is so often to be found between intention and outcome, between creative capacity and creative expression. It is this creative expression – what may be called 'doing our being' and in doing so, building a personal and spiritual practice, which is the goal of psychosynthesis.

The Act of Will

As a model for practical use, the Act of Will represents a chain, which is as strong as its weakest link. Will must be applied to working with the individual's internal psychology. This means becoming aware of and paying attention to points of individual strength and weakness. If I find myself frequently stuck in deliberation, unable to move on to make choices, then I know I need to work to release whatever is causing this block. If I find myself constantly failing in my attempts to carry out a plan of action, then I may need to pay more attention to the planning stage. When an act of will falters at a certain stage we may need to be willing to go back to an earlier stage, including right back to re-defining the goal or purpose, in order to release the block.

Also, of course, there are some stages which will be more relevant or more important depending upon the context; long deliberation will not be appropriate in deciding the best route out of a burning building; in understanding a difficult challenging action about which one has fears or reluctance, it may be very important to devote considerable time and energy to affirmation. In avoiding getting stuck in different stages, in maintaining a willingness to work flexibly with the model as a practical tool, a sense of disidentification is the key.

Purpose

A sense of Purpose is fundamentally necessary. It entails clear vision of an aim or goal to be reached. At the same time, as long as it remains a vision, it is not yet 'will in action'. First the aim must be evaluated and assessed; then it must arouse the motives which generate the urge as well as the intention to achieve it. This gives the zest or impulse to achieve; otherwise the person will lack drive and will be a dreamer rather than a doer.

Motives are aroused by the values that we attach to the goals we seek to attain. They therefore come from a sense of meaning and purpose in life rather than from unconscious drives of subpersonalities which serve a part rather than the whole picture.

Once aroused, motives need to be used otherwise the setting of goals remains academic. Psychological energies must be set in motion and used with clear intent in service of a higher good.

Deliberation

Assagioli talks about this stage as an 'act of restraint'. It represents a time to contain the impulse to act, to give it space in order to consider it carefully and employ wise counsel. This is not repression, but conscious control; consciously holding back the impulse or the tendency to act whilst deliberating on how best to deal with it. Therefore, it has a discriminatory function and an inhibiting function.

Psychosynthesis

It is an inclusive stage, opening to all possibilities. In order to make a choice we must determine which amongst the possible goals is preferable. It may include consulting with others, and it means being willing to take the time necessary to decide rather than going on impulse.

This stage is Will focused through the mind. A body of awareness is built which serves to generate feelings within the personality. Some will be cooperative to the chosen aim and others will be reactive. Making conscious these responses ultimately serves the direction of the chosen act.

Choice

Choice often feels like the Will itself. But it is only a stage in the whole act. The hardest thing about making a choice is to let go of all the alternatives. Letting go of them is like an Act of Renunciation. There is always a Yes and a No to every choice.

Being in touch with values or purpose gives the person a predisposition to choose one way or the other. Choice also includes the quality of freedom, of acting or not acting; of deciding yes, no, or not for now.

Affirmation

This stage activates and fosters the dynamic and creative energies needed to ensure the achievement of the goal. It is the command and authority function and 'musters the troops'.

Affirmation is the pivotal stage. What has been chosen must be achieved. It needs to come into expression and requires a further impulse to do so. It requires a synthesis of two inner attitudes: faith and conviction leading to certainty. An emotional body is built, aligning feelings with the mental affirmation. Let others know what you are choosing to make it present in your life and to engage them as witnesses and gain their cooperation.

There are numerous different techniques for affirmation including using evocative words, ideal model exercises, mudra or symbolic gestures, repetition, drawings, images and ritual.

Psychosynthesis

Planning

Careful elaboration of a programme is needed, assessing 'what is' in terms of means, and having a sense of timing. This is where we choose 'the right programme', and adjust to limitations using all the available resources.

Skilful will is important here. This stage represents 'the how' and has a relationship to deliberation. We need to keep the goal in mind to avoid means becoming ends, thus losing sight of the goal itself.

Planning should always include planning for what will be likely to go wrong, including how I might sabotage myself. Being willing to drop the plan is important, without dropping purpose. Is the timing off? Have I missed a step? A frequent problem is wanting to carry out the programme oneself whereas others with greater resources may be more capable. So we cooperate and don't duplicate acting with wisdom and humility.

Implementation

This means directing the implementation of the plan. Assagioli uses the analogy of the driver of a car taking the right actions to ensure that the car goes where we want it to go; this is a reminder of the fact that an act of will may not mean huge effort but rather choices made which are then enacted in a disidentified way cooperating with available resources.

It entails a skilful use of other psychological energies existing in the personality. The Will is the director of the entire production, but normally is not one of the actors. The direction includes constant supervision; watching the development of the programme to see it follows the right course and is aligned to purpose. This entails a subordination of the various means to the underlying purpose.

Exercises Following this Section

The following exercises on the Psychological Workbook and the Ideal Model Technique provide a series of very practical activities which together with the 'Evening Review', the 'Disidentification' exercise and the 'Who am I' exercise, can help develop a personal discipline and psychospiritual practice.

Psychosynthesis

Further Reading

Assagioli, Roberto, *The Act of Will*, David Platt, 1999

Ferrucci, Piero, *What We May Be*, Thorsons, 1995 (Chapter 15)

Psychosynthesis

Psychological Workbook

One of the most useful instruments for long term self-development is a workbook, diary or journal. We use the term 'psychological workbook' because many people tend to associate the word 'diary' with memories of adolescence in which often trivial and burdensome accounts were kept of one's daily activities.

The type of workbook suggested here has as its purpose the recording of your inner life and its developments. Outer events may be recorded in as much as they are related to inner events (feelings, thoughts, observations), but the focus should be on the unfolding awareness of oneself and the world, and on the new meanings, values, and inter-relationships one is able to discover.

There are many purposes for keeping a workbook of this sort. One of the most important is to help ourselves formulate our thoughts, feelings, and observations with greater clarity. And in the act of putting something on paper we tend to commit ourselves to a greater extent. We are taking a step beyond simply thinking or saying something when we make the effort to write it down. Also, in the process of thought clarification through writing, we are obliged to choose between alternate points of view; we are thus less likely to deceive ourselves by holding contradictory views without being aware of it. If there is a problem to be solved or an area of real confusion, we are better able to define it and thus take the first step towards its resolution.

The act of writing is also a great stimulus to the creative process. When we are trying to grapple with a problem, it is a common experience that in writing down a few thoughts on the question, other related thoughts begin to stream in through a process of association, and these ideas in turn open up new avenues of thought, new possibilities we may not have considered before. If we can learn to let our minds range freely in this manner, we will be truly amazed to discover the depth of the insights already within us – just waiting to be liberated.

Keeping a workbook as a technique of self-development also functions in other ways. It gives us an opportunity to express in a harmless way any powerful and disruptive emotions we may have bottled up inside us. If we can learn to let off steam through writing, we will have a useful means of discharging tensions, and of becoming aware of what underlies them. Writing is also a useful exercise for developing the faculties of

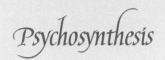

concentration, attention, and control of the will. It may help a person who is somewhat shy, and reluctant to express himself in a face-to-face setting, to explore certain aspects of himself more freely.

For all these reasons keeping a workbook can be an important aspect of the psychosynthesis process in that it is a method which one can employ on one's own initiative, as one takes the process of one's growth and self-realisation increasingly into one's own hands.

In addition to written material, one can make drawings and other visual aids a part of the workbook. These may be of various kinds. In one category are images – which may come to you in the form of dreams, fantasies, or visualisations. In another category are diagrams, more abstract symbols, or visual aids which we can use to express our ideas in graphic form. This is useful in developing clear concepts and in communicating these concepts to others. A final category is what one might call 'spontaneous drawing'. This should be done when we are in a relaxed state of mind and when our attention is fixed on something else – as when we are doodling. Such drawings reflect the activity of the unconscious mind and may be of value in self-understanding. Thus, drawing as well as writing can be part of a complete workbook.

Here are headings of possible areas for inclusion in your workbook. It is suggested you choose among them the ones that, according to your own needs and experience, are likely to be of greater value. But, of course, your choice can be revised at any time. It is important to date each entry, in order to provide a developmental perspective.

Dialogue with ideas Include a heading for any area of vital intellectual interest in which you are trying to advance your own understanding (e.g. education, religion, mathematics, systems theory, ecology, etc.).

Dialogue with persons Insights into or questions about your relationships.

Dialogue with events Your response to meaningful events in your life; note occasions on which you are aware of 'synchronicity'.

Inner dialogues Miscellaneous thoughts, musings, intuitions, questions, or speculations which do not fit under other headings.

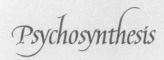

Dreams Description, context, associations, and amplifications of your night dreams (which are most easily recorded immediately upon waking).

Imagery Visualisations, or experiences in other sensory modalities. This may include images which come spontaneously or while using one of the guided mental imagery techniques. These can be recorded in writing and/or through drawings. It is helpful to record the feelings and associations you have in response to the image, or to different parts of it (form, colour, etc.), its meaning for you, and a tentative interpretation if possible.

Imagination Fantasies, stories, situations, etc. which might serve as the seed for an imaginative work. This category is best limited to those fantasies which have some creative potential.

Diagrams Graphic models of theoretical constructs (though you may wish to include these under the headings of the various areas of intellectual interest instead). These will help you express your thoughts visually, and this may be useful for purposes of clarification and visual communication.

Meditation Notes on techniques of meditation with which you have experimented, seed ideas used, and results obtained. Note any insights or intuitions which come through.

Self Notes on your sense of personal identity, answers to the 'Who Am I?' questions, experiences with 'self-remembering' and other meditative techniques related to the question of essential being.

Will Notes on your experience with the various stages of the will, and evaluation of your areas of strength and weakness. Note any occasions and their distinctive circumstances in which you were aware of yourself making use of the will, and record your results with the exercises for developing the will.

Techniques for growth Your experience with the various approaches which do not fall under other headings. Please note as fully as possible the circumstances under which the various approaches were helpful or not and your opinion of the reasons underlying success or failure with a particular method.

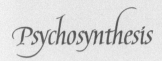
Psychosynthesis

Peak experiences Any 'high' or 'deep' experiences of peace, joy, love, expansion, awakening, etc. and their circumstances and effects.

Hangups Personal weaknesses of which you are aware and on which you would like to work. Particular emphasis can be placed on the techniques you can use to overcome them. Record also any strong negative reactions you have to other people as they may clarify your own unrecognised and projected problems.

Quotations Personally meaningful quotations from your readings.

Time perspectives To make the contact with your own movement through time, through the past into the present and toward the future. Stepping stones (bridges from where we were to where we are or hope to be), intersections (roads taken and not taken) and memories may be noted.

Ideal Model Technique

The creative imagination is a powerful tool for personal growth. It can be used to form an ideal model, concept, or image of oneself which provides energy and direction, and which is capable of being expressed outwardly in the world. Forming an ideal model means creating a realistic, and attainable self image which includes, or is substituted for the many already existing within us that may be one-sided, impractical, or restricting. These inner models of our personality – conscious or unconscious – are not only diverse in nature, origin, and energy level, but are often mutually exclusive, and in considerable conflict among themselves. The purpose of this technique is to develop the ideal model itself – the realistic vision of that which one can, and truly wants to become.

To do this we need first to recognise and understand the multiplicity of models which limit our appreciation of what we can be. Once these conflicting models have been understood, the exercise proceeds to the deliberate, purposeful construction and utilisation of the ideal model itself.

The ideal model is not an ultimate model of perfection, of complete psychosynthesis. It represents rather the next chosen step, or stage, in our growth, such as strengthening or integrating some undeveloped psychological function, building a desired quality or small cluster of qualities, establishing a more effective pattern of action, etc. It is therefore a realistic model of inner and outer living, toward which we can move, and which we can gradually modify and expand as we ourselves change and grow.

In the form in which it is presented, the exercise is intended for individual use. It can be easily modified to be used in groups. Suggestion for its use in groups and in therapy situations are given at the end.

Preparation

Have at hand your psychological workbook or writing paper and pencil, at least seven sheets of large sketching paper and a set of oil pastels, coloured pens or crayons. Number the sheets 1 to 7, and use them in that order. Select a place where you will be quiet and undisturbed for at least an hour and a half.

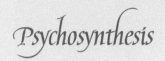

Psychosynthesis

Note: once you start, it is important to carry the exercise to completion without interruption.

Procedure

Sit in a relaxed position. Let your feelings become calm. Allow your mind to become quiet, but remain alert. Then read carefully the following words:

1 All of us undervalue ourselves in some way. We each have an image or model of ourselves which is *worse than we really are.* Sometimes we believe this model to be true.

Close your eyes and think about this model for a while. Let an image of it come into your mind. Try to see it clearly. Pay attention to your feelings about it; study it for a while, getting to know it as much as you can. Take some time to do this. Then open your eyes.

(After you have completed this first phase, continue reading the directions)

Now draw a picture of that image of yourself. Sometimes this is the image of a person, sometimes it may be a symbol, or perhaps an abstract pattern of colours. Or if you don't have an image, you can just begin to draw and let it come.

(After you have finished drawing, continue reading)

Write down the thoughts you had about the image, your feelings about it, the meaning you see in the drawing, the relation it has to your everyday life, and anything else that may be relevant.

(Continue reading after this)

Now recollect yourself; put aside this model; take a few deep breaths...again relax your body...let your feelings become calm...let your mind quiet down, but remain alert... Then read carefully the next statement, and deal with it just as with the previous one. After you are through with the drawing and the writing, go to the following statement, and so on until you have completed step 6.

2 I also over-evaluate myself in some way. I have an inner image of myself which is *better than I really am*.

3 There is in me some glamorous 'secret daydream' model or image of *how I would like to be*, one that is usually exaggerated, unattainable in practice, and therefore sterile.

4 I have also a model of myself as *I would like to appear to others*, as contrasted to how I really am.

5 There are also in me models of *how other people see me*, how they believe I am – the images they project to me; both images I like and images I resent (in working with this, take time to consider each kind, and draw both on the same sheet).

6 Finally, there is in me an image of *how other people would like me to be*, of what they expect of me, of how they would like to change me.

Take all the drawings and looking at them one at a time, in sequence, get in touch again with each model...name it... remember your feelings about it.

Now stand up and with your eyes closed get in touch with the weight of these images... feel how they limit and restrict you...how they hold you down...As you stand, let your body move to **shake them away**! Really shake off their weight and drop all these false, imposed models of yourself with an act of will...let go of them...and be still for a while experiencing how you feel. Then open your eyes.

7 Now sit down, again closing your eyes, and recollect and centre yourself. Think through what you really and realistically would like to be. Let an image of yourself, as this model, come from within you. Take time to do this. Examine this image, getting to know it as well as you can. See yourself that way. Then add to it any other aspect that you decide is appropriate, and drop anything that doesn't seem right or useful. Open your eyes and draw an image or symbol of it. And then write any thoughts or feelings you have about it.

(Continue reading after you have completed this)

Psychosynthesis

The next and last step of the exercise has the purpose of 'grounding' this model, of helping to make it a living and dynamic element in your everyday life. How to proceed with this step depends on how you feel about what you've already done, and particularly about the ideal model represented in the seventh picture. Its development may have been accompanied by the clear emergence of 'good' positive feelings, or perhaps by an insight or realisation such as 'of course this is what I want to be, why didn't I think of it before'. Or considering it now you may experience an inner certainty that this ideal model is 'right' and 'good', that it is what you want to be, and that becoming it will be a step forward in your growth. This does not mean it will be perfect, or complete in all details – you can always change it or improve it later.

If the model seems good to you, you can definitely proceed to the last stage of the exercise (if you feel tired, you can at this point take a break and continue later on, or perhaps the next day. But waiting too long will eliminate some of the positive feelings that have emerged, which can be used to vitalise the model).

On the other hand, as you reconsider the model you may feel that although it is generally in the right direction, it is not quite 'on', and that it may need further development, or changes, before utilising it. In this case you may want to spend 15 to 30 minutes a day, for the next few days, working on improving the model until you are satisfied that it is what you want. Or you may proceed with the exercise, but at first with caution, as an experiment, and as you do so you can keep improving the model on the basis of your experience.

But perhaps you may be uncertain about whether the model is actually right for you; whether it would be a step forward from the present; whether it would not be another limitation. If you feel this way, go back through the first six models you discarded, and consider whether some of them didn't creep back unnoticed, and condition your ideal model. If this seems to be the case, make sure you let go of them. Then focus on this model again, and ask yourself (on the basis of which beliefs, motives, values, aims, experiences, etc.) do you consider it to be your ideal? This last step may be quite valuable even if you feel satisfied with your model. Such an approach will often locate the causes of the impasse, and clear the ground for development of the true ideal model. You can then repeat step 7.

8 Once you feel good about your ideal model close your eyes, *visualise yourself as being that model*; see your face, your eyes, your posture, your expression, all embody-

---

ing the qualities of that model...spend all the time you need to do this. Then become that model; feel what it is like to be it. Visualise yourself dynamically in a number of everyday situations in your own life, possessing and acting out the qualities and attitudes of that model.

Now open your eyes, consider what happened, and write down any new insight, or anything you may want to remember. Then decide if you want to make any new changes to your ideal model.

This eighth part of the exercise gives a practical model of action which we can use more and more spontaneously when the need arises. It is quite useful if performed only once, but will be most beneficial if it is repeated frequently, preferably daily for a while. It is most valuable if done early in the morning, playing in the imagination the particular situations that are likely to occur that day. End the exercise by affirming your determination to act with the qualities and attitudes of the ideal model throughout the day, and especially during the situations considered.

A word of caution is needed here. There are occasions where attempting to act out a positive quality in our imagination may make an opposite one emerge. For example, imagining talking to an audience with calm and assurance, may cause anxiety to appear. Imagining acting lovingly toward a certain person, one may suddenly experience anger. This indicates that there is, in the unconscious, some emotion that needs to be brought to the surface and released before proceeding to utilise the ideal model. Specific techniques for doing this are available (Roberto Assagioli, *Psychosynthesis: A Manual of Principles and Techniques*, Harper Collins, 1993).

This fact that negative aspects sometimes emerge when we try to develop positive ones is clear evidence that placing emphasis on the positive – provided it is done in a wise and responsible way – does not in any way lead to repression of the negative in us. Rather it helps us get in touch with it and deal with it, but from a positive framework, that is, only as the negative becomes a real obstacle to further growth.

This exercise is also ideally suited to be done in combination with an evening review of your actual expression and application of the ideal model during the day.

The exercise can also be used effectively in groups, and by therapists and counsellors with their clients.

Psychosynthesis

Therapists and counsellors are urged to experience the exercise themselves before using it with clients. By doing so they will gain increased sensitivity in its right timing and use, and a deeper understanding of the dynamics involved.

In groups, it has been found helpful at the end of the exercise to form small clusters of three or four people, wherein each person in turn shows his drawings and shares and discusses what emerged, and gets feedback from the others.

Roberto Assagioli (adapted from 'Technique of Ideal Models' in Psychosynthesis: A Manual of Principles and Techniques, Harper Collins, 1993)

Psychosynthesis

YEAR BOOK

The Creative Process

"There is no finality in the presentation of truth, it develops and grows to meet man's growing demand for light." (Anon)

When we look at evolution, we tend to look at the forms through which the evolutionary process has been expressed. We try to understand the process through the eyes of history. However, history explains nothing about causality, it simply gives us a sequence of events in time. What we want to consider here is that the evolution of forms is a consequence, a response to the evolution of ideas and that by penetrating into the ideas themselves, we are more able to co-operate with the evolutionary process as it unfolds so that we as individuals become active partners with the creative principle rather than innocent bystanders and victims of fate. In this way, I think, we more effectively fulfil the destiny of humanity. The Human Being stands as a bridge between being a consequence of his past, helpless and impotent, caught in the chain of cause and effect, and being an active partner co-operating with his future.

In understanding the creative process, we find we need to have a vision which is able to hold two apparent dissonant views of reality; with one eye on the world of forms which are many and varied and often apparently opposing each other, and one eye on the world of ideas which are inclusive of many forms and can be expressed across many fields of service. For example, today, the language of physicists is sounding more and more like the Eastern Mystics' description of their view of reality. Also, people in many disciplines such as medicine, education, psychology and religion are able to communicate about needs which go beyond the boundaries of their own specific fields of service and which are common to each.

In aligning, therefore, with the principle of creativity, we need to acquire a synthetic view, so that this perspective becomes the arbiter of our actions, rather than the value judgements which so often determine the forms for our creativity in the world. The

Psychosynthesis

context for this perspective needs to be based increasingly on values which are beyond our individual personal needs.

Our bodies and physical environment; our feelings and emotional relationships; and our minds and our belief systems are the outer objective forms which are the consequences of our creativity and are all products of our conscious and unconscious processes – the consequences of our life energy manifesting itself. Over time, we become more or less identified with these forms and from them we derive our experience of our identity. As we learn to disidentify, let go of our attachments to these forms, so our experience of our identity expands until we awaken to our innate divinity and realise that we are the 'whole', we are all that there is.

As consciousness differentiates through independent points of view, we find ourselves the subject in relation to the objective world. The process of becoming more and more the subject of our consciousness and not identified with our concrete objective world is the bridge to creativity. Here we become the Thinker rather than the object of our thoughts – the process of disidentification leads to a consciousness of the whole and ultimately leads to the development of the faculty of discrimination – an aspect of Wisdom – beyond the judgements motivated by personality needs. With this consciousness of the whole comes the responsibility and the individual Will to act within that responsibility. There are many possibilities, many directions in which we can choose to invest our personal energy. However, as modern physics has shown us, until we choose, everything remains in potential, everything has probable outcomes and it is at the moment of choice that 'potential' enters into the dimension of 'space and time' and becomes actual or takes form. I can forever dream or fantasise and journey within the realm of ideas beyond the reality of my daily life, as beyond time there exist boundless patterns of probabilities – I can become a doctor, a teacher, a lawyer, I can create a business or build a home; all is possible. The moment (i.e. in time) I choose one or the other, the other possibilities vanish and potential actualises itself. It is as if the future is constrained and given a direction within the present – the many become the one and as soon as I perceive the outcome, I am determining its course.

At this point, what I am doing is choosing to take responsibility for my part of the whole. We are choosing consciously and unconsciously all of the time and therefore affecting the course of evolution whether we know it or not. We need therefore to understand what it means to surrender to the Future as it unfolds itself, which is not a passive act, but one which co-operates with the tide of evolution. It seems that the old

Psychosynthesis

Newtonian view of the physical universe is being challenged by quantum physics. We are not passive observers standing behind a glass screen. By the very fact of being in any one place, e.g. within a family, living in a country, being part of humanity, we are influencing our reality and to some degree we are actually creating it. The expansion of consciousness needs to serve our realisation of the greatest context of our identity. We are a part of humanity, not just English, French, American, or Russian and we are living on this planet, not just in England, France, America or Russia and we, by our very actions or non-actions, are willfully, within time, affecting the course of evolution.

In understanding the creative process, we find we have to free ourselves from our past conclusions on the nature of reality – not to disregard them, nor to dismiss them – but to include them as partial in relation to our present understanding, rather than seeing them as truth itself. A developing child internalises his environment as a way of understanding abstract principles, and modern biologists are describing organisms as embodiments, through the process of internalisation, of the ordered universe. This process gives internal reference points for the direction of their evolution and in this way they transform the environment. Our consciousness is riddled by polarities, by constructs which create duality in our consciousness and which are supported by feelings and rationalisations. They are relative to a particular point in time, decisions made in the past, so that there is always a polarisation between that within the constructs which we affirm or say Yes to and that excluded by the construct which we have dismissed or said No to. Einstein's General Theory of Relativity shows us that our mind forms structures which thereafter determine what it further will and will not accept freely, and we identify with that which we accept.

When making choices we are continually pulled between the conflicts set up by these polarities, and therefore our choices are exclusive in so far as we are choosing between alternatives, making one good and the other bad in order to appease our feelings. We are not taught to go to the 'vision' or to the idea beyond this conflict. It is not a question of what we believe, but one of continually re-examining our beliefs to be in step with evolution. It is a question of seeing whether or not the constructs we hold are still alive by the virtue of the value they contain. In order to determine whether or not something is still of value and aligned to evolution or the emerging order, we need to abstract to the level of meaning – which connects to whether or not there is a 'need' in society for that particular belief – whether or not it is still serving humanity. Then we need to abstract still further to Purpose to determine the context or the idea itself. For

Psychosynthesis

example, 'Make Love not War' was a familiar cry during the sixties and was instrumental in bringing an end to the Vietnam War. Inherent in that construct was a value that was emerging for humanity around Brotherhood and Goodwill to All Men, and the belief that 'I serve my King and Country no matter what' was being challenged. Inherent in any construct is authority. It contains a particular injunction which impels action in a particular direction and it is that authority which needs to be challenged to allow a more evolved principle to emerge. We need to re-evaluate our constructs, so that there is space in consciousness for a new idea to take shape and thus over time, our consciousness evolves. Any construct, therefore, is relative to a particular point in time and is the form that contains our consciousness, in space and time, rather than the larger vision which contains all the forms which are separated by time.

There are certain universal patterns or Archetypes which exist in the Abstract Mind which shape consciousness – Bohm speaks of a wholeness and the implicate order – these give rise to patterns in our consciousness through which we are able to perceive the emerging order. These patterns are abstractions; they are synthetic and are the contexts for the forms which appear as they manifest in space and time. Fundamental truths are contained within these archetypes such as Love, Power, Beauty, Wisdom, Unity, etc. These exist as synthetic wholes and over time they are revealed more and more to us as the forms which reflect our understanding of them continually evolve.

It seems therefore that Creativity involves mental processes whereby we have to bridge to the abstract beyond the value judgements of the intellect in order to penetrate into these fundamental patterns. One of the ways of understanding why the intellect exerts such a strong hold on us is to see that as we grow and develop through the various transitions of our lives from childhood to maturity, the external world imposes itself on us and we are forever reacting and responding to it, building for ourselves a 'safe dwelling house'. We become identified with the walls of our defences and we come to believe that our very survival depends on them. Our intellect, which contains the admonitions for our survival in the form of mental constructs, becomes 'God' himself. However, identity comes not from the mind, but from experiencing the greatest possible context of Being; the context of my totality, who I am, from the place of my causality and my knowing.

We need to learn to turn our mind away from serving only our personal needs towards serving the 'Meta needs' of evolution. We need to have our mind become receptive to the Abstract Mind; to be illumined by the light of the Intuition; to have insight and comprehension – for it to be truly the instrument of the Knower. We need to use our mind not to defend ourselves against a hostile universe, but to let go of 'victim' consciousness and to identify with being co-operators with a process that unfolds from within. And finally, within this context, there is understanding the right place of our feelings; our emotional energy holds tremendous power and is the very energy that carries life into form. In the days of the steam engine, steam needed to be compressed to drive the engine and we can describe our mind as being like the engine room with its direction programmed, focussed and concentrated and our feelings like the steam, harnessed and obeying the constraints put on them. In this way all of our energy is organised to flow in the direction of what we proclaim ourselves to be – co-creators in a purposeful and meaningful universe.

"For the essential in the being of a man of my type lies precisely in what he thinks and how he thinks, not in what he does or suffers. With this viewpoint, thinking is not a joy or a chore added to the daily existence. It is the essence of a man's very being, and the tool by which the transient sorrows, the primitive forms of feeling, and the other 'merely personal' parts of existence can be mastered. For it is through such thought that man can lift himself up to a level where he can think about 'great, eternal riddles'. It is a 'liberation' that can yield inner freedom and security. When the mind grasps the 'extra-personal' part of the world – that part which is not tied to shifting desires and moods – it gains knowledge which all men and women can share regardless of individual conditions, customs and other differences." (Einstein)

Joan Evans (reprinted from the Institute of Psychosynthesis Year Book, 1981, Vol 1)